# BREAKIN' IN
## TO THE MUSIC BUSINESS

# BREAKIN' IN
## TO THE MUSIC BUSINESS

## ALAN H. SIEGEL

CHERRY LANE BOOKS
PORT CHESTER, NEW YORK

Cherry Lane Books, Port Chester, NY 10573
First printing 1983
Printed in the United States of America

**Library of Congress Cataloging in Publication Data**

Siegel, Alan H., 1932-
Breakin' in—to the music business.

1. Music—United States—Vocational guidance.
2. Music, Popular (Songs, etc.)—United States—Writing and publishing.
ML3790.S55  1983      784.5'0023'73      82-17879
ISBN 0-89524-171-4 (trade)
ISBN 0-89524-156-0 (pbk.)

Art Direction by Franc Guerette
Cover Design by Jo Ann Gaynor
Cover Illustration by Dan Recchia
Illustrated by Dan Recchia
Photograph of Alan H. Siegel by Derek Photographers

*To Charlotte*

# Contents

### 5 Show Me The Way    151

The artist-manager relationship—the quest for a manager worth having—the typical management deal: duration, compensation, and exclusions—the hidden dangers of the traditional deal—both sides of the most often negotiated issues and some viable compromises. Interviews with four top managers, whose differing styles and attitudes will give you valuable insights.

Interviews with Shep Gordon, Miles Lourie, George Schiffer, and Jerry Weintraub.

### 6 You've Got A Friend    199

The choice of an entertainment lawyer—his functions—the various fee structures—how to best utilize the services of a lawyer.

### 7 I've Heard That Song Before    211

The mysteries and myths of copyright. Included is a reprint of U.S. Copyright Circular R1, *Copyright Basics*.

### 8 My Way    231

Major entertainment personalities tell of their experiences "breakin' in." The mistakes they made, the breaks they got, and what they learned along the way.

Interviews with Ashford and Simpson, Marvin Hamlisch, Barbara Mandrell, and Bill Wyman.

# *Preface*

Few fields of endeavor boast neophytes less prepared for what lies ahead than does the music business, and the least prepared of all are those seeking reward and fulfillment as songwriters and recording artists.

Although during the twenty-five years I have practiced entertainment law the "record contracts" I have used grew from two pages to forty pages, and although the recording-studio "board" has evolved from a "four-track" to a "sixty-four-track digital," the vast majority of aspiring songwriters and performers cling stubbornly to their abject ignorance of the business in which they seek success.

Why is this lack of knowledge endemic to novice songwriters and artists? Perhaps it is because there are few, if any, formal opportunities to obtain training. If you wish to pursue a career in motion pictures, television, advertising, drama, writing, or any other creative vocation, there are a slew of universities and professional institutions where you can seek training. For songwriters and recording artists, the school is "the business" and the street, and too often the lessons are learned too late, if at all.

Whatever its cause, ignorance spells disaster for the aspiring songwriter and performing artist. It prevents him from getting a start, and if he finally gets a toe in the door, he often succeeds in fouling up whatever opportunity may have been available to him, or ends up paying unnecessarily heavy dues. Ultimately, the pressures of family and the need to make a living, coupled with disappointment and frustration, drive many of them out of "the business" and into medical school, the local service station, domesticity, or to wherever else would-be "stars" fade.

"Why the lament?" you may wonder. Isn't that why they invented lawyers, managers, and accountants—so that the "creative" can be free to create? Ideally, yes, but few things evolve ideally. Too often artists and songwriters do not seek the aid of the attorneys, accountants, and managers they need until it is too late. When they finally seek the aid of experts, they are, because of a lack of understanding, unable to state articulately the busines terms they have discussed, or, even worse, what they have "agreed to." Why does this state of affairs exist, considering that artists and songwriters are, on the whole, bright and eager to learn?

The core of the problem is, I believe, a failure of communication on a technical and on a human level. The technical aspect involves the mastery of a new language. The vernacular of the music industry is studded with words that seem to have a simple and clear meaning, but which mean something more or something different in the parlance of the industry, and with words and phrases that are unique to the music business and hence totally alien to the uninitiated. The human component is more nebulous. Most neophyte writers and artists are young. Because of their youth and general eagerness to please, they are relatively easily intimidated. This, in turn, leads to shyness and a consequent reluctance to ask questions or to ask for explanations. Too often, they nod affirmation rather than ask the questions they have on their minds.

What, then, is the answer? Time and experience will take care of many of the problems for those who hang in long enough, and I hope this book will take care of many more. Knowledge is power, and power builds confidence.

Mastery of the contents of this book will provide you with a working knowledge of the language of the music business, how the business and the basic deals work, and how to acquire the professional help you will need. It will also afford you the benefit of learning from mistakes made by others, and will provide you with the answers the best professionals in the business have given me to the questions you are or should be asking yourself.

This is not the book I started to write last October. That book was to be a short, gemlike, pithy masterpiece intended solely for the aspiring songwriter and recording artist. Well, I either had more to say than I thought or was unable to say it succinctly enough. This is a much bigger book than I contemplated, and a much more complete one, which may well be of help to anyone associated with or interested in the music business. I hope it is one of those rare instances where more *is* more, rather than less.

If it helps you launch your career, or increases your understanding, or helps you avoid a mistake, it will have served its purpose.

Good luck! See you on the charts!

ALAN H. SIEGEL

*Scarsdale, New York*
*December, 1982*

# *Acknowledgments*

I wish to acknowledge with deepest gratitude and no small degree of pride the help and contributions of the following:

| | | |
|---|---|---|
| Nickolas Ashford | Lauren Keiser | Saul P. Pryor |
| Clive Davis | Miles Lourie | Linda Sargent |
| Jean Dinegar | Barbara Mandrell | George Schiffer |
| Shep Gordon | Billy Meshel | Irwin Schuster |
| Elizabeth Granville | Doug Morris | Valerie Simpson |
| Marvin Hamlisch | Milton Okun | Jerry Weintraub |
| Chuck Kaye | Rupert Perry | Bill Wyman |

AHS

# BREAKIN' IN
## TO THE MUSIC BUSINESS

# Lexicon Plus

This section was to be called a glossary, but I was advised that people don't read glossaries. I hope they read lexicons because this one is to the rest of the book what the Rosetta Stone was to hieroglyphics. It is the key!

But take heart. I found the spartan economic style of a true glossary (oops! I mean lexicon) as tedious for me to write as it would be for you to read. Consequently, this lexicon is liberally salted with observations and illustrations which I think make it more readable than it might otherwise have been—hence the "plus."

I recommend that you read it through once, and thereafter use it as a dictionary or glossary or lexicon or whatever.

## Aa

**A & R (Artists and Repertoire)** — The division or department of a record company traditionally charged with the responsibility for discovering artists and providing and selecting appropriate material for their recordings. The latter function has to some extent been diminished with the advent of the "singer-songwriter."

**"A" Side (of a 45-RPM Record)** —The side of a single that the record company believes is the hit. It is designated the "A" side on promotional copies distributed to disc jockeys so that they will know which side to play. Most of the time the record company is wrong. Most of the time it doesn't matter because the disc jockeys don't play it anyway.

**Accounting, an** — The periodic (usually semiannual) financial reports rendered by record companies to artists and producers and by music publishers to songwriters. In the event all recording costs and advances have been recouped, it is sometimes (depending on the solvency of the company) accompanied by a check in the amount of the royalties shown to be due.

**Administration Fee** — A fee charged by one music publisher to another for managing and "working" the latter's catalogue of songs. Such fee arrangements vary widely and are subject to extensive negotiation. See Chapter 2.

**Administration Rights** — The rights granted by one music publisher to another whereby the administering publisher acquires the rights, for a fee, to manage and "work" the catalogue of songs of the music publisher granting the rights. The structure of administration arrangements varies widely, and the contracts governing them are complex and contain subtle nuances with major economic ramifications. Beware! See Chapter 2.

**Advance** — A sum of money paid to an artist or songwriter in anticipation of, and chargeable against, the artist's or songwriter's future royalties. An advance, if granted, is usually paid on the signing of a contract, the exercise of an option, or on some other event such as asking for it. Advances, though recoupable out of future earnings, are not traditionally returnable if not earned. They are invariably welcomed and fuel the fires of creativity.

**AF of M (American Federation of Musicians)** — The musicians' union.

**AFTRA (American Federation of Television and Radio Artists).**

**AGAC (American Guild of Authors and Composers)** — A national songwriter's association, which performs various administrative, educational, and political functions for its members. It is funded by members dues and commissions on members' royalties, both of which are assessed on a graduated scale.

**Agent** — A person or organization licensed under state employment laws to procure employment for clients and to charge a fee for services rendered (usually 10% of gross compensation). Eventually artists utilize agents in connection with personal appearances. Songwriters rarely utilize the services of agents. Agency contracts are complicated and deal with many items. They should be carefully scrutinized and negotiated.

**Album Cut** — A song recorded for an album that is not anticipated to be a "single" or "hit" record. Such songs are not without quality, and are essential to the structure, continuity, and success of an album. All too often singles turn out to be album cuts and sometimes, though rarely, what are thought to be album cuts emerge as singles.

**AOR** — Album-oriented rock.

**Approval Not To Be Unreasonably Withheld** — Artists and songwriters in their negotiations with record companies and music publishers often ask for and receive the right to approve certain elements involved in the evolution of their work. Artists, for example, may have the right to approve their producers and the songs to be recorded; songwriters may win the right to approve arrangements. No one really knows what "not to be unreasonably withheld" means, but attorneys with well-earned paranoia insist on the language in case an artist or songwriter, without any real artistic motivation, refuses approval out of pique or as a hostage in a negotiation.

**ASCAP (American Society of Composers, Authors and Publishers)** — A performing rights organization whose sole and limited functions are the issuance and enforcement of licenses for the public performance of the nondramatic songs of its publisher and songwriter members and the distribution of the revenues derived from such licenses. ASCAP is not the other things you thought it was. It is not a union, it is not a music publisher, it does not administer or control copyrights.

**Audio-Visual Rights** — Rights to couple an artist's visual performance with his vocal performance — sometimes referred to as "Sight and Sound." This yet unmatured bundle of rights is fast evolving due to the popularity of video disc and video tape players. Earlier they could often be reserved to the artist, or at least a "standoff" requiring mutual acquiescence could be won during negotiation of a record contract. Now that what was the future is the present, and the scent of megabucks is high in the air, only established artists with considerable clout can alter what has become intransigence on the part of record companies relative to audio-visual rights.

**Audit Clause** — The provision in an artist's or songwriter's contract that enables him to have his accountant examine the books and records of the record company or music publisher in order to verify the accuracy of the accountings received. In the not too distant past such a clause had to be fought for. Now it is almost universally included as part of the "boilerplate" of all recording and songwriter contracts, although there is wide variety as to their limitations. Some are "cuter" than others. This is a key clause, and you might be advised to consider a change of counsel if a contract not containing an audit clause is submitted to you for signature.

# Bb

**"B" Side (of a 45-RPM Record)** — The "other" side of a single record. It is usually an album cut, since record companies are loath to press two "A" sides on the same single, only one side of which will receive air play. If an album has two potential "A" sides, one will be saved for release either when the first single proves to be a dud or when album sales begin to flag.

**Background Singers** — The singers that are heard in the chorus or background of a solo artists's record. If your forte is singing, this is an excellent way to put bread on the table while you are waiting to be a foreground singer. Background singers receive fees for their services but no royalties.

**BMI (Broadcast Music, Inc.)** — A performing rights organization with the same functions as ASCAP. It even isn't the same things ASCAP isn't. BMI and ASCAP are competitors and will fight over the privilege of giving you advances against your performance royalties, if and when you get something going. Until then you will find both of them to be niggardly.

**Boilerplate** — The provisions that are contained, with little or no change, in all record or songwriter contracts regardless of the luminescence of the artist or songwriter involved. These clauses are probably the only things your contract will have in common with Neil Diamond's or Billy Joel's . . . until your next round of contract negotiations. Boilerplate provisions are usually little negotiated and include such universal things as grants of rights, copyright notices, and other matters considered essential but mechanical, mundane, or otherwise without romance . . . the kinds of things a lawyer can't get a medal or a bonus for.

**Bottom Line** — No, not the Greenwich Village night club. When your lawyer and their lawyer have become sufficiently exasperated with each other in the negotiation of a particular point, one will say, "Enough of this nonsense (a euphemism). What's the bottom line?" Depending on what side of the table you're on, it's either the maximum they will give or the minimum you will take.

**Budget Line** — A record company's line of records that are priced substantially lower than the company's "top pop" line. A budget line usually consists of albums whose sales have so diminished as to render them no longer marketable as part of a "full price" line. Your attorney will (hopefully) obtain a provision whereby your albums will not be relegated to the budget line until a fixed period of time (18 to 24 months) after they have been commercially released as part of the company's "top pop" line.

**Bullet** — The black dot, star, or asterisk appearing adjacent to the titles of certain records on the charts of music trade publications. It connotes unusual activity in the growth of a record's popularity. The loss of a bullet is bad news, signifying that the record has peaked and is on its way down or off the chart.

# Cc

© — The international symbol for the word "copyright." It must appear with the year date of the copyright and the name of the copyright owner wherever prescribed by the United States Copyright Act and the Universal Copyright Convention. For an example, see the reverse of the title page of this book. I'm unduly impressed by all who have the © on their typewriters. Music publishers with such typewriters are apt to have more than one writer signed. See *Copyright*.

**Capital Gains** — A tax term meaning the gain from the sale of a capital asset. Music publishing companies, copyrights, and record masters are capital assets. You will pay a smaller tax on a capital gain than you would on gains that are ordinary income. Let's hope you have to worry about this real soon. Then pay your tax adviser to worry about it for you. His fees are deductible.

**Catalogue** — A group of songs characterized by something in common such as common ownership and/or common authorship as in, "Chappell Music's catalogue is studded with great show tunes."

**Catchall Clause** — Most record and songwriter contracts limit the liability of the record company and music publisher to pay royalties only with respect to those income sources specifically set forth in the contract. Since there are few psychic lawyers and an ever-burgeoning technology, it is wise to try to include a catchall clause at the end of the compensation clause. It should read: ". . . and fifty percent (50%) of all other income*, now known or hereafter to come into existence."

**Compulsory License** — Under the provisions of the United States Copyright Act, the copyright owner of a nondramatic musical work has the exclusive right to make and distribute phonorecords of such a work *until* a phonorecord of the work has been distributed to the public under authority of the copyright owner. After public distribution, any person may,

*from all other sources

by complying with the requirements of Section 115 of the Copyright Act, obtain a "compulsory license" to make and distribute phonorecords of the work. In other words, once a voluntary license is issued by the copyright owner, he can't stop anyone else from recording the song. The monopoly supposedly ends. Actually, compliance with the compulsory license provisions is so onerous that few would go this route unless they absolutely had to. When might one have to? When one has followed the tradition of recording first and licensing second, and has pressed and packaged a large quantity of albums containing the unlicensed song. When would a copyright owner refuse a voluntary license? Usually only when he finds the contemplated recording so aesthetically offensive as to be damaging to his valuable copyright.

**Controlled Composition** — In the parlance of record contracts, a controlled composition is one recorded under the contract and owned or controlled directly or indirectly (as through a corporation) by the artist, his producer, his wife, his parents, his aunts, uncles, cousins, children, or pets. Record companies compete for the most comprehensive and all-inclusive language in this clause. It seeks for the record company a reduced mechanical royalty (music publishing royalty as opposed to artists' recording royalty — don't confuse the two) with respect to controlled compositions and total exemption from mechanical royalties in those instances where there is no requirement to pay the artist a record royalty (for example, on records distributed for promotional purposes or on records given away free). It is a negotiable clause, but how well your lawyer does will be more a function of your clout than his skill (assuming he knows enough to fight like hell on this one). Artists with a track record can usually impose their will. Beginners may have to wait 'till the next time.

**Co-Publish(ing)** — The situation that arises when more than one publisher has acquired publishing rights to the same song. This is not at all uncommon, since collaboration in the writing of a song is anything but rare. If the lyricist is signed to one publisher and the music writer to another, both publishers own an *undivided* partial (depending on how the writers agree to share) interest in the song, and each can deal with the song as it sees fit, subject to sharing the income with its co-publisher and subject to an implied obligation not to "waste" or destroy wantonly the value of the copyright. Since each co-publisher can deal with respect to the song, neither can grant exclusive rights or licenses. Since exclusive rights result in the highest advances and other remuneration, it is usually beneficial for the co-publishers to enter into an agreement (a co-publishing agreement) governing how the song will be administered and exploited.

**Copyright ©** — A limited monopoly granted by Congress as an incentive to creators of certain literary and artistic works so that, subject to certain gobbledygook, they can control the destiny and enjoy the fruits of their creativity. It usually lasts for the life of the creator plus fifty years (séances are helpful). Did you know that you don't have to do anything to get a copyright on your song? That it's automatically granted you when you write your song? Well, it's true. See chapter 7 on copyright.

**Copyright Registration** — The legal formality by which the basic facts of a particular copyright are placed on public record. Registration is not a condition of copyright protection generally. Registration is, however, considered in the public interest; therefore the Copyright Act provides certain incentives to encourage registration. See chapter 7 on copyright.

**Coupling** — The practice of utilizing cuts or sides by different artists in conjunction with each other. Thus are made possible the plethora "best of" albums you see advertised on television. Your attorney will strive to bar or limit your record company's ability to thus use your recordings without your approval.

**Cover; Cover Record** — A recording by one artist of a song recorded and made popular by another artist. An artist covers a record he belives he can improve upon. Singer-songwriters who sing the definitive version of their songs are less often covered than singer-songwriters whose singing is weaker than their writing.

**Credit, Label** — There are two places where credits appear: on the label in the center of a record and on the liner notes on the album cover. While artists invariably receive both label and liner note credit, producers, if not protected in their contract, may find themselves relegated to the liner notes only. Why? Labels have little space, especially when an independent production company must also receive credit.

**Cross-Collateralization** — The application by a record company or music publisher of an artist's or songwriter's royalties from one source against unrecouped recording costs or advances from another. The novice is subjected to cross-collateralization in two situations. Beginning artists who sign record contracts with independent production companies are often required to simultaneously sign an exclusive songwriter contract with its affiliated music publishing company. The artist is very disappointed when songwriter royalties he is anticipating receiving are instead applied against advances or recording costs still unrecouped by the sister record company. The other cross-collateralization snare befalls the songwriter who from time to time assigns individual songs to a particular publisher. When at last he meets success and is looking forward finally to paying his lawyer, both he and the lawyer are chagrined to find the royalties applied against an unrecouped advance the writer received two years before and had forgotten about. The remedy is simple. If you ask for a "no-cross" clause, you will probably get it. The trick is to remember to ask.

**Crossover Record (or Artist)** — A record destined for a limited market, such as "R & B" or Country, that finds success in the pop market. After a few crossover records an artist may, to his delight, find himself a crossover artist: one whose career, though launched in a limited market, now enjoys across-the-board popularity. Diana Ross and Kenny Rogers come to mind.

**Cut in** — The interest and economic benefit derived from the practice of ascribing to a person (usually an artist) writer credit with respect to a song not written by that person. A cut in is usually extracted as a condition precedent to the artist recording the song in question. It is also applied to the practice of assigning a copyright interest in a song from one publisher to another for similar reasons. You may make any moral or ethical judgments you wish, but be assured they will become tempered with success.

**Cut out** — A record that has been deleted from a record company's active catalogue. An artist should strive to have a contractual provision barring his records from being cut out until a fixed period of time after release. Cutouts are sold at much reduced prices and do not add luster to the artist's reputation, especially if they are of recent vintage. To add injury to insult, no royalties are paid on records sold as cutouts.

# Dd

**Demo (Demonstration Record)** — A record made by an artist for the purpose of inducing a record company to record him; or by a songwriter or music publisher to induce an artist or producer to record the song "demoed." Demos must be tailored to your talent and their intended purpose. The demo studio is the graveyard of careers. That's why there is a chapter devoted to the demo. It's important. Study it.

**Derivative Rights** — The rights the Copyright Act of 1976 says remain with the publisher of a song after its writer has exercised his right of termination and has taken the song back. This Copyright Act of 1976 is so new that no one is quite sure what derivative rights are. Possible examples might be the right to continue to print and sell arrangements created by the publisher prior to termination, and the right to collect mechanical royalties derived from licences issued prior to termination. The question is being tested in the courts. Since a writer cannot exercise his right of termination for 35 years, there is optimism that the question will be resolved by the time you need to be concerned with it.

**Distribution** — The process by which a record finds its way from the studio where it was born to the ultimate consumer. Most major record companies have their own distribution systems, and distribute their own product and that of other record companies. Some companies rely on independent distributors. Distribution is a key factor in the success of a record company. Find a record company that doesn't have to worry about it.

**Domestic** — As used in conjunction with words such as "rights" and "sales," "domestic" is used to distinguish between the United States (and sometimes Canada) and the rest of the world, which is referred to as "foreign." For example: domestic sales as opposed to foreign sales.

**Drilled Records** — When a record company sells cutout records at a price much below its usual wholesale price, it literally drills a second hole through the label (and through the jacket). This is done to protect the record company from having the record returned for credit at the original or full wholesale price.

# Ee

**Earned** — Most record and publishing contracts have provisions whereby the artist or songwriter receives as part of his royalties a percentage of the record company's or publisher's income from certain sources. The word "earned" is usually inserted before the word "income" to relieve the record company or publisher from an obligation to pay a share of advances received by it over to the artist or writer until such time as portions of the advances are actually earned. This practice serves the record companies and publishers well on two levels: first, they retain the use of the artist's and songwriter's share of such advances for a period of time at what are today very substantial interest rates; and second, since advances are often paid with respect to entire catalogues, they avoid the problem of apportioning the advance among many artists or many writers, which apportionment would be speculative at best and would assuredly engender the enmity of certain of their artists or writers.

**Educational Music** — Usually printed editions of music arranged for and designed to be used by schools and other educational institutions, either for the purpose of teaching or for the needs of specialized users of music peculiar to schools, such as glee clubs, choirs, school orchestras, and marching bands.

**Employee for Hire** — Although a seemingly innocuous term, this one is fraught with ominous significance for songwriters. If it appears in one of your contracts, it should inspire a knee-jerk spasm in your colon (no small anatomical feat). The Copyright Act of 1976 provides that if you write a song as an employee for hire of a publisher, the publisher, *not you*, is considered the author for the purposes of the Copyright Act "and owns all of the rights comprised in the copyright." As an employee for hire you will have forfeited your right of termination, and neither you nor your heirs may look forward to the return of the song at the end of thirty-five years. If the song has become a standard, this is a very substantial economic loss. As might be expected, the Copyright Act of 1976 has prompted attorneys for music publishers to revise their songwriter contracts so as to cast their clients as employers for hire. You are forewarned!

**Engineer (Recording)** — An engineer has the responsibility for the technical (as opposed to artistic) content and excellence of a recording. He twists the knobs and adjusts the levels and does whatever else is necessary to assure that the tape reflects what the artist and the record producer wish captured. Engineers are usually employees of the studio in which they ply their craft, and many studios owe their clientele to the regard in which their engineers are held. Engineers often aspire to become producers — and do so.

**EP (EP record)** — Extended-play record. Usually a 10-inch 33 1/3 rpm record containing more songs than a single but fewer than an LP. Never before of commercial significance in the United States, EPs are popular elsewhere in the world, and are fast growing in importance in the United States.

**Exclusive; Exclusivity** — Exclusive means to the exclusion of all others. You will meet the term in the form of contract provisions making you a record company's exclusive recording artist, or a music publisher's exclusive songwriter, or making someone else your exclusive manager. Although there are songwriter agreements for individual songs, I have never come across a nonexclusive recording-artist agreement or management contract. For the duration of such exclusive contracts, you cannot record for another record company, assign songs to another music publisher, or use another manager.

**Execution (of a Contract)** — Legal jargon for the formal completion or signing of a contract. A contract drafted but not signed is termed "unexecuted." A fully signed contract is termed "executed."

# Ff

**First Record Sold; Payment from first record sold; Payment from first record sold after recoupment** — Traditionally, although the record company initially pays the costs of recording a record, such costs are charged against the artist's royalties, if and when earned, as if they were advances to the artist. When an individual producer is lured by a record company to produce an artist's record, he is paid a royalty on sales of that record. For obvious reasons the record company would prefer not to pay the producer a royalty until after it has recouped its recording costs. The scenario usually goes like this: the record company's first contract draft provides that the producer will receive a royalty only on those records sold after the record company has recouped its recording costs at the artist's royalty rate. The producer's attorney then takes the position that his client insists on receiving his royalty from the very first record sold. The usual compromise results in no royalty being paid to the producer until after the record company recoups its recording costs, at which point he receives his royalty retroactively from the first record sold. Whether the recoupment takes place at the artist's royalty rate or at the combined artist's plus producer's royalty rate (faster!) is the subject of additional negotiation. And you thought it was a simple business!

**Folio** — A bound collection of songs usually with some common element or theme. "Matching folios" parallel, or match, the contents of particular record albums and usually feature the same cover art. "Personality folios" contain songs, biographical material, and pictures associated with a particular artist and in-variably feature that artist on the cover.

**Foreign** — As used in conjunction with words such as "sales" or "rights," "foreign" is used to distinguish between the rest of the world and the United States (and sometimes Canada), which is referred to as "domestic." For example: foreign sales as opposed to domestic sales.

**Free Goods** — The term refers to records purportedly given away free by record companies to their customers in proportion to the number of records purchased by the customers—thereby providing the customer with an incentive to buy more records. Your record contract will provide that you will receive no royalty with respect to records distributed as free goods. It is incumbent upon your attorney to negotiate a limitation on the quantity of free goods the record company may distribute (usually 15% on albums and 30% on singles). Some record companies give no actual free goods, but, instead, reduce their wholesale price by the percentage provided for in the artist's free-goods clause. Such companies nevertheless withhold the artist's royalties as if free goods were in fact given. Where is the sales incentive, in such instances, that is supposed to justify withholding the artist's royalties? The point hasn't been litigated *yet*.

It is important to note the distinction between free goods and other records given away free for promotional purposes, such as those given to disc jockeys to induce air play.

**Front Money** — Another term for "advance." Your lawyer will need little inspiration to pursue front money for you. It is often the only money he can look to for the payment of his fees.

# Gg

**Gig** — A single professional engagement usually of short duration; a play date. Of jazz origin, gig has come to mean a job, even one not related to music.

**Gold Record** — A gold *album* is one certified by the RIAA (look under "R") as having had a minimum sale of 500,000 units. A gold *single* is one certified by the

RIAA as having had a minimum sale of 1,000,000 units.

**Grand Performing Rights** — "Dramatic" rights as opposed to "nondramatic" rights, which are known as "small performing" rights. Simple? Were it so! Unfortunately, it has yet to be determined with any degree of consistency what constitutes a grand performance. The distinction between grand and small rights is important because if the use to be made is small, the user's already existing ASCAP or BMI license is all that is needed. If a grand right is involved, a separate license must be negotiated, at additional cost, with the owner of the copyright of the song being used. The courts have from time to time held different and conflicting views as to what constitutes the exercise of a grand right. Different criteria have been applied, such as whether costumes and scenery were used, whether the song was woven into and carried forward the plot. What is thought to be the better view, although it does not dispose of the question, is that a performance of a song is dramatic (grand) if it aids in telling a story; otherwise it is nondramatic (small). In the negotiation of a songwriter contract it is often possible, and always desirable, to reserve to the author the grand performing rights.

**Gross Income** — The total income from a source without deduction of expenses or other costs of earning that income. Gross income less such expenses and costs is known as "net income."

# Hh

**Harry Fox (The Harry Fox Agency, Inc.)** — The Harry Fox Agency issues licenses on behalf of its music publisher clients for the use of their songs on phonograph records (mechanical licenses) and in connection with motion pictures, commercials, television films, and video tapes (synchronization licenses). It also collects and distributes to its clients the income from such licenses. Harry Fox charges a commission for its services which ranges from 5% to 3½% of gross collections with respect to mechanical licenses and up to 10% in connection with synchronization licenses.

# Ii

**Independent Producer** — An independent producer or independent production company can be thought of as a mini record company in that it discovers talent, signs artists to record contracts, and produces the artist's records. Because it lacks the financial and personnel resources of large record companies, it cannot manufacture, distribute, or promote its product. Often it cannot afford recording costs. Consequently, it must obtain those services from a large record company. The usual route is for the independent producer to produce a demo or a few master quality sides of an artist's performances and to "pitch" these to a record company, which, if it is "sold," will enter into an independent production contract with the independent producer. The record company will provide the funding for an album and its manufacturing, distribution, and promotional services. The independent producer will provide the exclusive recording services of the artist for a period of time measured by years or albums delivered and its production services, in exchange for which it will receive a royalty on records sold. The independent producer pays the artist's royalties out of the royalty it receives. There are infinite variations on this theme, some of which we will explore later on.

**Individual Producer** — The person who oversees the actual studio recording by the artist. He acts as the artist's coach and director, plans the recording sessions, and helps choose the songs to be recorded. He bears the responsibility for the artistic and commercial quality of the recordings made and for completing them within a pre-scribed budget. Great producers are rare, highly compensated, and in great demand. They receive a royalty on records sold and quite often substantial advances.

**Infringement of Copyright** — Anyone who violates any of the exclusive rights of a copyright owner under the Copy-right Act is an infringer of the copyright. Infringement makes available to the copy-right owner one or more of the following remedies: an injunction against further infringement, impoundment of infringing articles, damages and the profits of the infringer, and costs and attorney's fees. In addition, there are infringements that constitute criminal offenses and are pun-ishable by fine and/or imprisonment. I have observed that my clients consider it an infringement of their copyrights when someone else's work bears the slightest resemblance to one of their copyrighted songs—as opposed to an unconscious, subliminal, and minimal borrowing of public-domain material when the shoe is on the other foot. Infringement is "law-yer country" and need not be pursued further here.

# Jj

**Jingle** — Jingles are musical composi-tions written for, and as part of, advertis-ing material. The writing and singing of jingles can be a sustaining source of income for aspiring songwriters and artists. Barry Manilow, Melissa Manchester, and Ashford and Simpson are just a few of the "names" who supported themselves by doing jingles until they made it. Some jingles you may recall are: "*You Deserve a Break Today,*" "*Have a Coke and a Smile,*" "*Fly the Friendly Skies,*" "*It's the Real Thing.*"

**Joint Work** — A joint work, according to the Copyright Act, " is a work prepared by two or more authors with the inten-tion that their contributions be merged into inseparable or interdependent parts of a unitary whole." If you, a composer, write a song with a collaborator who is the lyricist, you both jointly own the resulting song. You own an undivided half-interest in his lyric and he owns an undivided half-interest in your music. The two are "merged." If, however, a piece of instrumental music had been in existence for some time and the copy-right owner caused you to write a lyric for it, the question of who owns and can exercise dominion over the separate elements and the combined elements is still subject to judicial determination. See *Co-Publishing*.

# Kk

**K-Tel** — K-Tel Music, Ltd. pioneered the practice of licensing record masters from different companies and creating compilation albums. With the aid of extensive TV advertising, the resulting albums were marketed by mail order and through chain stores. The concept proved so successful that K-Tel's name became an almost generic term for that type of record. See *Coupling*.

# Ll

**Lead Sheet** — A copy of a song con-taining the melody line, the lyrics, and no-tations indicating the harmonic struc-ture. Prior to the Copyright Act of 1976, lead sheets were required to register a song for copyright. Under the Copyright Act of 1976 a recording can be filed in lieu of a lead sheet.

**Liner Notes** — The copy on the back or inside cover of a record album. "Liner notes" are a nice thing to have "approval" of. They afford you an opportunity to say thanks to people who ordinarily do not receive credit—your musicians, the engineers, background singers, etc. I will confess to an inordinate amount of pleasure at finding I was "executive producer" (without justification) of a client's album. People, including lawyers, love to see their names in print.

**Liquidation (of reserves)** — In the United States, records (and to a lesser extent printed music) are sold on the basis of "a 100% return privilege." If a record seller has bought one hundred copies of your album and it "bombs" and he is left with ninety-five copies, he can return the ninety-five copies to your record company for full credit against his outstanding bill or against future purchases. All record contracts provide that the record company can withhold from the artist's (or producer's) royalties "a reserve for returns." The record company does this so that it will not find that it has paid out royalties that subsequently prove, by virtue of extensive returns, to be unearned. High interest rates provide an incentive to record companies to be quite conservative (pessimistic) in setting up their reserves against returns. It is therefore incumbent upon your attorney to limit the amount of that reserve to a "reasonable" amount or to a

specific percentage of the records shipped (30% is about right for albums and 50% is permissible for singles, which are considered a promotional device more than a profit producer). It is even more important that your attorney provide for the liquidation (the payment to the artist of the unused portion) of the reserve after a specific period of time. Three accounting periods (1½ years) after the reserve is set up is usually acceptable to both sides. Reserves usually provide fertile ground for your accountant to till while conducting an audit of the record company's books. This is a long section of the lexicon, but it will also serve to explain *reserves* and *returns* . . . so read it again!

**Litigation** — A lawsuit. Although the subject of much posturing, relatively few lawsuits are instituted or progress beyond the initial stages. The risks and expense to both sides usually result in a settlement, either before the suit is started or before the trial itself is commenced. Keep in mind that in the United States, unlike England, the "winner" is not usually awarded attorney's fees. There goes your "profit"!

**Loanout** — Often, for tax purposes, it is recommended that an artist or songwriter act through a corporation he owns or controls. In such instances the artist or songwriter enters into a personal-services contract with his corporation, which then enters into a contract with the record company or music publisher whereby it "loans out" the artist's or songwriter's services. That contract is called a "loanout agreement."

# Mm

**Manager, Business** — If you are lucky, you will have need of this chap down the road. He is the expert you will call upon to structure and manage your financial empire. It's his job to make sure you don't end up as the Joe Louis of the music business. Business managers usually have an accounting background and may serve as accountants and business managers.

**Manager, Personal** — The person charged with the responsibility for molding and overseeing an artist's professional and artistic career . . . the Henry Higgins to your Liza! Your manager can be your salvation or your destruction. This is the key relationship of an artist's career and worthy of the chapter it receives. See Chapter 5.

**Master (Record)** — The finished, mixed, and polished tape from which the parts necessary to manufacture records are made. It is the ultimate synthesization of everything you've done in the studio.

**Matching Folio** — See *Folio.*

**Mechanical Royalty; Mechanicals** — The royalty payable to a copyright owner for the use of its song on a phonograph record. The first "records" were piano rolls for player pianos. These were referred to as "mechanical devices" under the Copyright Act of 1909—hence the term "mechanical royalty." Although player pianos are almost gone, as is the word "mechanical" from the new Copyright Act, the term "mechanical royalties," or "mechanicals," persists in the record industry. Mechanical royalties can be either "statutory" or "negotiated." Statutory royalties are those prescribed by the Copyright Act for those who wish to avail themselves of its compulsory licensing provision. The copyright owner and the user may, and often do, agree to abide by the statutory royalty rate (in cents) without invoking the compulsory license provisions. When the user negotiates a mechanical royalty rate that is less than the statutory royalty rate, the user is said to have received a "rate." A mechanical royalty rate can be negotiated on two levels: a diminution of the statutory rate and/or by exempting from the calculation of royalties certain classes of records, such as records distributed free.

Under the Copyright Act of 1909 the basic statutory rate was 2¢ per song. Under the 1976 Act it was 2¾¢. In 1981 it was raised by the Copyright Royalty Tribunal to 4¢. No, there was no increase from 1909 to 1976! In January 1983 it will be raised to 4¼ ¢ . The statutory royalty rate is subject to continuing change by the Copyright Royalty Tribunal. For the sake of simplicity, we shall assume throughout this book a statutory mechanical royalty of 4¢.

**Mixing; Mixing Down** — The combining or blending of all the "tracks" made during the recording of a record into the final master recording. Most new studios now have the capability to record on sixty-four separate tracks.

**MOR** — Middle of the road. This is mellow popular music, usually ballads or melodic instrumental music—the music your parents enjoy.

# Nn

**Name And Likeness** — The term used to describe the exclusive right of an artist, songwriter, or other personality to grant to others the right to use his name and picture in connection with the commercial exploitation or marketing of products or services. A typical example would be the licensing by an artist to a music publisher of the right to use the artist's picture and name on the cover of a personality folio.

**Net Income** — See *Gross Income.*

**New Copyright Act** — The Copyright Act of 1976 (which became effective in 1978). Usually the term is used to distinguish the 1976 Act from the 1909 Act. The 1976 Act will probably be referred to as "new" until the next copyright act is promulgated—probably in 2043, if the past is precedent.

# Oo

**Old Copyright Act** — See *New Copyright Act.*

**One Hundred Percent Of Sales** — The old 78 rpm records were heavy and brittle. Some invariably broke in transit. The shards were expensive to return for credit. The practice therefore evolved of factoring a 10% "breakage allowance" into the record company's invoice. The artist, with justification, was paid a royalty on only 90% of the records sold. In 1948 the vinyl, unbreakable record was introduced. Invoicing at 100% of sales resumed. Payment of royalties at 90% of sales persisted and still persists in some record company contracts to this day. If your attorney requests "payment on 100% of sales," it will rarely be refused. The record company's representative may even blush.

**One Nighter** — A gig that is limited to one night.

**Option** — Although there are other options, the one you will be primarily concerned with is the record company's or music publisher's option to extend a contract for additional periods of time should they, *not you*, choose to do so. Most record contracts proffered new artists provide for an initial term of one year with four consecutive options, whereby the record company may extend the term for up to four more years (a total of five years). Of late record deals are being cast in terms of albums rather than years. The same principle applies. Record companies utilize this structure to avoid the obligation to spend more money on additional recordings and annual advances should they lose faith in an artist's ability to be a commercial success. Understandably, they won't sign an artist for just one year, lest they "break" him only to find themselves in a bidding war with their competitors for the artist's future services. Songwriter contracts do not usually have option provisions unless the publisher is required to pay an annual advance. When you have some clout as an artist or songwriter, you can insist on "firm" (that is, no options) deals.

# Pp

℗ — The symbol for copyright to be incorporated in the copyright notice appearing on phonorecords of sound recordings. The notice should also contain the year of first publication of the sound recording and the name of the copyright owner. It will be found on the record label: ℗ XYZ Record Co. 1983. It is the record company's problem, not yours, since it is their copyright. Your demos should not bear a notice, because they are not "published" in the context of the Copyright Act. You need not worry about a ℗ being included on a record to protect the underlying song. The ℗ is only fixed to visually perceived copies of published versions. If, however, your lyrics are printed on the album cover, they should be accompanied by a © copyright notice.

**PA** — Personal appearance.

**Packaging Costs** — Purportedly, the costs of the jacket in which your album will be marketed. They are set forth in your record contract as a percentage of the retail or wholesale selling price of the album, depending upon which price your royalty is based. They rarely bear any relationship to the actual costs of packaging, and are much higher than such actual cost. This is especially so when an album is successful and one-time costs such as artwork can be spread over many records.

| | |
|---|---|
| $7.98 | album retail selling price |
| -1.59 | packaging deduction/ |
| | (20%, assuming a cassette) |
| $6.39 | |
| x    5% | your royalty rate |
| $ .32 | your royalty? |

Well, almost. There are other deductions factored in, such as "free goods" that we need not go into at this time. The packaging deduction varies from company to company and is not subject to much negotiation, especially at your stage of the game. The record companies take the position that it all "washes"; that it's the way the industry grew and that if they lowered the packaging deduction, they would have to lower the artist's royalty rate to emerge with an acceptable profit. When you're a star, you can negotiate for a dollars-and-cents royalty on a per-album basis and avoid "shrinkage" in the record company's accounting division. If you read your record contract, you will note that packaging costs are deducted from the retail (or wholesale) price before applying your royalty rate to it.

**Pass** — Congratulations? Wrong! In the music business, "pass" means fail, as in: "Although the artist has talent, we do not hear a hit single, so we'll pass at this time. When the artist has additional material, please do not hesitate to . . . " Record companies never just say "Ugh!"

**Pass Through** — This expression characterizes a contract or a contract provision whereby one party "passes on" to the other party the benefits contained in an already existing contract. It is a device most often used by independent producers who sometimes pass through to an artist the benefits of the independent producer's negotiations with the record company, or pass through to an individual producer the benefits of the artist's contract with the independent producer. The device avoids embarrassment to lawyers and shortens a 40-page agreement to three pages, since the royalty provisions of the prior contract are "incorporated by reference." Whether a pass-through arrangement is requested or granted depends on the relative strengths of the parties. For example, a very "heavy" producer who is engaged to produce an unknown artist may well feel he can negotiate a better contract than the artist could extract from the independent producer. In such an instance, the producer would be disdainful of a pass-through provision.

**Performing Rights** — The exclusive rights granted by the Copyright Act to copyright owners of certain works, including musical works, to perform their copyrighted works publicly.

**Performing Rights Societies** — Organizations, such as ASCAP and BMI, that license to users, on behalf of copyright owners of songs, the right to perform their songs publicly. See *ASCAP* and *Public Performance Right*.

**Personality Folio** — See *Folio*.

**Platinum Record** — A platinum *album* is one certified by the RIAA as having had sales of 1,000,000 units. A platinum *single* is one certified by the RIAA as having had sales of 2,000,000 units.

**Points** — Royalty percentage points. In lieu of saying "3% of the retail selling price," the more Runyonesque might opt for "3 pernts."

**Pop** — Derived from the word "popular," "Pop" refers to that genre of music appealing to the largest listening audience. Pop music is generally youth-oriented and targeted for Top Forty play lists and AM radio. Pop can best be described by what it isn't, for example, jazz, AOR, Country, MOR, R & B, Adult Contemporary, or Hard Rock. A song initially characterized as belonging to one of the catagories other than Pop can become Pop if it "catches on" and "crosses over."

**Power Of Attorney** — This has nothing to do with your lawyer's ability. A "power of attorney" is what you give to another person (or business entity) when you authorize and empower him to act for you and in your place, for example, to sign a contract for you. There are limited powers of attorney and general powers of attorney. They are what their names imply.

Rule 1.  Never sign a general power of attorney. Not even for Mom!

Rule 2.  Same as Rule 1.

Rule 3.  Same as Rule 2.

There are two limited powers of attorney that are legitimate and justified. The first is the one in your songwriter contract that makes the publisher your attorney to sign necessary documents to perfect the copyrights you assigned to the publisher, if you are not available or if you refuse to do so. The second is a power of attorney to your manager to sign contracts for short-term personal appearances when you are unavailable to do so yourself. Most management contracts, which are traditionally prepared by the manager's attorney, contain general powers of attorney whereby, if he chose to do so, your manager could sign you to a ten-year recording contract. Such powers are abusive and entirely unnecessary. They should be deleted.

**Premium Records** — These are not better-quality records, but, rather, records that are given away with a product to induce sales of that product. The usual record contract provides that the record company may do this. It will also provide that the record company may pay you a much reduced royalty with respect to such records. There are many products on the market with which you may not wish your name or records associated. It is therefore up to your attorney to cause the record company to surrender the right to use your records for premium purposes or to give you an *absolute* right of approval. This is a situation where "not to be unreasonably withheld" is not acceptable.

**Print, Print Rights** — Printed copies of musical compositions as typified by sheet music; folios; collections; teaching, band, choral, and orchestral editions; books, and an almost infinite variety of other forms. Although somewhat eclipsed by mechanical and performance income, print is a highly underrated source of income for songwriters and publishers.

**Producer** — See *Individual Producer.*

**Product** — The creative output of a record company or independent producer, as in "We'll talk about a deal after I hear the product."

**Promotional Records** — Records distributed for no charge by record companies to disc jockeys, radio and television stations, trade publications, magazines and newspapers and similar media outlets to stimulate interest in and sales of a record. Promotional records should be distinguished from so-called free goods, which are purportedly given by record companies to their customers for sales-incentive purposes. No royalties are paid to an artist with respect to promotional records.

**Public Domain (PD) Works** — This is generally how your lawyer characterizes the music you've been accused of infringing. Actually, PD works are works that do not enjoy copyright protection. Works may attain this status in a variety of ways. They could have been created before copyright protection was available. The copyright owner may have failed to observe a formality under the old copyright act or "blown" the renewal under the old act. Or the copyright may have expired by passage of time. Caution, however, must be observed if you intend to use a public domain work. There were extensions of the copyright term under the old act, which make the expiration date of certain copyrights a matter of conjecture. In addition, there are copyrights in arrangements that survive the underlying song's copyright.

**Public Performance Right** — The Copyright Act grants to the copyright owners of certain works the exclusive right to perform the copyrighted work publicly. Musical works are included but sound recordings are not. Hence the copyright owner of a song on a record would be entitled to compensation for public performance, but the copyright owner of the sound recording (the record itself) would not be. To perform a work publicly means performing it at a place open to the public or at a place where a substantial number of persons outside of a normal circle of a family and its social acquaintances is gathered. The definition also includes transmission of a performance by any means or device to such a place or to the public. "Perform" includes live face-to-face renditions, renditions from recordings, broadcasting, transmissions by cable, microwaves, etc.

**Publication** — This ordinary word owes its place in this lexicon to the Copyright Act. Many things in the Copyright Act, such as the copyright notice date, and the loss of certain rights, are keyed to the date of publication of the copyrighted work. The Copyright Act of 1976 defines publication as "the distribution of copies or phonorecords of a work to the public by sale or other transfer of ownership, or by rental, lease or lending. The offering to distribute phonorecords to a group of persons for purposes of further distribution, public performance, or public display, constitutes publication. A public performance or display of a work does not of itself constitute publication."

**Publisher's Share** — The income from a song retained by a music publisher after paying the writer his share. In the traditional deal where the writer assigns 100% of the copyright in a song to a publisher, the writer's royalty is supposedly equal to the publisher's share of income. Publishers have rather universally maintained an "edge." That advantage is in the area of sheet music (and to a lesser extent in other printed editions), where, although the publisher receives 35¢ or 40¢ from its print publisher, it still offers only 6¢ to 10¢ to the writer. This is negotiable, but not usually up to the vicinity of 50%. It is wise to ask for 50% of the publisher's profit from print—with a tight definition of the word "profit."

**Publishing** — This term has come to mean ownership of the copyright of a song. When you make your first deal, your friends will ask "Did you have to give publishing?" Your answer will be either "No" or "Yes, but . . ." If your answer is yes, they will shake their heads mournfully and seemingly knowingly. Sometimes you just have to give to get. It's known as paying dues. If you're good, you won't have to give for long, and if your lawyer is good, you'll get it back in time for your "prime of life" via the thirty-five-year right of termination.

# Rr

**R & B** — Rhythm and Blues, Black music.

**Rate** — See *Mechanical Royalty*.

**Recording Budget** — Pursuant to the terms of an individual producer's contract with a record company or independent producer, he is usually required to prepare and submit for approval a detailed budget setting forth what the project will cost. This will include studio time, musicians, arrangers, instrument rental, background singers, etc. In dealing with independent producers, record companies will sometimes waive a detailed budget and stipulate a sum as the recording budget. Then it is the responsibility of the independent producer to bring the record "in" under the budget or to pay the excess. Usually, as a practical matter, the record company picks up the excess, too. After all, what good is two-thirds of an album?

**Recording Costs** — The costs of making a recording. Since all recording costs are charged as advances against the artist's royalties, the record company's contracts have very comprehensive recording-costs clauses. In general, they include all costs of recording that are not part of the manufacturing process—and two that arguably are. These are mixing and mastering. If your lawyer screams, he may get a split: they may delete mastering.

**Recoupable** — This word invariably precedes or follows the word "advance." It means that when the record company or music publisher gives you an advance, they can recoup it from, or get it back from, your royalties.

**Recoupment** — If you become an individual producer, you will find the first draft of your contract will state that you will not receive royalties until "after recoupment of all recording costs." Whether there's a second draft, and how it reads, will depend on your bargaining strength and your representation. See *Individual Producer*.

**Release Commitment** — There isn't any fun in having a record deal, or making a record, if your friends and relatives never see it or hear it—and, even less money. First-draft record contracts usually state that the record company's only liability in the event they don't record you is to pay you union scale for sides not recorded; and they can keep you under contract! It is incumbent upon you to make sure your contract states that if a certain minimum amount of product (usually one LP) is not recorded *and* commercially released during the initial term, the record company may not exercise its option for a second year. At least then you are free to seek out a record company where you will be more appreciated.

**Reserve Against Returns** — See *Mechanical Royalty.*

**Retail Selling Price (RSP)** — Most records don't have a marked retail selling price. Since your royalty may be based upon your record's "retail selling price" it is important that some standard be established in your contract. Since retail selling prices are constantly rising, one would not wish a fixed dollar amount in the contract. The usual solution is to insert "suggested" before retail selling price. For each wholesale price there is an industry-accepted "suggested" retail price; hence some standard is effected. Many record companies are now abandoning even suggesting an RSP, and it appears that wholesale price will replace retail selling price as a royalty standard.

**Returns** — See *Mechanical Royalty.*

**Reversionary Rights** — Rights that come back to their grantor upon the hap-pening of a certain event or failure. For example, a contract may provide that the copyright in a song will revert to the writer in the event that the publisher fails to secure a commercially released recording within a prescribed period of time. Similarly, under the Copyright Act, a writer may terminate a grant after thirty-five years, whereupon the copyright reverts to him.

**RIAA (The Recording Industry Association of America)** — The main trade association of the record industry. In general it looks to the welfare of the record industry and serves as its spokesman in lobbying for legislation favorable to the record companies. It also sets the standards for, and certifies gold and platinum records.

**Royalties** — Compensation to the grantor of a right based on a portion of the income derived from the right. We're primarily interested in artist's and writer's royalties for the right to use the artist's performance and the writer's song.

# Ss

**Scale; Union Scale** — The minimum payment a user of talent is required to pay the talent under the rules of the particular union having jurisdiction. If you are a musician, the record company or independent producer is required to pay you scale for your services during recording sessions. If you are receiving an advance, your agreement will state that the scale payments are part of the advance. If you receive no advance, the scale payments will be part of the "recording costs" and recoupable from your royalties.

**Showcase** — A personal appearance (usually orchestrated by your manager) at a club to which record companies and publishers are invited to send A & R people to see how damn good you are before an audience. Your charisma quotient is important to record companies as a measure of your touring ability and sales potential. Many record companies, even if enamored of a demo, won't sign an act until they see the act perform live.

**Sideman Provision** — All record contracts are exclusive. There may, however, be occasions when you wish to perform as an instrumental musician (sideman) on another artist's record, either as a source of income or as an accommodation. To be able to do so you will require permission from your record company. It is easier to have such a clause inserted during the initial negotiation of your contract. A sideman provision usually requires that your performances will not be featured and that you will receive no credit or credit no more prominent than any other sideman.

**Sight & Sound** — Records or devices embodying both sound and visual images. See *Audio-Visual Rights.*

**Small Performing Rights** — See *Grand Performing Rights.*

**Song Sharks** — "Operators" who through small ads in small magazines offer for large fees to copyright your song, print it, and attempt to have it recorded. They may even offer to set your lyric to music. No legitimate music publishers function this way. One might characterize these operations as scams. Many a family has enjoyed macaroni dinners over protracted periods of time as a result of a song shark's efforts.

**Soul** — R & B, Black music.

**Sound Recording** — This is the magic expression in the Copyright Act that finally, in 1971, gave copyright protection to recorded works. Sound recordings are defined as works that result from the fixation of a series of sounds (excluding those accompanying motion pictures or other audio-visual works) regardless of the nature of the material objects in which they are embodied. "Phonorecords" under the Copyright Act are the material objects, such as discs and cassettes, from which the sounds can be perceived.

**Source, at the** — Music-publishing contracts usually provide that the writer receive 50% of the publisher's income from territories outside the U.S. and Canada. It has been not uncommon for the U.S. publisher to assign its foreign rights to an affiliated company in the United Kingdom under an assignment which provided that the United Kingdom publisher would pay 50% of its income to the U.S. publisher. The United Kingdom publisher then assigned rights country by country to its affiliated publishers, similarly providing for the payments to the United Kingdom publisher of 50% of the income. Thus, if a song earned a dollar in Germany, the German subpublisher sent 50¢ to the United Kingdom publisher, who, in turn, sent 25¢ to the U.S. publisher, who, in turn, sent 12½¢ to the writer—instead of the 25¢ the writer was anticipating. Finally, writers' lawyers got smart and insisted on inserting "at the source" at appropriate places in publishers' contracts. The writer now got his quarter instead of 12½¢, and "Mister In-Between" began to fade. But beware! Although some publisher's contracts have "source" language, others do not.

**Staff Writer** — A songwriter who is employed by a music publisher. He usually receives a salary and a place to work in the publisher's office. A staff writer is a true employee for hire, and the publisher is usually the "author" of what the staff writer creates in the course of his employment. Relatively few publishers engage staff writers nowadays.

**Standard, A** — A song of great renown and enduring popularity; for example, "Stardust." One standard puts the kids through college and provides you with country-club membership for life. If you write one, you'll probably write more.

**Standard, as in Standard Contract** — From time to time you will be presented with printed form contracts bearing the word "standard" in their titles; for example, "Standard Songwriters Contract." Regard this as an attempt by the party proffering such a contract to seduce you into believing that "everyone" signs that same contract and that you needn't "worry about it" or try to better its terms. The word "standard" is also often used to describe a clause or provision you may question. Don't be intimidated by the word "standard." In your business, nothing is standard and everything is mutable.

**Statutory Royalty** — See *Mechanical Royalty.*

**Studio Musician** — A musician who earns his livelihood by playing on record dates.

# Tt

**Term** — The duration of a contract. For example, for a three-year exclusive songwriter contract, the term is three years.

**Termination, Right of** — The right under the new Copyright Act of the grantor of rights (songwriter) to terminate the grant at the end of thirty-five years, regardless of the terms of the grant. Even if a songwriter assigns his song to the grantee (music publisher) for the duration of copyright (the life of the songwriter plus fifty years), he can still terminate at the end of thirty-five years. The right of termination does not exist if, however, the song was written as an employee for hire. If the right of termination is exercised, the music publisher is left with only derivative rights. See *Employee for Hire* and *Derivative Rights*.

**Tight** — Unrelated to alcohol consumption, this term is used to describe a band that is really well rehearsed and playing exceptionally well.

**Top Forty** — Usually the first forty songs on the Pop charts. Most AM Pop stations play a fixed number of songs, repeating them at fixed intervals throughout the day. Stations whose play lists consist of the first forty or so songs on the Pop charts are called "Top Forty" stations. "Top Forty" has also become an adjective to describe a Pop song that has a good chance of attaining a high chart position.

**Tour** — A series of concerts or personal appearances through a geographic territory—U.S. tour, European tour, etc. A tour usually corresponds to the release of an album and is usually a device to promote sales of that album. Visits to and interviews by local radio stations usually are part of the tour routine. "Tour support" is the financial aid the record company gives (or advances) to support a tour.

**Trades** — The magazines devoted to the music business. Notably, *Cash Box* and *Billboard*. Read them. Although subscriptions are expensive, perhaps your library subscribes. They are also found in the reception areas of music publishers, record companies, and entertainment lawyers. Hang out.

# Uu

**Union Scale** — See *Scale*.

**Unpublished Work** — A work that has not been published in the context of the Copyright Act. See *Publication*.

# Ww

**Wholesale Price** — The price at which a record company sells records to its customers. It varies a bit from company to company and is subject to some manipulation. In general, it is approximately half of the suggested retail selling price. Artist's royalties are keyed accordingly; hence the numerical royalty given by a company that pays on wholesale will be twice that of a company that pays on retail. For example, 10% WSP roughly equals 5% RSP.

**Writer's Share** — That portion of the income from a song that the publisher pays to the writer under the pertinent songwriter contract; the writer's royalties. See *Publisher's Share*.

*Merry Christmas! May I see your ASCAP License?*

# I

# *Pennies From Heaven*

Music by Arthur Johnston
Lyrics by Johnny Burke
© 1936 Chappell and Co., Inc.

I t is an inescapable fact that it is essential to have at least a rudimentary comprehension of the economics of the music industry in order to understand the forces at play while you try to break in. This is true no matter how idealistic you may be, no matter how devoted you may be to your music, and no matter how insignificant financial reward may seem relative to your hunger to be heard or to have your songs heard. So find an uncomfortable chair and "listen up."

Never easy, it is now more difficult than ever to break in as a songwriter or recording artist. In the late 1970s, after enjoying an unprecedented boom and expansion during the 60s and early 70s, the record industry experienced the fall for which it had been riding. Earlier, with no end to the good times in sight, clever managers and lawyers had been able to seduce or coerce record companies into bidding wars for established artists, which resulted in low-profit, high-risk deals. Whether it was due to a lack of new and exciting talent, record piracy, the facility with which home taping could be accomplished, or just inflation and a failing economy, record sales plummeted. The low-margin deals made with the artists who were still selling records didn't provide enough ballast for many record companies to ride out the storm. Record companies folded, independent producers closed their doors, and a lot of good people, from company presidents on down, found themselves seeking new employment. As a natural result, the market for new songs dried up, and the music publishers, especially those without catalogues of established copyrights, often suffered the fate of their colleagues in the record industry. Retailers searched their basements, warehouses, and shelves for salvation in the form of records to return to the record companies for credit against their accounts payable. Many of the records thus returned were excellent recordings by established stars, which, in the halcyon days gone by, would have been retained in inventory in the valid belief that they would ultimately be sold. But the wolf was at the door, and returns inundated the record companies. In one year, returns approaching one year's total industry output found their way back to the record companies' warehouses. Desperate for cash, many record companies dumped their returns into the marketplace at ridiculous prices. Sometimes this was done even though prohibited by contract. In one instance, thousands of eight-track cartridges of an established artist were sold by a major record company for a nickel apiece.

Thus, the suicide cycle was completed. An abundance of high-quality product was available to the consumer at bargain prices. With money tight, many record buyers took advantage of the plethora of records by established artists at bargain prices rather than risk their shrunken dollars on new and still unproven artists.

Apparently flies, boils, and pestilence were not enough. As in the case of the Egyptians of Biblical times, another plague was deemed necessary to drive the message home to the record companies. The locusts were provided by the radio stations, the arbiters of what music is played, what we listen to, what sells, and, consequently, who will be the stars of tomorrow. The radio stations' already limited play lists were further trimmed. Stations that were already down to forty or fifty records a day reduced their lists until some were playing only twenty-five songs a day. And these cuts reflected a trend toward conservatism. The stations "got on" the "A" sides of super groups and established artists—the records they were sure their audiences and therefore their advertisers would appreciate. There was damn little room to take a shot on a new artist. The competition for the few available slots for new artists was brutal, and a lot of good artists and a lot of good songs never had a chance to win acceptance. The situation was further aggravated by the advent and apparent success of stations with a format exclusively of "oldies but goodies" records.

The record companies were taking a beating on new artists, and many, exercising business prudence, felt that their promotion dollars were better spent "bringing home" records by established artists, where the odds were more favorable.

Having reaped what they had sown, the record industry took stock. A wave of conservatism engulfed the industry, and signings of new artists dropped dramatically. For a new act to be signed, almost universal agreement by the A & R department and a high degree of company-wide excitement and enthusiasm had to be present. Whereas in the past a "could be" artist often got a record deal, now he had to be a "sure." Even with signings limited to what the record companies believe to be sures, it remains to be seen whether the record companies' batting average will rise much above the 18% success rate they enjoyed in the past. As you may surmise, the deals being offered new artists are not extravagant.

What does this mean to you? Tempted to break your pencils or sell your guitar? Well, if you are, perhaps you should. It is clear that the laws of natural selection are going to be more heavily enforced. Only the best *and* the strongest will emerge as the stars of tomorrow. Note the "and." It is not going to be enough for you to be talented. You will also have to be incredibly hungry for success, tough as nails, and uncommonly tenacious and determined to make it in today's music business.

Frustrated by hours of fruitless listening, a record company A & R man once slammed a cassette to the floor of his office and exclaimed, "When the hell are they (meaning you) going to realize that this isn't a hobby!" He was registering frustration over the welter of "garbage" he had to wade through in the course of a day. A litany of complaints followed, including: tapes so bad technically that if they contained "Stardust" there would be no way of knowing; tapes containing such patently impoverished pap that he couldn't hit the eject button fast enough; the good idea stillborn; the lyric in search of a melody, and the melody bereft of a worthy lyric. What he was really saying was that there is a pervasive lack of professionalism demonstrated by those aspiring to be recording artists and songwriters.

Well, if it isn't a hobby, it must be a business. Business means money. Perhaps a businesslike attitude can be inspired by discussing money, music money, as it relates to you.

Myopia, the inability to focus on distant objects, is not a condition that confronts only ophthalmologists. In its nontechnical context, short-sightedness is also a concern to those who deal with not yet established artists and songwriters. Very often an artist can't understand why a record company won't risk the modest advance and meager recording budget it would take to give him his chance. Looking through the wrong end of the telescope, he doesn't realize that those expenditures are just the tip of the iceberg for the record company. The artist is oblivious to the costs the record company must incur in order to transform the masters he records into the records he eyes enviously in the racks of the local record store.

Each released album by a new artist involves an investment of approximately $250,000 by the record company. On top of the advance (if any) and recording costs, there are the costs of pressing an initial quantity of albums (usually 30-50,000), and the obligatory single, preparing the cover art, manufacturing jackets, shrink-wrapping, packing and shipping the records, distribution, and, last but not least, promotion—without which a record, like the tree falling in an uninhabited forest, doesn't make any noise. Of course some costs diminish relatively when amortized over large sales. The cost of a one-time item such as cover art becomes of small moment when it is for a platinum album, but one must appreciate the considerable risk a record company takes whenever it commits itself to an album for an untried artist— especially when they bet wrong 80% of the time. Why do the record companies take such risks? The question is almost rhetorical. The answer is obvious. When they bet right, the profits are large enough to cover the wrong bets and still pay a dividend to the stockholders.

As interesting as the problems of the record companies may be, I suspect you are more interested in how your income is going to be derived from your activities as a singer and/or songwriter.

Let's turn the clock ahead and assume you are a singer-songwriter whose first LP has been out about six weeks. Your recording contract is with a small label, which, because of its size, didn't have to worry about antitrust problems and therefore was able to extract half of your publishing interests, which you assigned to the label's affiliated publishing company as a condition of getting the record deal. Your record royalty is 7% of the retail selling price; the packaging deduction is 15% on discs and tapes; the free goods allowance is 15%; your LP bears ten songs (all of which were written by you), and its suggested retail selling price is $8.98. Because you have surrendered half of your publishing interests, your attorney had been able to withstand the record company's insistence on a mechanical rate, and it has agreed to pay the full statutory mechanical royalty of 4¢ per song (but only on records with respect to which they must pay a record royalty, that is, not on free goods). The recording costs were $75,000 (you learned the folly of rehearsing in the studio), and your lawyer, to make sure his fee is paid, negotiated a $10,000 advance for you.

Okay. I warned you about the Lexicon. Go back and study it till you understand your deal. I'll wait.

Well, your first LP didn't go gold, in spite of the assertions by all your friends and relatives that it couldn't miss. But you are getting over your disappointment as you realize that your sale of 250,000 units was very respectable indeed for a first album. Besides, you've noticed that the president of the record company is taking your calls and the promotion people have stopped being rude to your manager.

Your first royalty statement and check are due in a few weeks, and you enter your accountant's office to get a handle on how much money you may anticipate. While in his waiting area you clip an ad for a Porsche 928. The accountant sees the ad in your hand, and you hear him mutter through clenched teeth, "Here we go again." He treats you to fifteen minutes of Toyota talk (at $150.00 an hour). Fiscal responsibility is his game, and he knows from experience that you're not yet inclined to play.

He suggests that you work up the figures with him. First he warns you that the record company will probably hold a reserve against returns of 30%; therefore your sales of 250,000 units must be reduced, at least for the present, to 175,000 units. He demonstrates this for emphasis:

| 250,000 | units | | 250,000 | units |
|---|---|---|---|---|
| x    30% | | | -75,000 | reserve units |
| 75,000 | | | 175,000 | units |

"Easy come, easy go," you quip, still smiling. After all, 175,000 units isn't chopped liver either.

He then performs the following bit of arithmetic:

| 175,000 | units | | 175,000 | units |
|---|---|---|---|---|
| x    15% | | | -26,250 | |
| 26,250 | | | 148,750 | units |

"Wait a minute," you protest. "You already deducted 30% for the reserve against returns. Give me back the 15%."

"You don't understand," he responds. "This 15% is for free goods. They *always* take the 15% for free goods, whether in fact there are any or not."

Your smile has now waned but you manage a firm "Oh."

He now explains to you that the $8.98 retail selling price has to be subjected to the 15% packaging deduction provided for in your contract. Out comes his pencil again.

| | | suggested retail |
|---|---|---|
| $8.98 | $8.98 | selling price |
| x  15% | -1.35 | packaging deduction |
| $1.35 | $7.63 | net retail selling price |
| | | for royalty computation |

Since your royalty rate is 7%, your accountant now multiplies:

```
$7.63    net retail selling price
         for royalty computation
x   7%   royalty rate
$.534    royalty per record
```

Your Porsche is looking good. What color? you wonder. You follow your accountant's next operation with pleasure.

```
148,750    units
x  .534 ¢  royalty
$79,432.50 royalty due
```

You're home! You're trying desperately to think of where the nearest Porsche showroom is. As you rise triumphantly from your chair, your accountant motions you to sit down. "You forgot a few things," he says. "Like your $10,000 advance and your recording costs of $75,000." Here comes that damn pencil again, you think. He doesn't disappoint you.

```
 $79,432.50
 -85,000.00
-$ 5,567.50
```

You realize you're in the red ("unrecouped," in the parlance of the business; see "Recoupable" in the Lexicon, please) to the tune of $5,567.50. What the hell, owning a Porsche would be pretentious anyway!

As the tears stream down your cheeks, the accountant relents and reminds you that you are also the writer of the songs and that your lawyer managed to retain half the publishing for you. (He's paying back your lawyer for having recommended you to him. Otherwise there might have been an "only" before the word "managed.") Out comes the pencil again. this time it looks friendlier. He scribbles:

```
 4¢    per song
x10    songs
40¢    mechanical royalty per record
```

You understand that half of that is yours in your capacity as songwriter.

```
148,750    units
x    20 ¢  writer mechanical royalty per unit
$29,750    net writer mechanical royalty
```

You're feeling better. Of the remaining twenty cents (the publisher's share), half goes to your own publishing company and half goes to the record company's affiliated publishing company. Thus another dime a unit can be added to your coffers.

```
148,750    units
x    10 ¢  your share of publisher's mechanical royalty
$14,875    net publisher's mechanical royalty
```

You borrow the accountant's calculator and rapidly punch in the numbers.

-$ 5,567.50    net record royalty
29,750.00    writer mechanical royalty
14,875.00    publisher mechanical royalty
$39,057.50

"Not bad," say you proudly (you're thinking that a 924 isn't bad either).

Now you notice your accountant is sporting a malevolent leer. "According to your contract with your manager, I have to deduct 25% and pay it directly to him." That damn pencil again.

| $39,057.50 | | $39,057.50 | |
|---|---|---|---|
| x      25% | manager's percentage | - 9,764.39 | manager's commission |
| $ 9,764.38 | manager's commission | $29,293.11 | your net (perhaps) |

Once again you rise, extend your hand cheerfully to the accountant, and offer gamely, "Well, they make some good-looking Toyotas." He doesn't release your hand. "Indeed they do," he responds. "But you will have more income this year from performance royalties, and your price for personal appearances will rise substantially. We'd better put $15,000 in a money market fund as a hedge against taxes." His hand feels cold as he releases yours. As you turn to leave, you hear him say, "And then there is my fee. . . . "

In the lobby of the building you find a pay phone with a directory. Your fingers do the walking . . . Su . . . Suz . . . Suzuki.

Actually, as you think of your assorted creditors, who have waited patiently for your first success, you realize that your dreams can wait a while. You take comfort in the knowledge that finally you no longer have to worry about breakin' in. The Rolls isn't far off.

The above scenario is subject to many variables. If your lawyer had not excluded recording costs from commissionable income under your management contract, as was presumed above, you would have owed your manager another $18,750 ($75,000 x 25%). If your record company's affiliated publishing company had insisted on a 10% gross administration fee, your publisher's share of mechanical royalties would have been lighter by $2,975. Puzzled? Don't fret about it now; we'll work out the arithmetic in the chapter devoted to publishing.

If it's of any comfort, you now know more about your business than 99.9% of the lawyers in the USA. If you reread and master the Lexicon, you can raise that to 99.95%. There's a chapter on lawyers, too.

*Happiness is many covers*

# 2

# *I Write The Songs*

Music and lyrics by Bruce Johnston
© 1974 by Artists Music, Inc.

O nce upon a time songwriters only wrote songs, singers only sang songs, dinosaurs roamed the earth, dodo birds and virgins were in abundance, and a nickel pack of Kleenex cost five cents. There was also a time when record companies hounded and badgered music publishers for their best songs.

Today many singers write their own songs, music publishers hound and badger record companies to record their songs, a nickel pack of Kleenex costs 35¢, and we all know what happened to dinosaurs, dodos, and virgins.

There are many knowledgeable people in the music industry who feel that the songwriter who does not perform (a euphemism in this context for record) his own songs is well along the path taken by the extinct species cited above. To adopt this position would cost me half my readers and undoubtedly my publisher. In fact, I do not subscribe to it, but to discount it entirely would be akin to the behavior of ostriches, which bury their heads in the sand when being overtaken by pursuers, because they cannot distinguish between seeing and being seen.

Anyone who denies that the writer who performs his own songs has an edge over the writer who cannot or does not do so is similarly out of touch with reality. If you are a writer who doesn't perform, should you throw up your hands and abandon songwriting as your profession? Perhaps, for if one quintessential trait necessary for success as a writer or artist became apparent in the course of preparing to write this book, it was commitment. Each and every one of the experts interviewed, formidable individuals all, whether publisher, record executive, man-

ager, artist, or songwriter sooner or later hit on "character," "persis-
tence," "drive," or a similar quality as being the indispensable element in
the success formula. For you, writing must be what winning was for
Vince Lombardi—everything!

If it isn't, see if you can't exchange this book for a novel—before it
becomes too dog-eared.

Still with me? Good! Get a cup of coffee and stick a bookmark in
the Lexicon; you've got a lot to absorb and master in these pages.
Although this chapter will be of equal importance and spellbinding
interest to the singer-songwriter and the writer who doesn't perform (to
whom I may allude from time to time as the "naked writer"—"naked" in
the medieval sense of being without a weapon), the focus may well be on
the latter, since the singer-songwriter already has his ability to perform
as a vehicle to drive down the road to recognition.

It's a cold world out there, Mr. Naked Songwriter. Let's get some
clothes on. Mr. Singer-Writer, don't gloat; we'll put things in perspective
for you in Chapter 3.

How often have you heard someone you know say, "I ought to
write a novel," or "I could write a novel," or "I could write a better movie
than that clinker we saw last night," or words to that effect? Well, when
the first sheet of paper is in the typewriter or on the table, and it's still
half blank after several hours, enthusiasm wanes. Eventually, the realization dawns that there are about three hundred and ninety-nine more
sheets to go, and *that* literary masterpiece invariably comes to an end.
All is not lost, however, for at the next cocktail party there is an
"unfinished novel" or a "work in progress" to dazzle people with. Just
the awesome bulk of a novel, the climb to the top of a mountain so high
that its peak is shrouded in clouds and unattainable, is enough to
discourage most amateur novelists and abort their efforts. Ah, but a
song, one lousy page, a little ditty easily completed, a mere ant hill as
opposed to the Annapurna (26,503 ft.) of a novel, lends itself to
completion, satisfaction—and incredible competition. That kind of
competition, though not formidable or threatening in the quality sense,
is nevertheless a killer when it is for the ear or attention of a publisher or
other professional user of songs. When the amateurish (note the "ish,"
because most of you are probably still amateurs in the dictionary sense)
cassette arrives at a publisher's office, there is no way to distinguish it
from the cassette containing songs of professional and commercial
quality. If you could invent a device, such as the metal detectors used at
airports, that, when receiving a cassette, would announce either "BS" or
"BINGO," your fortune would be assured. The demo cassette that sings

"BINGO" is the subject of Chapter 4; be patient. The singer-songwriter has the same problem, but he experiences it at the record companies rather than at the music publishers. The singer-songwriter usually doesn't start hitting on the music publishers until after he feels he has struck out, at least for the time being (the hunger never dies), at getting a record deal. For the singer-songwriter, the music publisher is ofttimes thought of as the back door. For the naked songwriter, it is the front door, indeed, pretty much the only door—and the trick is to open it.

Unfortunately, I am not unique in harboring the belief that the emergence of and subsequent domination of the pop-music scene by the singer-songwriter and self-contained groups has so diminished opportunity available to the naked songwriter as to eclipse the possibility of substantial success for all but the most talented and hardy.

A talented young singer-songwriter was recently referred to me. I listened to his tape and loved it. The songs were literate and melodic and his voice was inordinately good. In addition, he was charming and extremely attractive. His previous attorney had "shopped" him without success and had apparently lost interest.

I sent his tape to six record-company executives who had not previously heard him. The results were uniform, six for six—all "passes." The responses represented a typical cross section of passes:

| | |
|---|---|
| one | "wimpy" |
| one | "nice but too MOR for us" |
| one | "would take a shot if business were better" |
| one | "I'd sign him if we were signing—but we're not signing. . . . I would be interested in one of the songs for another artist" |
| two | "thanks, but not for us, at this time . . . try again" |

Actually, there was cause for a little encouragement. I felt that the two companies that indicated that under different circumstances they would have signed the artist meant it. To the artist, however, after a while a pass is a pass, and encouraging words become just so much rhetoric.

At this point we had exhausted our supply of record companies. To the artist's credit, he had no intention of folding. I must confess I might not have been as stalwart had he not set an example by his courage and perseverance.

It was decided to work on the songs. Perhaps if he could break in as a songwriter and attain some recognition in that capacity, a record deal might follow. I arranged to play the demo for a major music publisher. The interest was real and immediate. An exclusive songwriter deal was discussed which involved a modest weekly advance. A meeting was set up, and the publishing company's people met with the artist. Enthusiasm abounded. The artist conceded on the last open issue and agreed to give all of his publishing interest to make the deal (we had tried to retain a half-interest). The publisher indicated that it was going to send the tape to a producer with whom it was just about to close a deal. Great—we might get a record deal too! We left the publisher's offices buoyed by the belief that in principle we had a publishing deal and the possiblilty of a record deal *too*. The publisher maintained phone contact with the artist, but nothing was "happening." After several weeks I called and was told that the publisher's deal with the producer had foundered, and that without it, the publisher was not prepared to go forward. Sorry!

Shortly after this disappointment, the artist's demo was played for the president of a newly founded record company, who appreciated it. Happily, a deal was negotiated between the artist and the record company and its publishing affiliate, and the record company announced the signing of the artist in the trades.

The day after the deal was announced in the trades, the publishing-company executive who had aborted the deal we thought we had struck called; "Are you interested in doing a publishing deal?" "Where were you when we needed you?" I queried.

All of the elements one would think necessary for a publishing deal had been present: a talented and reasonable writer willing to make whatever concessions were demanded of him and an established and well-funded publisher having great enthusiasm for the writer's songs. How come no deal?

I believe that because of the shrinking need for new songs due to the self-contained nature of most of today's artists, many publishers have lost faith in their ability to nurture and develop a new writer to the point where the investment in time and money is economically justified— unless there is a built-in record outlet for the material. I say this not in a pejorative sense. I am not implying that their lack of faith is indicative of a lack of courage or, indeed, unjustified. More ominously, I am fearful that it is well placed and that it is reflective of experience and considered judgment. The publishers realize something most of you don't yet appreciate. Without a successful record to popularize it and make it a viable economic commodity, even the best of songs may as well not have been written. Even if you are fortunate enough to have a song "accepted" by a publisher, its only immediate value to you is as encouragement. The advance, if any, will be just enough to constitute consideration necessary to sustain the contract in the eyes of the publishing company's attorney. Not one additional penny will inure to your benefit until and unless the song is recorded. No song is printed today unless it is a hit or part of a matching folio. There are no performance royalties until the song enjoys air play, which obviously it cannot have till it is recorded. If the publisher can't place it soon after its acquisition, while it is "in mind," it will probably turn to dust in the publisher's archives.

The following *Cash Box* excerpt is from a feature entitled "*Cash Box Spotlights Music Publishing*" (January 30, 1982). "*The predominance of the self-contained artist and slumping unit sales have brought about the current trend wherein publishers negotiate sub-publishing and split copyright deals with artists and production companies. Artists who perform solely outside material like Steve & Edie Gorme [sic] and Andy Williams have diminished 60-70% over the past 15 years, and the striking of administration and subpublishing deals has become a necessity.*"

The article was really about how the publishers were reacting to the diminished need for new songs caused by slumping record sales, paucity of new record acts, and the prevalence of the self-contained artist. Each publishing executive contributing a quotation to the article waxed enthusiastic about the health of publishing's future and indicated that the slack, if any, would be taken up either by exploiting existing catalogue through the new technology, such as video software; through repackaging; through increased efforts to revitalize underutilized areas of exploitation, such as motion pictures, commercials, and print; or through liaisons with writer-performers who have been or could be groomed for record or video-software exploitation.

I couldn't help think, just a little, of the time-honored concept of whistling aloud to buoy one's courage while passing a graveyard.

You naked guys seem to be left out simply because the publishers can't find outlets for the material they already have stockpiled. Theirs is not an irrational position, especially when they've been trying to soothe a bunch of writers who are asking in rather strident tones, "What the hell are you doing with my songs?"

Before we both become despondent, I should state that I soon came to the realization that, as in everything else, the difficulties of the naked songwriter are relative, and that a lot of us were spoiled rotten during the 60s and 70s, when music and records were a dominant influence in our society. During those years a lot of chaff went gold and platinum along with some wheat. More winnowing is going to take place in the 80s, but a lot of "bread" is still going to be made.

The second realization was that real songwriters, ones with the right stuff (to borrow from Tom Wolfe), are going to write songs whether there are a thousand publishers or ten publishers; whether naked or armed; indeed, whether their music is commercial or not. Considering all the great standards that were written during the Great Depression, when opportunities for success were almost nil, I shudder at my presumption in thinking that what I write might discourage a writer of merit. Enough apologia—back to work.

Let's turn back for a moment to my client with the aborted publishing deal. In the context of all of the above, do you perceive what was happening? I didn't, until I started putting this chapter down on paper. My attempt to create a marriage between that particular writer and that particular publisher was preordained to be a failure. As perceived by the publisher, the writer was naked. "No!" you say. "He was a singer-songwriter—not naked according to your definition." Right, but wrong. The publisher knew that he had failed to get a record deal notwithstanding many attempts. So, for all practical purposes, from the publisher's vantage point he was naked. Remember, the publisher itself was trying to cover its nakedness by closing a deal with a record producer, thus assuring an outlet for its product. Had the publisher succeeded, it could, it felt, have handled my writer. When the production deal fell through, everybody was still naked; hence no deal. When my client's record deal was announced, he became clothed, and, even though its situation had not changed, the publisher felt it could handle a contract with my client, because as a signed record artist he represented an assured record outlet for the songs he wrote.

About now a light bulb should appear over your head, as in a cartoon. Naked plus naked, although terrific in bed, doesn't produce progeny in today's music business.

It's a brand-new theory. Congratulations! You helped formulate it. I suspect everyone in the business has known it for years, but nobody ever said it before, out of either self-interest or lack of focus.

Okay, so what now? You singer-songwriters can skip a few pages and wait for us where we talk about the various kinds of publishing deals. I want to work a few minutes with the nonsingers.

Let's assume, as you must, that notwithstanding all adversity, you have the magic and will ultimately prevail. No harm in giving destiny a hand, is there?

While in Los Angeles recently, I managed to arrange a meeting with a well-known and long-established singer-songwriter—a real star! The meeting took place during a rehearsal break, and its purpose was to solicit an interview for the last chapter of this book. The meeting started badly and got worse rapidly. I had sought the interview because my past experiences with the performer indicated to me that he was an extraordinarily intelligent and articulate man from whose experience you might profit. The fate of the interview was sealed when I mentioned, perhaps unwisely, that one of the things I was exploring was the effect of the singer-songwriter on songwriters "coming up." His reaction was immediate, passionate, and defensive. Paralleling Marie Antoinette's rejoinder "Let them eat cake!" when advised that the citizens of France had no bread, our star responded, "Let them learn to sing!" Although his imperious tone belied any constructive motivation, he may unwittingly have been of great help—at least to some of you.

You needn't be a Placido Domingo to sing in the pop idiom. Perhaps some of you might give this some thought. A certain unique and indefinable majesty is often bestowed upon a song when sung by its creator. It's worth a try—and it is certainly the least expensive way to make a demo.

I would be a Pollyanna if I did not impart to you the following anecdote. An extraordinarily handsome writer of uncommon talent sought my services. I immediately had visions of sugarplums, platinum albums, and a TV career. I asked if he could sing—after all, I thought, anyone who could write a song should be able to carry a tune. His response was a forlorn negative shake of his head. He was adamant; I was insistent. Persuasion is my business, and I ultimately persuaded him to do a demo tape. A week or so later he brought in a tape. We put it on the deck. Two choruses later, I hit "Eject." I looked at him gravely and intoned, "You were right." We both laughed good-humoredly. Ultimately, one of his co-writers secured a record deal, and he is now looking forward to the release of an album that, though it doesn't bear his voice, contains several of his songs. A classic example of a naked writer finding a way to secure some cover. And he didn't even have this book!

Let's see, having propounded this super theory, how it can be put to use by you.

As you will learn in a later chapter, naked recording artists (artists who do not write and who are not equipped with a source of material) have an even tougher time getting their foot in the door than naked songwriters. It would therefore seem of mutual benefit for a songwriter and an artist of complimentary talents to merge forces—object, synergism and a simultaneous withdrawal from the nudist population. An apt example was the triple platinum album *Bat Out of Hell*, which resulted from the writing strength of Jim Steinman and the performing power of Meatloaf.

Similarly, you can scout local performing groups whose ability and style is compatible with your songs. Every town and city has bar bands or groups that have a local following and big-time aspirations. Work on having them perform some of your songs. Usually, a lack of good original material is their main weakness. An audience's reaction, or the absence thereof, is a good teacher and will greatly aid in honing your abilities and enhancing your professionalism. Such an alliance will also provide exposure for your material and enlarge your chances for success. Besides, you may cadge a ride on their coattails.

If you play well enough, and have the disposition for it, you may attempt to join a performing group or, indeed, form one, with you and your songs as its nucleus.

Another possibility is to think in terms of specific projects rather than random songs. Perhaps you are equipped to write for the musical theatre. Try working on a theatre idea. If you are in college, ample access to would-be book writers (and lyricists) is available. Cast about (no pun intended).

In 1694, William Congreve said in *The Double Dealer*, albeit in a different context: "As to go naked is the best disguise."

If you wish to disguise your talent, going naked is as good a way as any. You see, I practice what I preach: I would feel very naked without a copy of Bartlett's *Familiar Quotations* at my side.

If you resolve that you are a songwriter pure and simple, and that you have neither the inclination nor the ability to utilize any of the foregoing devices, or to conjure up your own, you will have to go naked. Please keep in mind while doing so that the random broadcasting of cassettes, like the random sowing of seeds, in addition to being very expensive is sure to be less fruitful than careful planting in the right soil and climate. Till the soil of the clothed publishers first, those with record outlets for your material. Virtually all of the successful individual producers of artists who don't write have publishing satellites and are searching for hit songs that are suitable for their acts and that they can own (not necessarily in that order of priority).

Although it would be logical to assume that a music publisher that is part of the same corporate family as a major record company is not naked, it would more often than not be an erroneous assumption. The larger the corporate family, the less likely is there to be a close and productive interrelationship between the music-publishing and the recording branches of the family. Not unlike brothers and sisters in most families, jealousies and rivalries seen endemic to the relationship. They seem to vie for paternal recognition and their respective shares of the family budget. The larger the respective operations are, the larger the gulf between them seems to grow. This natural rivalry, when coupled with the omnipresent specter of antitrust prosecution, serves to maintain the separation. There are, however, exceptions, but the nuances are subtle and you will have to do a great deal of research to appreciate them.

For example, Warner Communications, a giant conglomerate, boasts several major record companies, the three best known of which are Warner Bros. Records, Electra Records, and Atlantic Records. Warner Communications' major music-publishing arm is Warner Bros. Music, whose relationship with Warner Bros. Records, Electra, and Atlantic, while familial, is still very much at arm's length. Elsewhere in Warner Communications' table of organization, one finds Cotillion Music, which is part of Atlantic Records and obviously enjoys a close relationship with it.

How do you, operating out of Duluth, Terre Haute, or Oshkosh, garner the information and expertise necessary to make a choice? It would be easiest to refer you to the myriad little books and pamphlets of a "how-to-do-it" nature which sport lists of record companies, music publishers, managers, etc. (I have suspected that such lists are promulgated by the U.S. Postal Service in order to bolster the sale of stamps.) The lists are often out of date by the time the book is on sale, are undifferentiated, uninformative, and misleading. What is the benefit of sending a tape to a "music publisher" culled from the rolls of ASCAP and BMI which exists only as a repository for songs written by a particular writer (who is struggling, as are you, to have his songs recorded) and whose address is a file drawer in some accountant's office? A rhetorical question, to be sure.

I'm afraid, like the Smith-Barney of the television commercials, you, too, are going to have to "earn it." Having songs placed is not a shotgun operation; it requires research and targeting. Not only do you have to beat the competition musically, you have to beat them in a business sense. You must learn not only your profession, but also the business in which you hope to ply it. The research sources are available to you wherever you are located. A prime source is your local record shop. Album jackets are loaded with information of use to you. Zero in on artists for whom you believe your songs are suitable but who don't write their own material. How do you know who does and who doesn't?

Check the album cover and the label. On one or the other you will find the names of the writers of the songs and the names of the publishers. Don't be dismayed or discouraged if you find that the artist is a co-writer of several of the songs. It doesn't necessarily mean that he wrote them. There is a very strong possibility that the acknowledgment of the artist as a co-writer was merely a "cut in," a quid pro quo for recording the song. A slightly changed lyric or the turn of a musical phrase is often utilized as a rationale and permits both the "cutter" and "cuttee" to sleep better.

Let's assume you've targeted a likely artist. Study the artist's albums. (Don't worry about the proprietor of the record shop; when you're famous, you can come home and do a promotion for him.) The chances are that one publishing company's name will come up with curious frequency. Find a bookie and make a wager that that publisher is owned by either the artist or the producer. Guess where to send your demo!

The other research tool that you must avail yourself of is a trade magazine. If your local library doesn't have a subscription to either *Cash Box* or *Billboard*, you should subscribe to one of them. They are both excellent but to some extent duplicative, and either one should suffice your needs. An annual subscription (about $100.00) is not cheap, but quite reasonable in the context of "professional equipment." It is not sufficient for you to just read or browse through them. Study them and absorb each issue, especially the charts—not just the song titles and the artists, but the publishers and the writers. You must learn the music business if you are going to enjoy so much as a whisper of success.

Did you notice that in the parenthesis above dealing with the record-shop proprietor I used the words "come home"? Well, it was intentional. This brings me to a subject I have put off because of the potential havoc it could wreak if not handled by you maturely, and from a proper perspective. What we have really been discussing up to now is "cassette roulette." For most of you, it's as far as you will go. In any profession there is attrition along the road to success. In the "glamour" fields such as music, theatre, and motion pictures, the attrition is most severe. When recognition and remuneration are high, the field is large but the winner's circle is small. The race therefore goes to the swift, the strong, and, most of the time, to the talented.

Playing cassette roulette through the mails can be fun for a while, but a little piece of you goes into the mailbox along with each demo, and it doesn't always come back along with the package marked "Return to Sender" (all the makings of a Country-and-Western song).

If you have great good fortune, you may place a song or two this way. This doesn't necessarily mean that the song will ever be recorded or heard by the public—merely that a publisher thought there was a possibility of having it recorded sometime, somehow.

If you ultimately determine that songwriting is to be your lifework, that it is through songwriting that you are going to support yourself and your family, pay for your kids' braces, put them through college, and amass your retirement fund, you aren't going to do it out of Duluth, Terre Haute, or Oshkosh. Sooner or later you are going to have to go to one of the music centers, New York, Los Angeles, or Nashville, hang out, make the rounds, get to know the publishers, producers, and artists, become known by them, and otherwise pay your dues. This is one of the rare instances where I firmly believe later is better than sooner. Don't go to write songs; you can write songs in Duluth. Go when you know you have something to sell. Study your business. Know it as thoroughly as you can before you make the pilgrimage. Don't go if you're still a "kid" either chronologically or emotionally. Go when you've done everything possible to learn your craft that can be learned without leaving your own turf.

One other thing: successful writers don't seem to be very young. The art of writing requires, besides a pencil and paper, something to write about. It takes time to store up the knowledge and experience you will have to draw on in order to write. It's akin to a reservoir that needs replenishing if it is to continue to supply water. Any would-be writer, whether he be novelist, poet, screenwriter, or songwriter, who gives up a minute of education he might otherwise obtain in order to get a head start on his career is very foolish indeed. Stay in school (play cassette roulette if the need is irresistible). Then, when you are ready, really ready—good luck!

Sooner or later, if you are as talented as you think you are, and if you have worked harder and been more persevering than you thought yourself capable of, someone, somewhere, is going to want one of your songs, or your services as a songwriter. At that point you may rely on receiving a contract with an accompanying letter indicating where you should affix your signature. Before doing so, there are several things you should do. First, revel in the feeling of accomplishment and vindication it brings to you. Enjoy it enormously; it is a feeling that comes but rarely in a lifetime. Flash it a lot to friends and family and develop an "I told you so" look, so you won't have to utter the words. Second, abandon any thoughts of an immediate or even distant dramatic change in your financial status. Third, read the contract. Fourth, read it again. Fifth, find this book, wherever you may have stowed it, and reread the chapter on entertainment lawyers, and this chapter. Now, remove the contract from under your pillow and let's take a look at it.

At this stage of your career as a songwriter, there are four situations that may confront you, three of which will entail a contract with a music publisher, one of which will not—necessarily.

Situation One: You've played cassette roulette and the little steel ball landed on one of your songs. This has resulted in your being proffered a simple *songwriter contract* for that one song.

Situation Two: Your talents as a master songwriter of the future have been recognized and a publisher wants to tie up you and your songs for the long haul. The book-length contract you receive is called an *exclusive songwriter contract.*

Situation Three: Your talent is so awesome and your bargaining position is, accordingly, so strong that the publisher in situation two above is willing to allow you to retain half the publishing of your songs. The likely scenario giving rise to Situation Three is that the publisher is the arm of a small record company or independent production company with which you are making a simultaneous record deal. The publishing here is a spin-off of and a condition precedent to the record deal. The leverage you have as a desired recording artist, while probably not strong enough for you to retain all your publishing, may very well be strong enough for you to walk away from the table with half your chips. The contract covering the split of the publishing is called a *co-publishing agreement.* To work out the logistics of the relationship, it is usually accompanied by an exclusive songwriter contract.

Situation Four: This is the most blessed of all. You have secured a recording contract with a major record company which through benevolence or fear of antitrust prosecution has not hit on you for all, or even a piece of, your publishing. No contract, except an "internal" one, need evolve immediately. Any relationship with a publisher in Situation Four will be voluntary, advantageous, and probably, at least initially, lucrative.

All of the contracts alluded to above have much in common. It will be helpful to underscore the universal themes and clauses, thereby letting the differences speak more loudly. Not unlike a good song, which universally exhibits a beginning, a middle, and an ending, a good songwriting or music-publishing contract also boasts a certain universality of structure. They all contain the following elements:

1.   A grant of rights of a complete or partial interest in a song, and

the copyright thereof, to a publisher. This is what you give.

2. A promise to pay to the grantor of the rights in 1 above a portion of the income earned by the song. This is the royalty you've been dreaming about. This is what you get. There are several sources from which royalties are derived and which are subsumed in that general term. They include mechanical royalties, print royalties, performance royalties, foreign royalties, etc. It's Lexicon time again! When royalties are paid before they are earned, they are called "advances."

3. Warranties, which are affirmations that the grantor of the rights granted in 1 above owned them and was capable of granting them to someone else.

4. A term. This is the period of time for which the rights in the song are granted. At your stage of the game, the term is universally for the duration of the copyright. If the contract is for a writer's exclusive services as a songwriter, there is an additional term, which is the period of years for which the writer is bound to the recipient of his services. The two terms are mutually exclusive. For example, if a writer enters into a five-year exclusive songwriter's contract with a publisher, the term of that contract is five years, at the end of which period the writer is free and may enter into another exclusive songwriter's contract with a different publisher. The songs written during the five-year term of the exclusive songwriter's contract will continue to be owned by the initial publisher for the term of the grant of rights, which was the duration of the copyright in each song (presumably, the life of the author plus fifty years). Thus, even though the writer may leave after five years, he cannot take the songs with him.

5. An accounting provision that states when and how often the royalties must be accounted for (explained) and paid; the period of time after receipt during which the recipient can protest that the royalties thus paid were less than should have been received (there is yet to be demonstrated a single recorded instance of a royalty recipient complaining of an overpayment); and usually, but not always (so be careful), when and under what circumstances the royalty recipient's accountant can audit the publisher's books to make sure the royalties are accurate.

6. Lots of boilerplate, which should be your lawyer's concern and which is beyond the scope of this book.

Now, let's perform an experiment. Close the book and hold it before you, right side up, with the unbound long edge pointing at your nose. Do you perceive that about a 3/16-inch section of pages on the left is a few shades darker (dirtier, if you will permit the indelicacy) than the remainder of the pages? No? Well then, you either are playing Lady Macbeth or you aren't using the Lexicon. Use it, dammit! If you don't you've wasted your money and my time.

With the foregoing in mind, let us look a little closer at the contracts begat by the "situations" alluded to above. It would be perhaps more prudent of me to shunt you off to an entertainment attorney at this point and move on to something else. Indeed, with respect to the exclusive songwriter contract and the co-publishing agreement engendered by Situations Two and Three respectively, I shall do just that— after you have a little more awareness of the issues involved. Let's, however, spend some time on the Situation One contract, the so-called simple songwriter contract. Why single this one out for attention? For several reasons. It involves only a song or two, not years of your life. Moreover, it is the type of contract that you are apt to receive while you are still situated in Duluth or Oshkosh, where entertainment lawyers do not abound. Since the advance, if any, will be minimal, the trip to an entertainment center and the retention of an entertainment lawyer are neither economically practical nor justified. (Of course, if you are already in an entertainment center, it's a fine excuse and opportunity to start lawyer shopping.) It is the simplest contract to understand and negotiate, and it serves as the basis for all the music contracts, which are, for the most part, extensions, expansions, and embellishments of the basic songwriter agreement. Finally, the Situation One writer is not in a position to extract major concessions from a publisher even if represented by the ablest of entertainment counsel. Remember, this book is for you now, not when you have become established and your songs are in demand. At that career stage, even a contract for one song can become quite esoteric.

Every contract has to be read in a dual context. First, it must be read for what it contains, then, for what it doesn't contain. It's relatively simple to read it for the former and very difficult to read it for the latter. In the first instance, red flags pop up after each comma. In the second, the silence is deafening. It takes a great deal of experience with many different contracts dealing with the same subject matter before your brain develops an intuitive check list and the little white flags of omission begin to wave at you. Although most attorneys prefer their adversaries to prepare a "first draft" (it's a lot of work), we who are more insecure (or devious) volunteer to do it—experiencing along the way our "rights of omission." If your songwriter contract provided that you would deliver your first-born child to the publisher, all of you would pick that up immediately, and would probably consider it a bit over-reaching. (Of course, those of you with the requisite drive for success would probably start packing the kid up unhesitatingly.) If, however, it stated that you will receive a royalty on "X" and "Z" but was silent on "Y," I can guarantee that you will be oblivious to the omission. I can also guarantee that you won't receive a royalty on "Y." How could you be expected to perceive the omission? At this stage of the game, you don't even know "Y" exists. Even when you are more experienced and know that "Y" exists, you probably won't pick it up because your business is writing songs and you will never read enough contracts to develop a white-flag-intuitive check list—nor should you.

Songwriter contracts come in all shapes, sizes, and, indeed, colors. They can be typed double spaced on letter-size paper, in which case they are "fat"; or commercially printed in tiny type on two sides of a long sheet of paper, in which case they are intimidating. They can be in the form of a letter that is kind of folksy and friendly, or they can be in strict and forbidding legalese. Pastel-colored paper is sometimes used, which the more cynical think is part of a publisher's plot to lull the reader into somnambulance (which is unnecessary, since the text effectively accomplishes that). Sometimes a songwriter contract bears the word "STANDARD" in its title, which term's only significance is as a pallia-tive to induce the recipient to believe that the contract in question is the same one "everyone" receives and signs and hence it is unnecessary and fruitless to attempt to tamper with it. Whatever the form, color, or label, they are all going to say pretty much the same thing. "Why are the damn things so long?" you may wonder. Well, you have company. Publishers and record companies are constantly asking their attorneys the same question and beseeching them to shorten the contract. They believe, quite logically, that the shorter the contract is, the easier and cheaper it will be to close a deal. The beleaguered attorneys' response is simple: "Guarantee that the song or artist involved will be a 'flop' and I'll give you a short contract!" Songwriting and recording artists' contracts are not unlike insurance policies, which start out as very concise documents but which have annexed pages and pages of riders to cover each unanticipated contingency with respect to which the insurance com-pany was at some time required to pay. The same is true of songwriting and record contracts. Each time the publisher or record company got "burned," a new clause had to be added to cover the situation. In addition, as the music industry prospered and grew more sophisticated, more possibilities had to be anticipated and conjured with.

Be that as it may, whatever the size, form, or style of your contract, it is not immutable. All contracts are negotiable under certain circumstances

The first principle (and the second and third as well) of contract negotiation was perhaps best stated by Archimedes, to whom is ascribed the statement "Give me a lever and I'll move the world." Want to see a "great" lawyer? In any given situation, he's the one with leverage, the one representing the client who has the guns, the client who is less in need of the deal and more prepared to "walk" if his requirements are not met. Alas, the Situation One songwriter has relatively little leverage. If it were economically feasible, and you were to retain an entertainment attorney, he would, if he were worth his salt, attack the Situation One contract as if you were Paul Williams or Billy Joel, asking for every concession ever made by a publisher to a writer, including a demand that you retain half of the publishing. He will at all times, however, have in the back of his mind the fact that you aren't Paul Williams or Billy Joel and he will be ever sensitive to the necessity of pulling back just short of "blowing the deal." If you are able to enjoy the luxury of professional aid in this situation, so much the better, but the most important thing at this stage of your career is that you "blood your sword," "break the ice," "open the door," or whatever other expression suits your fancy but means "get started." For the moment, assume that your first basic songwriter agreement is going to be a "do-it-yourself" negotiation. Accompany me on a walking tour through the highlights of a typical songwriter's contract for a single song and spot the red and white flags that may indicate contract changes that a reasonable and benevolent publisher may be willing to make for the asking. After all, you do have a little leverage—you have written a song the publisher believes may make money. What if the publisher says, "That's the deal; it's not negotiable. Take it or leave it"? My gut reaction is sign the damn thing and get on to your next song. As you prove yourself, your contracts will become more and more "negotiable."

First stop on the tour is the very beginning of the contract, which we'll call the preamble. This identifies you as the "writer," your song as the "composition," and the publishing company as the "publisher." Poke around a bit. If you see yourself characterized as an "employee" or "employee for hire" of the publisher, or, indeed, if you see any word beginning with E-M-P-L-O-Y, you have found your first red flag. Although I do not believe that a Situation One contract can be legally sustained as an employment-for-hire contract within the context of the

Copyright Act, you don't want to risk losing your right to terminate the contract thirty-five years hence. Since courts are somewhat unpredictable, you should try to secure deletion of any employment language. Confused? Look up "Employee for Hire" and "Termination, Right of" in the Lexicon, and all will become clear.

Pretty soon we come upon your warranties and representations. This is the part of the contract where, in perhaps rather formal language, you state the song was created by you, was original, and that you haven't given any rights in it to anybody else. Any red flags here will be those hoisted by your conscience.

The paragraph dealing with your grant of rights to the publisher will probably soon appear. This is where you give all rights in the song to the publisher for the full length of copyright, for the entire world! Publishers' lawyers seem to compete to compound the most comprehensive all-inclusive grant of rights possible. With characteristic paranoia, the clause usually says the writer grants all rights . . . including but not limited to all copyrights, renewal copyrights, etc., etc., etc. There follows a litany of every conceivable right. Occasionally overzealousness backfires. From time to time, there may be included in the rights granted, the right to use the music of the composition with another lyric, or the lyric with different music. It's conjectural whether the broad general grant would give this right anyway, but when you see the specific language, it earns a red flag, and deletion of the provision should be requested. It's much more desirable to pick, and work with, your collaborators than to have them visited upon you.

Now we start walking uphill. The royalty provisions loom before us. Philosophically, or perhaps I should say theoretically, the publisher and the writer are supposed to share in the income from the song equally. Although most songwriter contracts attempt to deal fairly with writers in this regard, there is one area where all publishers seem to take an "edge" and another where some take a contractual edge whether or not they actually intend to avail themselves of the possibilities it affords them to unbalance the theoretical equation. The first involves a red flag; the second, a white flag. You are going to have to use the Lexicon if you are to appreciate and understand what follows. Usually the compensation provisions of a songwriter contract consist of several paragraphs setting forth the royalties to be paid. These paragraphs are either preceded by or followed by a sentence or paragraph that in more elegant prose says that all that the writer is entitled to are the specific royalties set forth. What you see is what you get!

Royalties are usually broken down into three general catagories.

The first is print royalties, which are royalties from the sale of printed copies of the composition. These, in turn, are divided into a "¢" royalty for sheet music and a percentage of wholesale selling price for folios and other editions. The ¢ royalty is the red-flag edge the publishers universally (in my experience) take. Most songwriting contracts are sent out by the publisher with a 5¢ or 6¢ sheet-music royalty. Twenty-five years ago, the royalty was 3¢ to 5¢. Not a hell of a change! And notwithstanding the fact that the publisher's royalty from his print licensee is 40¢ to 50¢, depending on the retail selling price. If you question whether the publisher will raise your royalty to the theoretical "half," the answer is "No," but the publisher may blush and raise it to 10¢ or 12¢. The usual royalty on the folios and other editions is a proportionate share of 10% of the wholesale price, and there is little chance of improving this. Your share of the royalty with respect to a folio containing your song and nine other songs would be 1/10th of the 10%, or 1%. There is a white-flag situation here that is worth a shot. To illustrate the point, I am going to use an admittedly unrealistic hypothetical situation. Assume your song is a big hit. The publisher, seizing on your song's popularity, combines it with nine public-domain songs (songs he can use without paying a royalty). The total writer royalty the publisher has to pay on this folio is 1%, and the success of your song is being used to peddle the folio. If you were to ask the publisher to modify the contract to provide that your 10% royalty be prorated only with copyrighted songs, the publisher might just agree; they do so quite often. Granted this concession, your royalty in the hypothetical situation above would be the full 10% instead of 1%.

The next general categories of royalties are those emanating from mechanical rights and performance rights. They are traditionally 50% of all net royalties actually earned by the composition from those sources. This is usually quite straightforward and is not fertile ground for you to till. The contract will provide that the publisher need not pay you performance royalties with regard to those performances with respect to which you receive a writer's share of performances directly from ASCAP or BMI. This is fair, usual, and consonant with industry practice and should not be a cause for alarm or anxiety. Sometimes the language goes a bit too far and uses ASCAP and BMI payments directly to writers to exculpate the publisher from any obligation to pay performance royalties, notwithstanding the fact that there are performance areas that ASCAP and BMI don't deal with, such as the performance element of a motion-picture-use license. This does not occur too often, and, in all candor, if you are talking to a publisher rather than his lawyer, you might be thought of as a bit overzealous.

This is perhaps the appropriate time to deal with the major white-flag edge taken by publishers that was alluded to earlier. I am now referring to what, for want of a more legal term, is generally referred to as a "catchall" clause. Keeping in mind the concept that the publisher and the writer are to share equally in the earnings of the song, there must be royalty language that provides for the sharing of the myriad income sources that are not usually listed with specificity in a songwriter contract because they are too "minor," too "numerous," too "rare," too "unimportant," too "obscure," or, indeed, not yet invented or evolved. What might some of these be? Well, of late, the title and the theme of songs have been licensed as the basis for motion pictures or television programs. "Ode to Billy Joe" and "Harper Valley P.T.A." are two examples that come to mind. If a song is licensed for use in a TV commercial, in what pigeonhole does the income nest? When satellite transmission of music and the so-called new technologies burgeon, will the income sources fit the existing royalty categories? If a catchall clause is in your contract, you can revel in each new exploitation device rather than stew about whether you arc going to get your fair share of the income. Few publishers will balk at a request for a contract provision providing a royalty of "*Fifty (50%) Percent of any and all net income earned by the composition and not otherwise provided for herein.*" You will sleep better.

The third and last major royalty category involves income from uses of the composition outside the United States and Canada. Foreign royalties are traditionally 50% of what the publisher receives and usually need little touch-up except for the addition of "source" language, which is dealt with extensively in the Lexicon.

Phew! The hill has been crested, and the rest of our ramble has the aid of gravity. Now that we know what the royalties are, how do we get them? The contract will have an accounting clause. Usually the publisher will account to the writer twice a year, or semiannually. Quarterly accountings are rare but not unheard of. If you ask for quarterly accountings, you will be told that the computer is programmed for semiannual accountings. I forget what the excuse was before the advent of computers. Oh, well, you can't win 'em all. Your contract's accounting provision may or may not grant you an audit right. That is the right to have your accountant examine the publisher's books to ascertain the accuracy of your accountings. If an audit right is not included, ask for it; it will not be denied and it is a white-flag point that should not be passed over. Without an audit provision, it will be necessary to institute a lawsuit to verify your royalties. Even if you are successful, absent a huge hit song, the expense of the litigation will render your victory a Pyrrhic one.

There remain but two more stops on our tour, one of which isn't on the contract map, and one of which may or may not be. Let's look for the latter first. If your contract provides for an advance payable to you on signing, the problem is solved. You may not rejoice in its amount, but looking at your cup as half full rather than half empty, you must revel in the fact that you really did "sell" a song. What, however, if you see what was conceived as an advance clause on the publisher's form contract, but it has been crossed out? Ask for an advance! Many publishers feel that they will probably have to invest in a demo, and the risk of not earning back demo costs and an advance is too great to take. If you are persuasive, perhaps the publisher will relent and reinstate the clause with a modest sum inserted in the appropriate blank. How modest? One hundred to 250 dollars seems to be the range in Situation One contracts. The actual amount will depend upon whether the publisher believes he can use your demo rather than have to produce one. The crossed-out advance clause is a red flag. The nonexistent advance clause is a white one. The more artful publishers (or, more likely, their attorneys) have two sets of form contracts, one with and one without an advance clause, thereby avoiding the red-flag reflex of a "cross-out." Red flag, white flag, the bottom line is the same; if there is no advance provided, ask for one—politely, of course.

The last stop on our tour is a traditional white flag. Few, if any, Situation One contracts have this provision, yet, if requested, it is usually granted. It is a clause whereby if, after a specified period of time, the publisher has not caused the composition to be recorded, or effected some other substantial use of it, all rights in the composition revert to the writer. That's right, you get it back! The time period varies. Of late, publishers are requesting more time because they say it is harder to get a song placed. They are right. The times for reversion vary from two to five years. Take what you can get, gratefully.

Let's take a moment to distill the above and formulate a little check·list.

1. Employment for hire—red flag
2. Sheet-music royalty—red flag
3. Prorate print royalty with copyrighted songs only—white flag
4. Catchall clause—white flag
5. Foreign royalties, at the source—white flag
6. Audit clause—white flag

7. Advance—white flag or red flag
8. Reversion if no activity—white flag

These are the points publishers are familiar with and which, whether you are victorious or not, will not cause you to appear unreasonable or "difficult." Moreover, it is extremely unlikely that any contract will be deficient in all eight areas.

We will not, thank God, go through Situation Two and Situation Three contracts in the same way. Such an exercise would be beyond the scope of this book. When faced with Situation Two and Situation Three contracts, you are in lawyer country. The most we can hope to do is arm you with a smattering of ignorance, or, phrased more positively, enough knowledge to keep you out of deep trouble until you find the help you must have.

Okay, master songwriter of the future, you got your demo listened to, and much to the publisher's surprise (of course not to yours) it was found to contain not just one but three good songs. The publisher called you and asked if you had more material. You sent another demo, and the promise of the first demo was fulfilled—three more good songs. The publisher thinks you could be a "winner" and proposes an exclusive arrangement. Welcome to Situation Two! The word "exclusive" should charge you with emotion. You're not a "one-night stand"; they're talking about "going steady." Much as it would in a personal relationship, this opportunity must engender mixed emotions. You have to be flattered that you're wanted, yet there is a gnawing anxiety about being tied up. I know that right now you can't contemplate the slightest hesitancy. You believe I am out of touch with reality (a polite euphemism). Wait till you have the slightest affirmation that the world is aware of the burden of that massive talent you have been bearing. See how rapidly the manure of flattery can nourish the garden of your dreams, and, let us hope, you will entertain the following considerations with appropriate solemnity.

Exclusivity is not to be taken lightly. It means what it implies. Every song you write during the term of the exclusive songwriter agreement will belong to the publisher. Indeed, all the songs you have theretofore written will also belong to the publisher. The agreement may take the form of a true employment agreement, whereby you receive a salary, work space ("office" is usually too grandiose to be an accurate description), and are expected to maintain regular working hours and work under the direction of a supervisor. It may, on the other hand, be a very loose arrangement whereby the publisher lays claim to whatever, if anything, you write, during the term. Regardless of the form it takes, the following factors must be reckoned with:

How long is your commitment for? How long is the term? Is it a firm commitment or is it an option deal? How much of an advance will you receive? Will you receive a monthly or weekly stipend? Will it be just a guarantee, that is, will the publisher agree to pay you just the difference between some annual sum and what you have earned at the end of the year? Will the advance be enough for you to survive on, enough to enable you to pursue your writing without worrying about eating?

Are you satisfied that the publisher has the capacity and willingness to "work" your songs so that they will be recorded? Is the publisher one with access to producers and artists? Is it "naked"?

Will the publisher undertake, in your contract, to professionally demo your songs?

Will the publisher entertain your retaining a partial interest in the publishing?

If you are a singer-songwriter, is it a propitious time for you to enter into an exclusive arrangement? Is a record deal sufficiently remote for you to abandon the co-publishing or self-publishing options it will make available?

Do you respect and believe in the abilities of the publishing company's personnel? Can they polish your talent? teach you your craft? And, most important, will you have access to them?

You will have to ponder all of the above; you will have to spend time with the people with whom you will be dealing; you will have to ask questions, consult with your attorney (who may be familiar with the publisher in question), and make a decision. "Act in haste, repent in leisure" is the aphorism that comes to mind.

Situation Three contracts involve "co-publishing," which is defined in the Lexicon. These are the most complex of all publishing agreements, not necessarily by virtue of their length or intricacy, but by virtue of the many possibilities engendered in their conception. There are just too many ways to skin the cat. Although you are going to have the help of a lawyer on this one, let's give that poor soul a little help by preventing you from giving the store away before he is on the scene. There is nothing more disheartening for an attorney to hear in response to a proposal than "Sorry, Counselor, that's not negotiable; your client already agreed . . ."

There are two main issues that have to be resolved before a co-publishing deal can be concluded, and they are both concerned with administration. The first issue is which of the two publishers is to administer the copyrights. This one is relatively simple. Your publishing company is not. The other publishing company is presumably the more established, knowledgeable, and competent of the two. "Wonderful," you say. "They do the work and we get half the money." Almost correct. Two factors militate against this. The first is the question of advances from publishing-income sources. Remember the usual scenario. You are retaining half of your publishing because your career as a recording artist is about to be launched. In the usual co-publishing situation, the nonadministering publisher receives half of the net *earned* income of the compositions involved. The word "earned" excludes advances. Furthermore, your compositions will be commingled with the rest of the administering publisher's catalogue, and when it makes foreign deals for substantial advances there will be no way of apportioning a share of those advances to your songs, with the net result that the administering publisher will keep the advances, enjoy the use of the money at 20%, and pay your share as *if*, and when earned. If your records should take off, the advances from foreign licensing can be substantial. The only viable solution to this problem is to insist that your compositions be segregated from the rest of the administering publisher's catalogue (in a separate joint company) and be dealt with separately, as a unit. Whether you and your attorney can pull this off will depend on your leverage at the time the deal is "talked," on the "buzz" that exists about your record potential at the time, and, in no small part, on your being able to insinuate the concept of segregating your catalogue early on in the discussions, as early as possible.

It is traditional for the administering publisher to charge a fee for administering the catalogue. This is the second factor militating against an equal split between co-publishers. It is appropriately called an administration fee. It is usually 10% to 15%. The concept of an administration fee is not an immutable law, and it has been successfully challenged. The degree of success in such a challenge once again depends on leverage and, to a large extent, on timing and negotiating skill. If you hang back on acquiescence to a co-publishing arrangement in general, ofttimes the deletion of the administration fee can be won as a "clincher" in making the deal. It is always best for a neophyte to decline to discuss these esoteric details until he has the benefit of knowledgeable counsel. Too often I have had clients announce that they have agreed to an administration fee of 10%. When I ask, "10% of what?" the only response is a questioning stare. What I am trying to determine is whether it's 10% of gross income or 10% of the publisher's share of income after the writer's royalties are paid. If it hasn't been discussed, you may be sure that the first draft of the agreement proffered by the administering publisher will provide for an administration fee of 10% of gross income. What in effect has happened is that the deal that was sold to you as an equal-sharing 50-50 deal has, through a "book-keeping" clause, been converted to a 60-40 deal, with you on the short end. Let's see how this works. Assume that one of your songs was recorded and the administering publisher receives a mechanical royalty check from a record company of $1,000:

TABLE 2.1

|  | No administration fee | 10% of gross administration fee | 10% publisher's share adminis- tration fee |
|---|---|---|---|
| *You as songwriter* | $500.00 | $500.00 | $500.00 |
| *Administering pub-lishing company* | $250.00 | $300.00 | $275.00 |
| *Your publishing company* | $250.00 | $200.00 | $225.00 |

In the course of a long and successful career, we are talking about a great deal of money. It is therefore important that you understand the stakes in this poker game.

Where the co-publishing deal is part of a record deal, which we will assume is the case here, two things must be established immediately. They can be won if raised and disposed of immediately. If they are left till later on, they become chips in the negotiation and will have to be paid for. They are the term of the co-publishing contract and the question of cross-collateralization. Assume that your record contract is for five years. The co-publishing deal with the record company's publishing arm should also be for five years. You can bet that's what it will stipulate. What you may have forgotten is that the record deal is traditionally an option deal whereby the record company has the right to end the contract at the end of each year. Unless the co-publishing contract provides that it is coterminous with the record deal, you will find yourself in the unhappy position of being tied into the record company's publishing company after you are no longer signed to the record company. That's not good! Especially when you have a subsequent record opportunity that is contingent upon a co-publishing deal.

The problem is even more important when you are signing a straight exclusive songwriter contract (no share of publishing) with a record company's publishing company.

Unless you are very vigilant, you will find that the record contract and the co-publishing agreement are cross-collateralized. (It is time to hype you about the Lexicon again.) That is to say, any advances paid you under one will be recoupable out of income from the other. Recording costs under your record contract are treated as advances to you. Therefore, if you are still in the red under your record contract, any earnings from the co-publishing agreement will be paid to the record company to diminish the unrecouped advances, including recording costs under the record contract. This is particularly vexing if the publishing income being thus applied is not even from your record!

As stated briefly above, each co-publishing arrangement also requires, as part of the package, an exclusive songwriter agreement in order to tie you as a writer to one of the publishing companies involved as co-publishers. It is desirable that your contract be with your own company. This is best effected if that agreement is presented as a *fait accompli*.

It is unlikely that you, as a somewhat awed, intimidated, and anxious novice, will sit down with the record company president or the publishing company president and negotiate these points. What is hoped is that by studying this material, you will acquire enough knowledge, enough buzz words, enough red flags, at least to deter you from acquiescing to some of the more distasteful contract provisions that have been visited upon your predecessors. Your job is to fight a holding action until the Mounties (your entertainment attorney) arrive. So much for Situation Three.

We'll make short shrift of Situation Four. You have a brand-new record deal with Columbia Records. Your publishing is intact. There has been a press release concerning your first album. Publishers are calling *you*! What do you do? Let your lawyer talk to them. You will get a sense of what is available to you, and it will set up "relationships" that will facilitate future dealings.

Whether or not you do anything at this particular moment depends on how badly you need cash and how much front money is being offered. If you can afford to gamble that you will have a hit record, it is obviously better to wait, because your bargaining position will certainly be stronger after a hit record. You will have the handle on ol' Archimedes' lever. On the other hand, if your record flops, you may have lost an opportunity to pick up a sizable advance—not an altogether unpleasant dilemma.

There is an awful lot in this chapter. Let's see if we can pull it all together with some $-and-¢ examples and a little quiz. This will be an "open book" test and you may use the Lexicon.

Your publisher has gotten your song, aptly entitled "At Long Last" (for which you wrote the words and the music), to the famous singer Kvetchan Grone. Kvetchan records "At Long Last" for what proves to be her first crossover album. "At Long Last" is released as the "A" side of the first single out of the album. The single goes "gold," selling one million copies. Larynx Records, Kvetchan's record company, insists on a "rate" with respect to all songs. Your publisher agrees.

When the album is released, you are pleasantly surprised to find that Kvetchan recorded another of your songs, "Better Late Than Never," which you wrote in collaboration with another writer. "Better Late Than Never" was the "B" side of the next single out of the album. It enjoyed exactly the same 1,000,000 sale as the first single. The album ultimately sold 500,000 copies, just winning a gold record. Sheet music of "At Long Last" sold 15,000 copies, and the album's matching folio sold 30,000 copies. The matching folio contained the ten songs that were in the album, which included an ancient hymn and the "Star-Spangled Banner." The folio's wholesale price was $3.13. When the foreign royalties came in to the publisher, they were $40,000 with respect to "At Long Last" and $15,000 with respect to "Better Late Than Never." Both singles had the same amount of air play. "At Long Last" earned writer's performance royalties of $40,000. "Better Late Than Never" was licensed as a commercial for a computer dating service. The fee was $20,000. "At Long Last" was dramatized as a motion picture about a man who is freed after spending one hundred and two years in prison, for which use the publisher received $20,000. Your contract with respect to "Better Late Than Never" was signed by you as it was received from the publisher. You received a copy of this book before you wrote "At Long Last," and the contract for that song was negotiated with benefit of an entertainment lawyer. Your sheet-music royalty with respect to "At Long Last" was 10¢. "Better Late Than Never" was never printed in sheet-music form. Incidentally, your advance for "Better Late Than Never" was $100. Your advance for "At Long Last" was $250. See, I told you to use an entertainment lawyer! (His fee was $500.)

Responding to the sudden success in typical fashion, you have been shopping for a beach house in the Hamptons (or Malibu, if you're L.A.-oriented). You found one you liked for a mere $750,000. The real estate agent asked you how much cash you were prepared to pay. You excused yourself, and, with a stick, you projected in the wet sand of "your beach" your earnings to date from "At Long Last" and "Better Late Than Never." Your response to the real estate agent will be $ _____ .

Don't rush! It's a typically unfair law school question! If you get a "C" we will both have done very well. Organization is the key. Let's track each income source.

---

### TABLE 2.2

| Source of Income | *"At Long Last"* | *"Better Late Than Never"* |
|---|---|---|
| *Sheet Music* | 15,000 copies<br>x  10¢  royalty rate<br>$ 1,500.00  your royalty<br>*Note: The 10¢ royalty was raised from the original 6¢ by your attorney.* | Having never been an "A" side hit, no print license was sought or issued. |
| *Matching Folio* | $  3.13  wholesale price<br>x  10%  royalty rate<br>$  .313  unit royalty<br>x  30,000  copies sold<br>$ 9,390.00  total writer's royalties<br>x  .125*  your song's pro-rata share (1/8)<br>$ 1,173.75  your royalty<br><br>*  Your attorney, in negotiating the contract, caused your royalty to be a pro-rata share of the copyrighted songs in the folio, hence the hymn and the "Star-Spangled Banner" were eliminated, reducing the number of songs to eight rather than ten.* | $  3.13  wholesale price<br>x  10%  royalty rate<br>$  .313  unit royalty<br>x  30,000  copies sold<br>$ 9,390.00  total writer's royalties<br>x  .10*  your song's pro-rata share (1/10)<br>$  930.00  your song's royalty<br>x.  1/2  **<br>$  465.00  your royalty<br><br>*  You signed the contract with regard to this song as it was submitted by its publisher, hence your royalty was a pro-rata share of all ten songs, including the hymn and the "Star-Spangled Banner," both of which were in the public domain.<br>**  You wrote this song as a collaborator, hence you receive only one-half of the royalty.* |
| *Mechanical Royalties*<br><br>*Single* | 1,000,000 copies<br>x  $.03  *royalty rate<br>$ 35,212.50  total mechanical royalty<br>x  1/2  writer's share<br>$ 17,606.25  your royalty<br><br>*  Remember Larynx insisted on a "rate" and your publisher agreed, hence the 3¢ royalty as opposed to the statutory 4¢.* | 1,000,000 copies<br>x  $.03  royalty rate<br>$ 35,212.50  total mechanical royalty<br>x  1/4*  writer's share<br>$  8,803.125  your royalty<br><br>*  The 1/4 represents the usual writer's 1/2 share, halved again by the fact that you had a collaborator. He will receive the other 1/4.* |

TABLE 2.2

| Source of Income | "At Long Last" | "Better Late Than Never" |
|---|---|---|
| **Mechanical Royalties**<br><br>**Album** | 500,000    copies<br>x    $.03    royalty rate<br>$ 15,000.00    total royalty<br>x    1/2    writer's share<br>$ 7,500.00    your royalty | 500,000    copies<br>x    $.03    royalty rate<br>$ 15,000.00    total royalty<br>x    1/4    your 1/2 of 1/2 writer's share<br>$ 3,750.00    your royalty |
| **Performance Royalties** | $ 40,000.00<br><br>*Note: Since ASCAP and BMI pay writers and publishers directly, there is no division of this sum. It was stated as the writer's share, and you keep it all.* | $    00.00<br><br>*I hope you fell for the trap and assumed that since the facts stated both singles had the same air play the performance royalties of the two songs would be the same. You didn't? Than you remembered that "Better Late Than Never" was the "B" side of the second single. As such, it received little or no air play (although the "A" side, which was not your song, received the same air play as "At Long Last") and hence no performance royalties.* |
| **Foreign royalties** | $ 40,000.00    total foreign royalties<br>x    1/2    writer's share<br>$ 20,000.00    your foreign royalties | $ 15,000.00    total foreign royalties<br>x    1/2    writer's share<br>$ 7,500.00<br>x    1/2    (that damn collaborator again!)<br>$ 3,250.00    your foreign royalties |
| **Other** | *$10,000.00, which represents one-half (writer's share) of the fee for the motion-picture use. This bit of income came under the catchall clause your sagacious attorney had added to your contract.* | *None! You signed the form contract submitted by the publisher, which omitted a catchall clause, hence the publisher needn't share with you his fee of $20,000 from the computer dating service. Paradoxically, if your collaborator signed a separate contract with a catchall clause, he would recieve $5,000.00.* |
| **Total** | $ 97,780.00 | $16,268.13 |
| **Less advance** | $    250.00 | $    100.00 |
| **Net income** | $ 97,530.00 | $16,168.13 |
| **Grand total** | $113,698.13 | |

Enjoy the house! While "Better Late Than Never" will probably bring you little future income, "At Long Last," by virtue of its extensive air play and success as an "A" side single, is probably now an established copyright and should take care of your maintenance problems for many years to come.

Incidentally, if you worked your way through the problem and the solution, give yourself an A.

Sir Isaac Newton may not have known beans about songwriting, but he sure knew about writers—and people too. His first law of motion, at least the half of it that states that bodies at rest tend to stay at rest, is one that every writer has to wrestle with from time to time; we call it writer's block. Although I had intuited the need for a book such as this, I couldn't overcome Sir Isaac's postulate until I perceived something unique to offer the reader. If this were to be my song, I was desperately in need of a "hook." Well, I could offer experience. Just the thought evoked a cloud of Zs. Then I realized there was something I had that you wanted and couldn't readily obtain: access! I could speak to the people in the music business that you would want to speak to and ask them the questions you would want to ask them and pass on the answers to you. That, I thought, should be worth the price of admission. What questions? The ones that newcomers have been asking me for years seemed appropriate, and some that I've been wondering about myself. In addition to slaking your thirst for knowledge, I'd find out if I had been giving the right answers. I hope they are among the questions you wanted to ask. Marvin Hamlisch's interview, which is contained in the last chapter, is very pertinent here, and I urge you to skip to it. I just couldn't bring myself to separate Marvin from the stars, where he clearly belongs.

Each of the gentlemen interviewed is a successful music publisher and each is a substantial human being. In their interviews they were not always consistent with each other, or, indeed, with themselves, but they were always sincere and desirous of helping you. Read those interviews included in this chapter and in other chapters for pleasure, enlightenment, and a sense of the flavor of your industry.

# Interview With
# Chuck Kaye

*Chuck Kaye has had a varied and extensive career in music publishing and is presently Chairman of the Board of Warner Bros. Music Publishing Co. Inc.*

AHS: What are the key things you look for when a writer comes in?

KAYE: Innovation, determination, and a willingness to work exceptionally hard.

AHS: How relatively important is it to you that a writer also be an artist, or have the potential of recording his own songs?

KAYE: It's a plus. I'm basically interested in the essence of the art of songwriting.

AHS: How many of the writers who come in here can actually write music? Musical notation?

KAYE: Difficult to say . . . I don't always look for composers, though; I'm very interested in lyricists. Ah, most musicians do know a little composition. As far as qualified songwriters who understand structure and can skillfully compound a song, I would say very few.

AHS: How significant is it to you in making or not making a deal whether the person can read music or not?

KAYE: Reading music is an academic skill; it's not an aid skill, one with which a composer can translate his feelings to his music . . . this isn't a classroom.

AHS: Okay. Do you have staff writers?

KAYE: Yes, always have.

AHS: Relatively few publishers do. What is the function of a staff writer? How do they work?

KAYE: They really work to write songs for contemporary artists, to have them recorded. They function to create new copyrights, which is the essence of what a music publisher is.

AHS: Do you supply them with a place to work and facilities?

KAYE: Yes, there's a demo studio here and there's a writers' room. Every company I've ever been associated with has had great success with staff writers.

AHS: When you hire a staff writer, it's as an employee for hire?

KAYE: Yes.

AHS: I assume you pay them a salary or an advance against royalties, and a regular songwriter's royalty?

KAYE: Yes.

AHS: I imagine publishers and record companies have a lot of material thrust upon them from various sources. Besides the ambitious young writer coming through the door, I'm sure there are attorneys and accountants who send you cassettes. To what extent is this a positive or a negative?

KAYE: Well, to get through material is a difficult problem only in the sense that no one has enough time to go through all of the unsolicited material. Most of the material you listen to is by referral. No one has the time to listen to all of the unsolicited material . . . . It's a shame, though. A very successful songwriter came to me via a tape in the mail, two of them actually; one is a fellow by the name of Rod Temperton. He has written an enormous amount of hits and had a successful band called Heatwave. The tape came in the mail to my English company. And another tape came to me in the mail from Minneapolis. The writer, whose name is Prince, is successful today.

AHS: Do you accept unsolicited material in the mail? Some publishers will return it unopened.

KAYE: You know, I'm having problems with it right now. I really have not been able to do it personally, certainly not. I'm trying to get the staff to get through it, but really, no one has enough time to do it. I think it's a sad thing. I have no answer for it.

AHS: Do you return it unopened, marked "Return to sender"?

KAYE: "Return to sender."

AHS: A lot of publishers are afraid of infringement claims . . . .

KAYE: I've been sued many times, it's cost a lot of money. Someone would walk into my office and sing a song . . . next thing I know, we're being sued for infringement. I mean, I'm talking about legal fees upwards of $20,000 that we've literally had to come up with to defend those claims, so it's a problem. The shame of it is, there's got to be some worthwhile material out there.

AHS: Is it fair to say that if an attorney with whom you're dealing sends in a cassette . . .

KAYE: I would listen.

AHS: You would have to listen?

KAYE: That's the state of the business. If any one of a number of people I do business with, attorneys, business managers, managers, present tapes . . . I listen.

AHS: The one advantage they can give is to get it listened to? . . . Chuck, in a time where young writers are advised of the value of their publishing and their lawyers are telling them how valuable publishing is, and their accountants are telling them that it's the annuity that's going to send their kids to school, do you find resistance to acquiring 100% of their publishing? Is there a lot of pressure for co-publishing?

KAYE: Yes, there is. Co-publishing deals are what predominately occur. I think the concept of one holding on to publishing in its entirety is an error. I think you need the professionalism of a successful company that can exploit your copyright worldwide. A publisher can be of immense help to talent in many capacities, whether it be in their recording career, in their songwriting, as an administrator, as a father-be-all . . . there are so many ways. We're the first ones to come in touch with people, creative people, and we can really guide them properly, or improperly, as the case might be. I don't know any writer who couldn't do with the benefit of a good publisher.

AHS: So, you would not be disinclined to enter into a co-publishing deal with a writer?

KAYE: If it's a writer you really want, and that was the way to get him or her.

AHS: Yes.

KAYE: I'd like to get 100%; sometimes I do.

AHS: How much time does your staff actually spend with a new writer?

KAYE: I have three or four people around here who spend a lot of time with them.

AHS: Listening?

KAYE: The majority of the professional staff, yes.

AHS: And advising?

KAYE: Right.

AHS: Do most of your deals with writers involve advances?

KAYE: Yes, either per song or on a weekly basis.

AHS: Do you pay these writers enough to support them . . . to keep them going?

KAYE: Yes. That's the idea.

AHS: So that they're earning from their art and . . .

KAYE: Yes. It's difficult, though; expenses are such today, it's very difficult. You have to be very careful when you're doing that.

AHS: If you were to advise any young writer, what would you say to him or her about the business today?

KAYE: Well, I would say it's a burgeoning business in the sense that there are lots of opportunities due to the new technology.

AHS: How would you suggest they break into it?

KAYE: Learn what the technologies are. Learn what the skills are that they must have and how they can utilize them. Study the masters. You know, it's like painting; they have to study the masters. I think songwriters have to study the great songwriters, whether it be a Cole Porter or an Ira Gershwin or a Paul Simon. Why were they good? What makes them good? What's the sensitive note that they ring? It's not just a matter of banging out three chords and a melody line. It's very difficult to write a song.

AHS: Then what do you suggest they do, ring on your doorbell, or find a manager, or . . .

KAYE: Find out how to get to me. Figure it out; you've got to be smart to get along in this business; you've got to be industrious. Creativity exists in many ways, you know, not only in the art form itself but you have to be creative in terms of your career and how to get it moving. Find the right people, understand the business, understand its pitfalls. Work harder than you've ever worked in your life, and make less money that you ever thought. And that's how you become a songwriter.

AHS: Thank you very much.

# Interview With
# Billy Meshel

*Billy Meshel, a former artist and producer, is now Chief Operating Officer of Arista Music.*

AHS: What is the first thing that pops into your mind when you're evaluating a writer?

MESHEL: Well, the first thing is the talent; after that, you evaluate the person. What kind of energy does this person have? How hard is he going to fight for his own success? Are they the type of person you have to take by the hand?

AHS: How relatively important is it to you that a writer also be an artist or a potential artist?

MESHEL: I would rather work with writer/artists because it's a shorter route to success for me. I've got more time to develop the relationship with the writer/artist and to exploit the material because they don't give you as much volume as the straight writer, and volume can, if it's volume for the sake of volume rather than high-quality volume, bury you. It can cost you a fortune. For me, the ideal thing is to find a writer who writes twenty songs a year that are great, rather than seventy songs a year taking shots at every idea that pops into his head.

AHS: Is the fact that the writer/artist will be recording and have records of your songs also a factor?

MESHEL: Yes. I feel that I can choose talent well and that my artist/writers tend to make it more often than those of most publishers.

AHS: How many of the people you sign can write musical notation, and how important do you consider that?

MESHEL: I don't consider it important at all; that's why I'm having a hard time even trying to remember who can actually notate. I know one who can.

AHS: Do you have staff writers?

MESHEL: I have, at this moment, two people who fall into the category of staff writers. That means they're straight writers. They're not artists. They were irresistible. They were so talented that I wanted to work with them as straight writers. Straight writers are very time consuming. They are in the office all the time, and you've got to have time for them, and there is not enough time in the day to do well everything that should be done. An integral part of the relationship between a publisher and a staff writer is time spent rapping and developing ideas; therefore, you have to be very, very sure that that writer has genius, because otherwise you are going to squander irretrievable time.

AHS: I assume you can squander some money on them also. I assume your staff writers are employees for hire or receive a salary or an advance, or a draw.

MESHEL: That's right. It's very expensive, but when you're convinced and commit yourself to a person, you can take the expense cheerfully provided the deal was made properly. The deal must be right because you know that it's going to cost you forty to fifty thousand dollars a year on one person for their weekly draw, the demos, and everything else that relates to this person. I'm not talking about recoupable sums, because we don't charge our writers for demos. We think that that is a very hypocritical thing to do.

AHS: What is your procedure with respect to unsolicited material?

MESHEL: We listen; most of the people in our company listen. There are seven people in the professional department, and then you discover other people in your staff who really have ears. So, when in an average week say forty tapes come in, everybody pitches in.

AHS: Is that about the number a week . . . forty tapes a week?

MESHEL: From one source or another. It seems to be about forty a week. I look for the ones that come from Oshkosh because I can make a better deal with them. I encourage them to take the contract to a lawyer so they know I'm not going to be able to rip them off. I cut my deals very sensibly. If I can make money, I make it. If I can't, I don't. No hard feelings.

AHS: You mean unsolicited material is listened to by you and your staff?

MESHEL: Oh, absolutely, absolutely. Every tape that comes in is listened to by someone in the professional department or somebody that we know has very strong musical acumen and can recognize good from bad.

AHS:       Your answer somewhat surprised me because the responses usually are otherwise. But a lot of publishers don't seem to have the time to listen to unsolicited tapes or in fact will send them back unopened because they are afraid of infringements.

MESHEL:    Yes, I know. I once had an infringement claim, but it was settled. That was eighteen years ago. I'm not worried, except I guess now that it's in print it will give the idea to people who would never have thought of it. But we write back a pretty nice letter if we don't like the thing. But I would much rather listen to unsolicited material because my chance of finding talent is exactly the same as with the referred material. Most of the time, the referred stuff is coming to you from a person that you don't have any confidence in artistically. It becomes a favor situation . . . a favor to listen. Then, I also find that a lot of people that we do business with, the businessmen, the managers, the lawyers, the accountants, who are trying to make deals for writers, use us just to find out how good the tape is. Then, when they think they have something, when they've used us to develop an opinion, they'll take it to a certain clique that everybody develops. You know, everybody develops their favorite people. So when a tape comes in unsolicited and I like it, I call the writer and I offer him what I consider to be the state-of-the-art deal.

AHS:       Then . . . it is "take it or leave it"?

MESHEL:    And it's take it or leave it. Right.

AHS:       Billy, in an era where young writers are aware of the value of their publishing and are being advised to retain it wherever possible, what incentive do publishers offer to writers to give up all or part of their copyright?

MESHEL:    First of all, the fledgling writer, the writer who you've got confidence in but hasn't accomplished anything yet (what I mean by "accomplished" is hasn't gotten a hit one way or another), doesn't, in my opinion, have the right to hold on to any portion of the publisher's share. They're not the publisher, they're not performing in any way as a publisher. So why should they have it? The writer/artist who is accomplishing something and isn't asking a tremendous amount of money is functioning in part as a publisher since he is helping to exploit the song by recording it. So there is justification for his retaining a part of the publishing. There is another aspect of that question that I think is very important. You asked why should they give away this valuable thing? Well, in their hands it's not valuable because they don't have the experience or ability to develop it. When I get tapes from the businessmen in the business, to me it's not exciting. I get the feeling it's been hacked around, that it's been everywhere, it's like buckshot . . . one pellet hit me.

AHS: Billy, I think when this book is published, you are going to be inundated with seven billion tapes from Oshkosh and you are going to be the only publisher in the business who's going to welcome it.

MESHEL: Well, I'm not going to hire people to listen to the tapes, because that's a losing item. If all of a sudden a hundred and twenty-five tapes start coming in a week, I'm sure we won't get to them all, and it will be a grab bag.

AHS: What is your concept of the ideal demo?

MESHEL: The ideal demo is just like anything else in the music business. It depends on the talent level of the people doing it. I know people who could cut a piano voice demo and absolutely knock you out. They're so good . . . they're so on target . . . the vocal and the piano. I know other demos that are done with four or five, six, seven instruments that are devastating . . . they're great. But, you know, as you start adding people to a demo, the chances of that happening really become slimmer and slimmer, because now you're into making a record, not a demo, and a record has a different objective than a demo. You want a song demo to appeal to the industry in general, so you try to stay away from a sound that's very identifiable. You try to find a spot where everyone can relate to the song.

AHS: A demo for a music publisher is probably different from a demo you would submit to a record company.

MESHEL: Oh, yes, to a record company you're submitting musicians, songs that they're involved with, a vocal sound and style, whereas for a publisher, the demo is designed to show off the potential of the song.

AHS:    How many songs would you put on a demo, Billy? How many songs do you like to see on a demo? I imagine you are turned off if there are too many songs.

MESHEL:  When you sit down and look at the tapes that you have to start playing, either in the office or at home or wherever you're listening, and you see a tape with ten songs on it, you do feel a sense of exasperation and frustration. Listening to demos is a demanding process and you can't think of anything else while you're doing it. If you're going to do yourself any good . . . if you're not just murdering your time, you have to listen and pay attention. I don't think that anybody can listen to more than twenty-five or thirty songs in one sitting, a sitting being about an hour. You know, you don't listen to the whole thing if you hate half of it or a quarter of it. You don't have to finish the pie if you don't like the first forkful . . . you know the whole thing is going to taste the same.

AHS:    How many songs do you think are ideal?

MESHEL:  Half a dozen. Half a dozen will serve the person who's sending the tape in best of all, because though it's a substantial amount, it's not too much.

AHS:    Back to your pie and the fork analogy . . . I assume it would be advisable to put your best shot first?

MESHEL:  Absolutely. That's selling. If they love the first song, they'll have a little patience with the second one, and so on.

AHS:    I thank you very much.

Because Billy Meshel was one of the publishers interviewed who expressed an affinity for unsolicited material, I called him after reading the interview and obtained the following additional information from him: Arista listens to about 240 unsolicited songs a week. Approximately one out of 500 is "liked" and approximately one out of 1,000 "makes money." Meshel indicated that 75% of the unsolicited songs acquired by Arista are recorded within two years, and that half of those recorded earn a gross of $1,000.00 or more. Meshel volunteered that many unsolicited songs are so bad that they are "nerve-wracking" to listen to, but that listening to unsolicited tapes is an investment in time that a publisher must make.

# Interview With
# Milton Okun

*Milton Okun, producer of, among other artists, Peter, Paul and Mary, John Denver, and Placido Domingo, is also the founder of the Cherry Lane group of music publishing companies.*

AHS:      Milt, what criteria do you take into account in evaluating a writer's merit or worth?

OKUN:      Just talent. In the case of the music, I look to see whether writers show individuality and creativity in composition or whether they merely use formula melodies and formula chords. I look for original ideas and for a sense of structure in both the lyrics and the music. If a writer can structure a song so that it has a beginning, a development, and an end, even if I don't like that particular song or the idea of the song, I know that it is written by a good writer. I am interested in good ideas and interesting development.

AHS:      I remember once, a long time ago, I played an artist for you and you asked me how old he was. When I told you I thought he was twenty-seven or twenty-eight, you said, "If he can't tune his guitar by now, forget it." That always stuck in my mind.

OKUN:      Right. I think for a singer or a musician there are certain elementary musical qualities that are needed to be a professional, and it would be hopeless for someone who doesn't have an ear for tuning an instrument to become a singer or an instrumentalist.

AHS:      But I think perhaps you and two other people in the world would have noticed that the guitar was a little bit out of tune.

OKUN:      Wrong.

AHS:      Wrong?

OKUN:      Most professionals are not perfectly in tune, and while I have a good ear, I would not have made that comment if the guitar was not grossly out of tune.

AHS:      How relatively important is it to you that a writer also be an artist or a potential artist?

OKUN:      Well, from my point of view as a record producer, obviously it would be much better to find a writer who is potentially a strong performer. I think, however, that people who have real writing and composing ability shouldn't be discouraged if they are not performers. It makes it a little tougher in the current musical scene to be a writer only, but if a writer has talent, that's the important thing.

AHS:      How many of the writers who submit cassettes to you, or whom you have come across in your day-to-day business, are trained in music? How many of them actually know music notation?

OKUN:      I don't think that knowing music is a prerequisite for being a good writer or performer, because I don't think that there is a much higher representation of trained musicians than nontrained musicians among songwriters. I get many cassettes from people who are good musicians, but most come from people who have no musical training. Training doesn't help if there is no talent or creativity. It is just that a person who can write good songs will be able to do more with his talent if he has a knowledge of sight reading, notation, and harmony. It makes the job easier if one has a sound basis in musical skills.

AHS:      Does Cherry Lane ever hire staff writers on a salary basis, and what is your attitude in general towards the economics of dealing with fledgling writers?

OKUN:      Cherry Lane is basically a company that works in tandem with my production activities. I do enough production, and we have enough writers without hiring staff writers, to have all that we can handle as far as promotion and development of material is concerned. We don't want to get into the mass business of signing writers and developing more copyrights than we can efficiently work, because we believe we have a big responsibility to our writers that must be fulfilled. However, since we're so strongly oriented towards record production, our situation may be unusual. Probably most other publishing companies are looking for talented new writers.

AHS:      It seems to me that what you just indicated was that you would be much more disposed towards a writer who is also an artist at this stage than you would if he were not an artist.

OKUN:      Yes, I guess for us that is the case.

AHS:     To what extent is the source of material that is submitted to you a factor? In other words, if something comes in unsolicited, what is the likelihood of its being carefully listened to, assessed, and evaluated, as opposed to material that is sent to you by producers or lawyers or people in the business? Do you actually listen to all the stuff that comes in?

OKUN:    No, I can't. I don't think I have ever found a viable piece of material that was submitted by an amateur writer. In recent years, I haven't gone through unsolicited tapes, but in my early years, when I started working with Harry Belafonte, one of my responsibilities was to go through all the songs submitted to him. I went through thousands and not one song ever got far enough to be recorded. Then, after Belafonte, while working with folk groups like The Brothers Four, The Chad Mitchell Trio, and Peter, Paul and Mary, I listened to hundreds and hundreds of submissions and while I liked a number of the songs and presented some of them to the artists, somehow they were dropped along the way. As far as I can remember, no unsolicited song has ever been recorded through my efforts. However, when I came across a writer who I believed had talent, even though I didn't like the particular song he may have sent me, I encouraged him to write more and send me other work. Sometimes, that would pay off and I would get some songs that I liked.

AHS:     What is the policy now at Cherry Lane with respect to unsolicited material? A lot of people are afraid of infringement claims and rather than run the risk of . . .

OKUN:    We're not afraid of infringement claims. I don't think we have ever had one. But that's not the reason for discouraging writers from sending unsolicited material. We know from years of experience how little chance there is of receiving anything usable that way. Our policy at Cherry Lane is to return all tapes from unknown sources without opening them. If we know the writer or recognize the source, we certainly consider the material.

AHS:     Milt, in an era where young writers are aware of the value of publishing and are being advised to retain it, what incentive does a publisher offer writers to part with all or part of their copyrights?

OKUN:     We prefer to have all of the copyright but will accept
          whatever part is available. If I have to have a song or have
          to use it, I think we are fortunate to get whatever part we
          can. I would never refuse a song because we cannot have
          all of it, although it makes much more sense to work on
          the songs that we own entirely or almost entirely, rather
          than on the others. However, I really don't think there is a
          dfference in our work on partially or on wholly owned
          songs. As a practical matter, I don't see the benefit to a
          songwriter of making an issue of keeping part or all of his
          copyrights at the beginning of his career. I think he loses as
          much or more than he gains, unless he is such an immense
          talent that people have to have his material. It strikes me
          that any publisher would be less interested in a writer who
          withholds part of the copyright. I believe that from an
          economic point of view, the publisher serves an important
          function and it is to the writer's benefit that the publisher
          prosper if he's going to be associated with it. I think, for
          example, the writers who have been with Cherry Lane
          through the years and who have assigned their copyrights
          to Cherry Lane have benefited by Cherry Lane's success
          as much as Cherry Lane has benefited.

AHS:      What do you mean by that?

OKUN:     If a company is successful and has a strong, well-paid
          staff, many more records go out to artists and many more
          records go to the radio stations for air play. More songs
          are printed, and more books are sent to foreign countries.
          The publishing company benefits and the writers benefit
          through the performance income.

AHS:      Sort of circular; having the copyright gives you the incen-
          tive, and having the success gives you the wherewithal to
          perpetuate the success.

OKUN:     That's true. Because we are a successful publishing com-
          pany, we have been able to go very strongly into print
          music, so that our writers benefit by having their songs
          extensively reproduced in chorals, and in piano and gui-
          tar books for school and other use. It strikes me that the
          long-term economic and artistic welfare of the songwriter
          is better served by increased use of his songs than by his
          getting part of the publisher's share of the income.

AHS:      Interesting. The question of demonstration records always comes up. Writers and artists want to know how to do a demo. If you could prescribe the ideal demo that you'd like to listen to, what would it be? Would it be different for Milt Okun/Publisher than it would be for Milt Okun/Producer?

OKUN: It strikes me that a well-done demo that sounds almost like a master would be very attractive to most publishers because when they send the demo out to record producers, there would be a better chance to get a record on it. Also, for producers who think the success of a record is based on production qualities, the more you can indicate on the demo, the better. However, in my case as either a publisher or a producer, I prefer a simple demo with one instrument, either guitar or piano, as accompaniment, and a clear, pleasant voice singing the song. I want to hear the song. I want to hear the melody, the chords, the words, and I want to make my own judgment as to whether it will make a record. For those producers who think success is based on the quality of a song, and I think the majority of producers do, a simple, very clear demo is best. As a matter of fact, I am often just as happy to see a lead sheet if it's properly done. There you have the melody, the chords, and the words in front of you and you can hear it in your own mind and decide whether you can make a record of it with the artists you have.

AHS: I think there are a lot of people in publishing houses and record companies who couldn't read a lead sheet if it came in.

OKUN: That's true. I think that what I said is only applicable to producers or publishers who are musicians, and since there aren't many, maybe it isn't the best advice to give to writers.

AHS: Okay. Please give me a little of your background. It's a rather interesting career and I think our readers would enjoy reading about it. You've been trained, haven't you?

OKUN: I always assumed that I would be a musician. I studied piano as a young child, then guitar, then majored in music education at New York University. I received a master's degree from Oberlin Conservatory. My main interests were in folk and classical music.

When I was young, folk music was esoteric, out of the mainstream. I didn't care for the popular music of the period, and it is ironic to me that today I am a supposed expert in popular music only because the music I did like, folk music, has evolved into today's popular music.

After receiving my degree, I became a music teacher and taught choral and vocal music in junior high school. There was so little curricular material applicable to the twentieth century for that age group that I did a lot of my own arrangements. Then, while I was still teaching, I began to work commercially as an arranger and a singer. I quit teaching and started my full-time professional music career as a pianist for Harry Belafonte and then joined the Belafonte Singers. Eventually I became his conductor and arranger, and would still be working for him today if he hadn't fired me. Actually, it was a blessing because it forced me out into the field, where I went on to full-time arranging, directing, and producing other folk artists and folk groups.

While working for Belafonte, I started a small publishing company to copyright my arrangements of traditional songs. Later on, when I was very active as a producer and arranger, I started finding original songs and signing writers. As a matter of fact, I signed my first important writer not because I was looking for a writer to sign, but as an act of compassion. While trying to find a replacement for a member of The Chad Mitchell Trio, one of the people I auditioned was a young Oklahoma songwriter, Tom Paxton. I really hired Tom for the Trio because of a song called "The Marvelous Toy" which he had written. I was so intrigued with the song and he performed it so well that I mistakenly thought he belonged in the Trio. After a week or two of rehearsals, it was clear that his future wasn't as a member of a commercial group, and I had to tell him so. He was very unhappy and upset, because the job with the Trio was his first break after coming to New York, and to have it taken away from him so quickly was a terrible blow. I remember sitting with him in my apartment and promising to help him if I could. I signed him as a writer and started trying to get records for his songs. From Tom's point of view it was the best thing that could have happened, because he sat down and started writing with ferocity and passion, and I think he has become one of the most important writers in his field. It might not have happened if he had gone with a successful group, where all his energies would have been directed towards performing.

AHS: You were his Belafonte?

OKUN: I was his Belafonte. But the difference was that Belafonte didn't offer to spend time helping me. He just fired me.

Over the years, my work as an arranger, conductor, and then producer of folk artists has been a natural development and a continuation of my work as a music teacher. I was really hired because of my training in music. The young people I worked with loved to sing and loved folk music, but didn't have enough training to do a professional job. I was the only professional musician, or the only trained musician, at that time who had a real interest in the folk-song movement and understood its roots. There were a lot of arrangers around, many of them much better than I, but they had no concept of the tradition out of which the songs came. When they did arrangements, they used sixths and ninths, and added embellishments to the chords which were marvelous and very beautiful but had no place in "Down in the Valley" or "On Top of Old Smoky" or in any folk-based melody. I had always loved folk songs. They were an obsession with me. I knew all the chords and I had a particular combination of abilities that were needed by performers and creators who didn't have musical training. I was lucky to be in the right place at the right time. I was a teacher to them. I gave them a sense of structure and a sense of music, the better to use their talents.

AHS: When you were firing Paxton from The Chad Mitchell Trio, was there another young fellow in the group that you ultimately teamed up with?

OKUN: You mean John Denver.

AHS: Yes, I was leading you.

OKUN: About four years later, when Chad Mitchell quit the Trio, I auditioned hundreds of people and picked John Denver to replace him. It was a good choice. John had a sense of rhythm and vitality that transformed the group. They were very successful and effective in performance, but they never made it on records. When the group disbanded, and it was the most gracious disbanding of a group that I have ever witnessed, John decided to start out on his own. Thanks to the fact that you and I were able to get him a four-record deal instead of the usual one record with options, he was able to have enough time for one of his records to take off. "Country Roads" was his first hit and it was on his fourth record. Think of how many talented young people who have only a one-record deal never get that chance.

AHS:      It doesn't happen any more. Those deals don't happen any more.

OKUN:      I know.

AHS:      You produced Peter, Paul and Mary also, didn't you?

OKUN:      Yes. At the same time that I was working with the Mitchell Trio, I was asked to work with Peter, Paul and Mary by their manager, Al Grossman. When I heard them sing, I didn't think much of their musical ability. I liked each of them individually as singers, but I figured it would be very difficult to get them singing together, and the only reason I agreed to work with them was that I hoped that if I did Al a favor, he might give me work for some of his more important artists, like Bob Gibson or Odetta. That shows how much I knew.

AHS:      That was before John Denver, wasn't it?

OKUN:      That was before John. I had ten years with Peter, Paul and Mary, from 1960 to 1970 approximately, and during those years I worked with other folk groups at the same time. At one point I felt as if I was the General Motors of the folk-song industry. There were days when I would rehearse with the Mitchell Trio in the morning, Peter, Paul and Mary in the afternoon, and The Brothers Four in the evening, with time in between for The Phoenix Singers or Leon Bibb. The three major groups all had a significant success in different degrees and all disliked knowing that I worked with the others, so there were many difficult moments during entrances and exits, especially when rehearsals ran overtime. They were all talented, creative singers and performers who were not well trained musically, so they needed me. I served a purpose and had many good years with them, but if they had been as well trained as they were talented, there would have been no place for me. When that era was over, I worked with Peter and Paul and Mary individually on their first solo albums and then went with John out of the Mitchell Trio.

AHS:    What do you have cooking now, Milt?

OKUN:   I've been extremely lucky over the years. Not only was I in the right place at the right time, but my career seems to have changed with the artists I have worked with, and the changes have always been to my liking. I was able to sing and arrange folk songs for Belafonte. Then the protest movement, really a folk movement, took hold and there were the folk singers and groups to work with. Then John, because of his sensibilities, became a part of the 70s' awakening to conservation and appreciation for the natural beauty in our country. It was a softening of the protest movement, a kind of a cry for a constructive point of view. It's part of John's great success that his songs speak to so many people. It's the reason why his songs, like Tom Paxton's, will be sung long after people will have forgotten the exact time that they were written, or even the contemporary events that led to their writing.

As to what I'm doing now. Well, I am still working with John as producer and publisher. And I am also working with Placido Domingo. Placido is a supremely talented musician, a gifted actor, and, I believe, the finest singer of our time, so this is a pretty stimulating experience for me. For a change, I'm the one who is being taught. He is already a giant star with a world-wide following in the field of opera. And what is unusual for an opera singer, and is apparent on his recently recorded tango, folk, and popular records, is that he sings ordinary songs with love and without condescension.

AHS:    You know, there are an awful lot of talented people who don't make it.

OKUN:   That's true. But I don't know of any great talents who don't make a mark or don't move people.

AHS:    Perhaps you haven't heard of them because they never had the initial success or the break?

OKUN:   In many years in music as a listener and as a professional, you hear many people. And it seems to me eventually the talented ones make it.

AHS:    I don't know . . . . All the masterpieces I've given you to listen to over the years . . . none of them have reached you.

OKUN:   True. But if I'm as bright as you say, you should have dropped them immediately.

AHS:      I did. Most of them.

OKUN:      Good. But you once played me something of someone who I really thought was talented. And I bet eventually he'll make a big mark.

AHS:      Who?

OKUN:      Peter Ivers.

AHS:      It's funny you should say that, because he's still trying.

OKUN:      Maybe the drive that keeps him trying is the most important ingredient, aside from talent, that makes a successful writer. Any really talented writer will eventually be heard if he just keeps working at it, developing his talent, if he just forgets about the "big break."

AHS:      I thank you very much.

# Interview With
# Irwin Schuster

*Irwin Schuster has enjoyed a long career as a music publisher and is now Senior Vice-President-Creative of Chappell Music Company.*

AHS:      Irwin, what is your primary consideration in making a decision as to whether or not a writer belongs in the Chappell orbit?

SCHUSTER:      When listening to his songs, if he has one song out of the ten which is a quality song, a great song, I would be interested in trying to acquire only that song for the company. If he has four, five, or six songs out of ten which are quality songs, I would be more interested in signing him as a writer, because that percentage of quality songs shows me that he is a quality songwriter.

AHS:      How relatively important is it to you that a writer also be a potential recording artist?

SCHUSTER:      It's very important only because I believe that the better a writer sings his own songs, the better chance we have of getting good recordings on it. It's always more difficult with a writer who writes well but then presents you with the problem of finding a demo singer to fit a specific song, an R & B song, a country song . . . you're always searching for a different kind of singer because the writer doesn't sing well. If the writer sings well, no matter what kind of song he writes, there's a validity to his singing his own song, and the song is going to be sold much more readily. If the writer then goes on to become an artist, like Carole King, who was a smash songwriter for many years, had one semi-hit record called "It Might as Well Rain until September," but really was not considered an artist until she did the *Tapestry* album, which was a monster . . . that's an added plus, of course, but the fact that they can sing, and sing their own songs with conviction and with feeling, that to me is extremely important.

AHS:      So a writer need not feel barred from Chappell merely because he doesn't have the potential to be, perhaps, a hit recording artist, as long as he can sing his own songs and get his own songs across well?

SCHUSTER:   Oh, sure, even if he can't sing, okay, I'm not even making that a requirement.

AHS:   But that's helpful?

SCHUSTER:   Most writers sing, but there's a difference between being able to sing a song so that it will be appreciated by your publisher, who is on your side, and singing it so that it will be appreciated by a producer or an artist three thousand miles away listening to a cassette in a car, or with the shower on, making a judgment . . . "Is this the song I'm going to cut?" That voice or rendition which may be acceptable within the publisher's office is not necessarily acceptable or even liked when heard under those other circumstances.

AHS:   How important is formal music training to you? How important is the ability to read and write musical notation?

SCHUSTER:   I think the importance is dependent upon the talent of the individual. There are people like Burt Bacharach and Marvin Hamlisch who have had great musical training and are greatly talented people and are greatly successful . . . but there are probably people who were in their classes at the same places, who studied the same things and maybe got higher grades, but didn't have the talent to create. On the other hand, there are people who do not read music, but who successfully write music. It's the creative force and the ability to sing or to play or to write words that count. The fact that you cannot then make a lead sheet really doesn't mean anything, because making a lead sheet is a technical function that someone else can do.

AHS:   Marvin Hamlisch is giving me an interview. I'm going to ask him the same question and see what his answer is.

SCHUSTER:   I think Marvin will probably be the first to admit that although training is fantastic to have, it doesn't necessarily mean you're going to be a great songwriter. I just want to say one other thing. If you're a writer who knows four chords on a guitar, your scope of writing has to be narrower than if you know many chords and many variations, because you then have a wider scope as far as melody and melodic possibilities are concerned, and when melodic possibilities open up, the lyrical possibilities open up. So it's all important, but great musical training does not make a great songwriter.

AHS: Does Chappell sign staff writers?

SCHUSTER: Yes.

AHS: I think you're one of the few remaining publishers who do.

SCHUSTER: I don't know what the answer to that is, but I know we do, and I know there are other publishers who do also.

AHS: Tell me how somebody could become a staff writer for Chappell. What deal he would get if he were a staff writer? Do you pay him a salary?

SCHUSTER: I'm not going to name a dollar figure, but what we would probably do is try to sign someone for X dollars, for six months, with options after that. Usually those options, if we were to pick them up, would entail some kind of an increase. This money would be an advance against earnings.

AHS: Your staff writers are employees for hire, and you own the copyrights of the songs they write?

SCHUSTER: Yes, we own the copyrights in that the songs are published 100% by Chappell, but they are the writers . . . and receive full writer's royalties.

AHS: Do your contracts provide that they are employees for hire?

SCHUSTER: When you say "employees for hire," that has a specific legal meaning, and I don't want to give you that answer because I'm not a legal person, okay?

AHS: To what extent is the source of material a factor to you? I'm getting to the question of unsolicited material, stuff that comes in over the transom . . . as opposed to material sent to you by someone in the business.

SCHUSTER: I think we're all human, and I think that if an attorney of great stature, if a manager of great stature, if a record-company executive of great stature sends me a tape and says, "Listen to this," I'm only human and I will listen to it before something that has come in from somebody I don't know. I think everybody would probably admit to that. . . . I hope they would admit to it because I think it's the truth.

AHS: In general, they do.

SCHUSTER: The fact is that everything that comes to Chappell addressed to someone is listened to by a qualified, and I underline that, a *qualified* person in our company, someone who has been taught what to listen for, by us, and knows that unless they feel that it is really something that has absolutely no value for us, they are then to give it to me or to someone with whom I work on a "higher" level for an evaluation. In other words, I cannot possibly listen to everything that everybody in the world wants to send in . . . I can't, okay, but someone in our company does.

AHS:          You said something very fast.

SCHUSTER:   What?

AHS:          It slid right past, and I want to underscore it. You said anybody who sends something addressed to *someone*.

SCHUSTER:   Right. I think that anyone who wants to be in the music business should have initiative enough either to make a phone call, or read a trade paper, or find out who the people are at the publishing company to whom a cassette should be sent. Find out, make a phone call or look in trade papers and find out the names of the appropriate people, and then address your tape to those people. I know, at Chappell, if something is addressed to me, I open it. I'm not going to open it if it's sent "Return Receipt Requested, Certified Mail," because I become leery, and if somebody sends it that way, they're going to get it back. But if somebody sends mail addressed to someone at our company, it will be opened, it will be listened to, and a reply will be given. We make no money, get no vicarious thrills and no kicks out of finding nothing. Our business is to find hit material, so when we reject something, it is no pleasure; it is a chore. We want to find hits.

AHS:          May I ask you a really tough question?

SCHUSTER:   Anything.

AHS:          How long have you been in the business? How often has unsolicited material proven of merit or value to you?

SCHUSTER:   Okay, in over twenty years in this business, I can only think of one instance. Someone who worked with me named Neil Portnow, who is now V.P., A & R of Arista Records, listened to an unsolicited song and he thought it was pretty good. He gave it to me to listen to. I called the writer, suggested some lyric changes, which were made, and took the song over to Clive Davis, because the writer wanted to be an artist too. Clive liked the song, but did not need another artist at the time. He had the song recorded by a group called Silver, and the song was called "Wham Bam

Shang-A-Lang." It wasn't a number-one record; it was a number-fifteen or twenty record on the pop charts, and it was successful, but that's the one out of . . . out of . . .

AHS: The only one out of how many thousands?

SCHUSTER: I can't begin to tell you because I don't even know how much I've listened to. I really don't. My life is spent listening to music, so it's got to be thousands.

AHS: It would appear that the odds are very low.

SCHUSTER: Oh yes, and the person, let me say this, the person who sent this unsolicited tape was not an amateur, though I didn't know him, and he had never had anything done before; he knew music and he knew how to write songs and he was working with a band down in Maryland.

AHS: Did he have any subsequent success?

SCHUSTER: Not to my knowledge.

AHS: I hear people telling me they never had anything that was ultimately successful come in over the transom.

SCHUSTER: Yes. Well, this is the only one that I can point to that, you know, made it . . . that was a chart record . . . and to me that's successful for an unsolicited song.

AHS: Just getting it recorded is successful for an unsolicited song.

SCHUSTER: Right. Right.

AHS: I'm going to ask you a question that came to mind in the last deal, or nondeal, we recently didn't make.

SCHUSTER: Sure.

AHS: In an era when writers are constantly being advised by their counselors to hold onto their publishing, what incentive do you as a publisher offer to writers to give it up? By their publishing, of course, I mean their copyrights.

SCHUSTER: Are you talking about 100% rather than a split company? Is that what you mean?

AHS: Well, you resisted my attempt to get a split company very, very strenuously.

SCHUSTER: Well, I think it's a matter of position, of strength, as in any business dealing. It depends upon what strength the new person has and what strength the company has . . . . Each tries to make the best deal possible. When it comes to someone who's established, and who says, "Hey, I want to be in business with you, but these are the terms," we then have to decide whether the terms are acceptable to us and whether to do it or not to do it. With someone who we feel is newer and needs us more than we need them, we will do what we feel is best for us. We will, however, work hard for everybody . . . . Let me say one thing, because I think it's important. When professional men sit down in their own room and say, "Okay, I've got to find some songs for Roberta Flack," or "I've got to find some songs for whoever it is that's recording," they do not say, "Well, we own 25% of this song or 50% of this song or 75% of that song or all of that song." They really don't. Their job is to get a song recorded. First of all, nobody can keep in his head how much of any song we own. We have songs on tapes, we have lists, we look through our stuff, and if the song looks like it fits the artist, we want to get a record, and it really doesn't matter how much of a song we own, and I want to make sure that everybody understands that. Getting the song recorded is what counts. We will try to make the best deal we can for ourselves, and if the writer believes that he's worth half the copyright and we don't agree, then we will say, "We think you're talented, but we can't work with you under those terms because they're not right for us."

AHS: That's what you said to my client last week.

SCHUSTER: God bless you, and good luck.

AHS: You didn't say "God bless you." You did say "Good luck," though!

SCHUSTER: No, I mean that's really it. It's like any other business.

AHS: The dues-paying part . . .

SCHUSTER: Of course. Of course it is. But "dues-paying" sounds like a rip-off, and it's not a rip-off.

AHS: I understand that. I didn't mean it in a pejorative sense.

SCHUSTER: Everybody starts out in this business and everybody, when he gets to be whoever he can get to be someday, then can say, "If you want to be in business with me, I'll give you 10% to administer and I'm going to keep 90%," and if some company wants it badly enough, they'll take it.

AHS: Leverage?

SCHUSTER: Exactly.

AHS: Okay. Now, assume you were in never-never land and you could have your every wish. What would you prescribe as your ideal demo record? How many songs, what kind of accompaniment?

SCHUSTER: Oh, you mean for a person sending in a demo?

AHS:          Right.

SCHUSTER:     I would say for their own, as well as for my, benefit
(because they are the ones who are outside pressing their
nose against the glass trying to get in), no more than four
songs, in keeping instrumentally with the kind of song it is.
If it's a funky song or a rhythm song, it's tough to do with a
guitar and vocal or a piano and vocal, because the rhythm
is needed and therefore you need three or four pieces to get
the feel of the song. Certain ballads can be done with
guitar/vocal or piano/vocal and it doesn't matter. Ah, I
think the mistake a lot of people who are trying to get in
the business make is trying to say, "I can write all kinds of
songs." I don't want all kinds of songs. If somebody writes
country songs, let him send four great country songs to
me. Variety is not what I'm looking for. So many times
writers have said to me, "Well, I can't send you just four
because I write so many different kinds," and I say to them,
"Send me four country songs, send me four black songs,
send me your best songs, I don't care if they're all in the
same bag, it doesn't matter." Variety doesn't mean anything. If you think about great writers, and I'm not going
to name any, you realize that the greatest writers have a
style. I don't mean they copy themselves, but I mean they
have a style, and they have found success in their style, and
the world loves their style and buys millions of records for
that style. They do what they do best. If the writer is going
to have to sing the song on the demo . . . if he can't get a
demo singer, then he should sing the kind of song he sings
best on the demo. If I'm white and if I'm a girl, I should not
be doing a demo of a song that I think is a Kool & The
Gang song, because I'm not going to sound right on it. I
would be better off doing a demo of one of my songs that's
more appropriate for Anne Murray, because that's closer
to me and to what I can do. So you have to keep in mind
what you sound like, what you write best, and the last
thing, the most important thing, is to say to yourself, "I am
now sitting in a room with Clive Davis or with Anne
Murray or with So-and-so; I am facing them. Am I
playing the best songs I have for them?" You have to be
extremely, extremely critical. . . . Don't be yourself when
you're choosing songs; be the opposition, and say to your-

self, "Is this song really good enough?" Be supercritical. Extremely critical.

AHS:    I have felt, and perhaps I'm wrong, and you're certainly in a position to correct me, that a lot of writers, a lot of artists, when they plan their demos, usually include too many songs. . . .

SCHUSTER:    Always.

AHS:    And when they do, they always save their really great song for the third cut. . . . You know, I'll tease them with one or two, I'll really knock them on their asses on the third cut. And they don't realize that you've turned off the machine by the time the third cut's come up.

SCHUSTER:    Sure, well, it's not so much that we turn off the machine. They have to realize that they are fighting for people's attention, and when the listener puts on your tape, that's when his attention is at the highest it's going to be for your tape. So put your best song on first! If you put your best song last, he has been turned off by *you* by the time your best song comes on. So, go with your best shot. You're doing this from far away, so hit them with your best shot first, right away, and you'll keep them interested.

AHS:    Is there any pearl of wisdom that you've been wanting to impart to writers that you haven't had a platform for? . . . Here's your chance!

SCHUSTER:    Quality! I think the only word that I could ever impart to anybody is when you're writing a song, write quality. Now, by quality, I don't mean you have to write a long, slow, beautiful ballad. Whatever the bag is, quality in lyrics, in chords, in music, in concept . . . quality is going to make it over junk every time.

AHS:    If it doesn't knock your socks off, don't think for a minute it's going to knock somebody else's off.

SCHUSTER:    Absolutely. Just to give you an example, and I don't want to overdo this, but it's important . . . melody is, you know, the vehicle that carries the song. I'm not saying which is more important, the melody or the lyric—they're both important—but . . . . when lyric writers are writing, they should have their hook. All these things have been said a million times, but one thing I think is very important for lyric writers to remember—in addition to all the rules about the AABA or the verse, chorus or the hook—you should strive, if you can, to have a line or two in a song that is not part of the title, but stands out. There are two songs that particularly come to mind, one which has been around a long time, and one which is new. There's a line in the *Arthur* theme which is not part of the title, but it's a line that says "... if you get caught between the moon and New York City." A line like that, even though you don't know what it really means, is something that stands out and is remembered. It adds a little extra spice. There's another song which was a hit called "I'd Really Love to See You Tonight," and there was a line in that that was "... there's a warm wind blowing the stars around," which is not part of the title or anything else, but it's a lovely line, it's an added picture in your song, and if you can get one or two of those in a song in addition to everything else you do, you've got an added plus; so try to do that, too.

AHS:       I think you're an incorrigible romantic.

SCHUSTER:  Oh, of course I am. You have to be.

AHS:       Thank you very much.

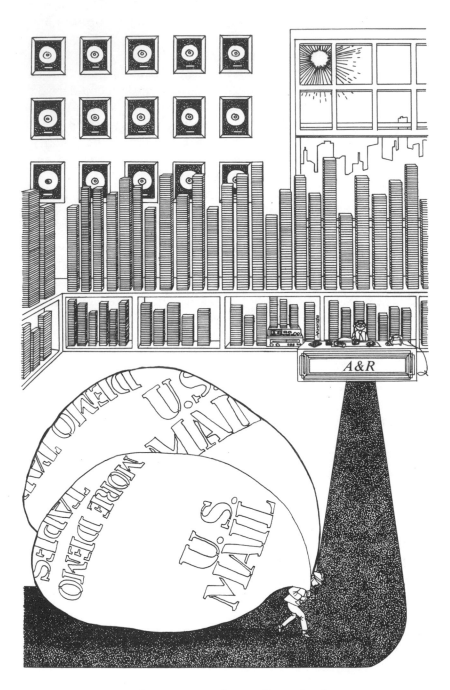

*Of course everything is listened to!*

# 3

# (Si Si) Je Suis Un Rock Star

**S**top! If, as I suspect is the case, your prime interest and major concern is the acquisition of a recording contract, you may, after having consulted the table of contents, turned directly to this chapter. If you have, it was a mistake . . . but an easily corrected one. Turn back to page three and start reading! This chapter will have infinitely more meaning and will be of significantly more benefit to you if you have read that which precedes it. Too many of the principles set forth in " I Write The Songs" are equally applicable to this chapter to be ignored and yet are too long to bear repetition. Similarly, the background information in the chapters that precede this one is needed to place this chapter properly in context. If you haven't yet read those two chapters, you will not have an adequate frame of reference in which to read what follows. Take my word for it, I planned it that way. Are you now thoroughly familiar with the Lexicon? If not, read it again—you will profit more from this chapter if you do.

If you knew nothing about the music business before starting this book, you probably have an edge. If you are possessed of a smattering of ignorance, I would beseech you to degauss that part of your mind as you would your tape heads.

Years ago, when I was into fishing, there were ads in the sporting magazines featuring a fisherman's "deliar." It was a little scale with a built-in tape measure. It shrank many a whopper (no, the word wasn't invented to describe a hamburger) to frying-pan size.

I used to think fishermen, golfers, and teen-age males had cornered the market on hyperbole in describing their "scores." They pale by comparison with rock-'n-roll bands describing the phantom record deals they turned down or the real record deal they finally landed. About three years ago I was told by a disc jockey in whom I had great faith with respect to all things musical (but not business) that a certain new group had received a million dollars for signing a recording contract with one of the major record companies. I told him that I didn't believe it. I would have bet a Ferrari that a new band couldn't get $1,000,000 from that record company with an Uzi submachine gun. My friend was so insistent, however, that I made a note to check it out. When I was able to buttonhole an executive of the company in question and confront him with the story, his response was as I had predicted. I think it was something like "What are you smoking?" The DJ called me a few days later and acknowledged that the group had been engaging in creative arithmetic in valuing their deal. They had received a $20,000 advance on signing ($5,000 a man). The remaining $980,000 was arrived at by adding up the advances they would receive *if* they were successful and *if* the record company exercised all of its options and extended the deal for a full five years, and by including all of the recording costs that would be spent *if* the record company recorded all of the albums it was entitled to record *if* it exercised all of its options. Well, if you figure the recording costs for from seven to ten albums at about $750,000, and if you assume, as you should, that the remaining $230,000 is advances spread out over the four remaining option pickups, with the larger portions allocated to the third and fourth option pickups (when success is assured and when the advances are in all likelihood earned before they are paid), it places the deal in perspective.

I would suggest therefore that, for the time being at least, you erase from your conscious mind all tales of sugarplum fairies you may have clung to in the past and be very skeptical of the scuttlebutt you hear in the streets. To do otherwise is very counterproductive. It's psychologically demoralizing; it renders you incapable of appreciating an otherwise satisfactory offer; it enhances the chances of "turning off" advisers who may feel they could never satisfy your expectations.

What are your chances of making it as a recording artist? If you are an awesomely talented performer *and* a great songwriter, your chances are excellent. If you are either of the above (and merely terrific at the other), your chances are good. If you are neither of the above, your chances are remote unless you are pretty damn close to being in both of those categories and, in addition, possess some unique qualities that will move a record company to believe you are salable. A sure-fire hit single never hurt.

What about all the successful recording artists you can name that are "none of the above"? Your assessment of their merit and talent is probably in error, or they possess some unique quality with which they are reaching, touching, and charming their audience.

I have been fortunate in that whenever I have difficulty with introductory material for a chapter, a suitable introduction seems to walk into my office. In this particular instance, it walked in on very good legs. A young man had sought an appointment to discuss my representing his band. At the appointed time he arrived, not alone, but with an exceptionally attractive young woman, who, it emerged, was the band's co-leader and lead singer. Their story, though unique to me, is probably not atypical. In fact, it is probably typical of many would-be recording artists who take their shot in the only manner they perceive available to them, fail, give up, and become assimilated into "normal" walks of life.

My visitors told me that they had mailed out seventy-five demo cassettes. They received responses from only a tiny fraction of those record companies and producers to whom their demos were sent. Only two of the responses were "encouraging"—inviting them to send more material. A & R people at two major record companies they approached in person told them that their demo would not be considered unless submitted under the aegis of an entertainment attorney, accountant, or manager. Hence their call to me.

They indicated that they had written some new songs that were better than the ones on the demo (an artist always perceives his new songs as "better") and would have a new demo in a few weeks. They gave me the "package" they had sent out, which included a picture. The picture was reminiscent of group club pictures found in high-school yearbooks. The lighting was harsh and the print was dark. The very attractive blonde lead singer was all but lost in the picture. The consensus upon subsequent listening to the tape was "not bad." The songs were "not bad," the vocals were "not bad," and the production was "not bad." In the 60s or 70s I imagine the seventy-five cassettes sent out would have borne more fruit. But in the 80s, with the record industry singing the blues, with some record companies "not signing" new acts, and some not even listening to new acts, "not bad" ain't good enough!

To break in as a recording artist today, you must have outstanding new material coupled with outstanding performances. Record companies have always searched for the elusive hit single. When the industry was booming, the record companies had the necessary profit margin to gamble on records that might have a shot. Today they must feel certain.

As you will learn from the interviews accompanying this chapter and the chapter entitled "I Write The Songs," most publishers and record companies profess to listen to all material sent to them. A careful reading of the interviews will indicate that some of the executives waffle a bit on this subject. Some indicate that they "try" to listen to all material thus submitted. Others indicate that material submitted "cold" receives a more cursory listening than material received from professional sources. A really careful reading of the interviews, with few exceptions, discloses that the publishers and record companies have found the mails to be a uniquely barren source of income-producing songs and records. Apparently it is considered un-American or undemocratic not to listen to unsolicited material, or at least bad public relations. With all due respect to the publishers and record companies, it is my impression that material submitted directly through the mails by writers and artists receives cursory attention at best. After all, who is apt to continue panning for gold in a stream that doesn't produce?

Why do record companies give preferential listening treatment to demos submitted by entertainment lawyers, accountants, and managers? Because they have great "ears" and know what is and what isn't a hit? Hell, no! If they had that capacity, they would have their own record companies or be on their yachts. The answer is twofold.

First, it's good business. The same lawyers, accountants, and managers who are hustling deals for unknowns are the lawyers, accountants, and managers who represent the stars now providing the record companies with their sustenance; the same stars whose current contracts will someday expire and who will be seeking new affiliations or renewals of existing affiliations. They therefore have a power base, and power begets "courtesy" and preference. It's just good business to keep such lines of communication open. Most reputable lawyers, accountants, and managers will candidly advise new acts that they don't hold out the promise of a deal—only the likelihood of a considerate "listen."

Second, the lawyers, accountants, and managers provide the record companies with an automatic screening process. Ninety-nine percent of the cassettes in the record companies' bulging mailbags are not of professional quality and hence of no interest at all to them. Usually an act whose tape is submitted by a lawyer, accountant, or manager has gone through a process of "natural selection" and paid some dues. The vast majority of the acts who have found an entertainment attorney, accountant, or manager have endured rejection at one level or another, and persisted. They have usually formed and reformed or been part of several bands, and, in general, have "been around." In all likelihood, they have become or are on the verge of becoming professionals. The easily discouraged, the dilettantes, the high-school bands, the hobbyists with delusions, and those bereft of any talent at all fall by the wayside before finding and investing in professional help. The record companies know that when a tape comes from a lawyer, accountant, or manager at least some screening has taken place. None of such sources are apt to risk their credibility with the record companies by submitting junk preordained for rejection.

With knowledge born of experience, most of us (at least those of us past professional pubescence) cast in this screening role have come to realize that we don't know what is or isn't a hit. By the same process, we have acquired a sense of what is "in the ballpark" of acceptability, or at least a sense of what isn't embarrassing. Of course we are all fallible and have politely discarded acts who subsequently "made it." They love to encounter us at cocktail parties and cast disdainful "I told you so" glances at us . . . and who wouldn't relish such an opportunity?

Is it tougher to break in as a recording artist than as a songwriter? Of course it is. The economics of the business dictate that it must be. For a music publisher to accept a song from you represents a minimal monetary investment. A very modest advance and the cost of a demo usually represent the maximum financial exposure of the music publisher. Very often there is no advance and your demo becomes the publisher's demo. Hence the publisher's financial exposure is limited to the costs of the form contract you have signed.

When a record company prepares to take the plunge, it is at considerably greater risk. You then represent an investment that can be modestly estimated at a quarter of a million dollars. No, I'm not out of my mind. Artists tend to think only in terms of what crosses their palms. What about the other palms involved? Besides an advance to the artist, which may very well be modest, there are recording costs for an album, the costs of pressing records, artwork, manufacturing jackets, shipping, distribution, and promotion. Accept the fact, therefore, that there are a lot of dollars' worth of "belief" in any record deal . . . and a lot of artists competing for that belief.

How do you go about securing your share? Well, all the things said above about getting into the business, getting close to people in the business, and paying dues, as true as they were with respect to songwriters, are even more applicable to the recording artist.

If the quest for a record deal can be analogized to basketball, sending tapes cold through the mail would be the equivalent of a shot from mid-court at the final buzzer with Kareem Abdul-Jabbar guarding you—a low percentage shot. If you have entrée to the record company through a third party who is championing your talent, the percentage rating of your shots is directly proportional to the clout of your sponsor. A supermanager with a heavy act already on the label may provide you with a lay-up; a hot producer, a shot from the foul line. On the other hand, it can be tougher to procure a supermanager or a heavy producer than it is to procure a record deal. Is there a slam dunk? Only if you can create a situation where the record company comes to you!

How do you do that? Ah, were there an easy or glib answer to that question. Unfortunately, you know the answer. You've got to create a "buzz" in the industry, and the only way to accomplish that is to work at your trade and to excel. You do this by performing and by keeping on performing and creating a following. The buzz follows and so will the record deal if you have "the right stuff." The right stuff in this context means hit songs and a quality that in the eyes of a record company is sufficiently unique to translate into that much abused word "charisma."

The message here is not to abandon all other avenues, but, on the contrary, to pursue all avenues; don't get so caught up in shortcuts, "edges," and "contacts" that you lose sight of the fact that to be a recording artist you must first be a performing artist. So, follow up on all your "contacts," court the powers that may be able to help you, play cassette roulette, but never lose sight of the fact that you are first and foremost a musician, a singer, and a performer. If you work at your art or craft or whatever else you call it, and if the talent is there, it will emerge and the pieces will fall into place and the record deal will happen, and the stardom . . . and the headaches.

At this point it would be appropriate for you to reflect on why you are reading this book. If you are anticipating a career as a performing artist as a means to an end—fame, fortune, and the good life—I would urge you better to invest your time, money, and energy in securing an education. Although fame may not follow, the chances of attaining a fortune and the good life are far greater. The entertainment road to those life goals is a low-percentage shot. If, on the other hand, a career as a performing artist is for you the end itself, then go for it! You can't lose.

You have probably heard the expression "record deal" so often and in so many contexts that you may even think you know what it means. You probably don't. Record deals come in so many shapes, sizes, disguises, and configurations that the term no longer has a definable meaning. There was a time in the not too distant past when the term had a very definite meaning. It was an exclusive recording agreement between a recording artist and a record label. The newest newcomer and the veteran star had essentially the same record deal. Oh, the royalties were different (but not that different) and the advances (if any) were different, but essentially their contracts were the same. You could track the paragraphs from contract to contract and, with a few minor variants, they were comfortingly or disquietingly similar (depending upon whether you were the newcomer or the veteran).

With the burgeoning of the record business in the 60s and 70s, huge profits were being made by the record companies. The cataract of cash stimulated the creative juices of the managers and attorneys, who proceeded to structure deals designed to alleviate the cash burden suffered by the record companies and to protect the recording artists from their resulting tax burdens. As the profits continued to flow, the arrogance and inventiveness of the artists' team kept pace. The record companies matched the artists' arrogance with their own greed and imprudence, and the fratricidal bidding wars for top artists (and even new artists) characterized the record industry in the 70s ensued. Mopping-up operations were led by the bootleggers and the equipment manufacturers, who placed tape-copying ability in the hands of every sixth grader in America. Pacman and his electronic hordes roamed the carnage administering the *coup de grace* to the wounded.

As the record companies folded one by one or were absorbed by the majors, new administrations pledged to conservatism grasped the reins of the survivors, and even where the hands on the reins were the same, they became tightly clenched. The net result is a reversion to the old days and ways, diminished opportunity for you, and, consequently, a greater need for you to excel in your art and to understand the business you are trying to break into. The deal structures invented during the boom years have persisted even though the boom hasn't. When you get your record deal, you will need an entertainment attorney to negotiate it for you. The contract will run from twenty-five to forty single-spaced pages and is not written in English. The language is jargon and it will be cast in a style I have just christened "fail-safe convolution." The style is born of paranoia (not necessarily undeserved) and provides for each unpalatable provision to appear twice, usually widely separated in the text, once in wolf's clothing and once in sheep's clothing. The theory is simple: if the artist's attorney knocks it out once, there is a chance he won't pick it up the second time and at least there will be an ambiguity that can be played with later on. If you want to leave this to your cousin with the real-estate practice in Mineola, that's up to you, but you've been warned. In running through the deals, I will not analyze each type of contract beyond what I think you should know to avoid "giving away the store" and to enable you to maintain intelligent discussions with record people, producers, and prospective managers before your attorney is retained. This is not a "do-it-yourself" course in negotiating a record deal!

Before dealing with reality, there is one fantasy that should be discussed and disposed of. If you follow a familiar pattern, you will begin your quest for a record deal confident that if you are just heard, you will be signed. When acceptance by record companies does not follow and your disappointment and frustration mount, your thoughts, as those of many before you, will turn to making your own record, having it distributed, and "showing them all." This is a way to go if you firmly believe that poverty is the fountainhead of creativity. It doesn't work, for many reasons. First, it is very expensive; second, at this stage your career, although you are capable of making a demo adequate to demonstrate your potential to a record company, you do not possess the skill to capture the production qualities required for a commercially competitive record; third, you won't be able to get national distribution worthy of the name; fourth, if you are able to get the record played on the air, you will not have the resources or expertise to exploit your brief success; finally, the resulting cartons of records will jam up your closet and will provide you with a "bummer" each time you open the door. The records thus pressed won't even make great demos—A & R people can't play them in their cars.

Let's now look at the basic record deals *you* will (a positive attitude is a prerequisite to success) be confronted with. We need not, and shall not, explore the exotic arrangements your attorney may conjure up when you are a proven platinum artist.

There is nothing wrong with a record company trying to give the most minimal deal possible to a new artist, especially during the early stages of his career when the risk is high and the chances of profit low. On the other hand, there is nothing wrong with the artist seeking the best deal he can possibly obtain. The point is that the words "right" and "wrong," "fair" and "unfair," have little place in the structuring of a record deal. The negotiation of a record deal is a balancing act. Both sides are constantly adding and subtracting from their side of the scale. The amazing thing is how often, when the artist is adequately represented, a balance is struck with which both sides feel comfortable. The process is a long one. Often months pass between the first draft and the traditional signing picture in *Cash Box* or *Billboard*.

Curiously, the consummation of a deal for an established artist usually takes much less time than a deal for a new artist. The reasons are threefold:

1.  The deal for an established artist will be thoroughly discussed before it emerges as a contract, and the contract will pretty closely resemble the deal.
2.  The contract will not be a form and will not contain any of the more offensive pro-record-company provisions that the attorney for a new artist has to struggle to have deleted or modified.
3.  The deal will not be put on the "back burner" by the record company's attorney while more important things are taken care of. There will be nothing more important! No record-company employee will look forward to Christmas if he knows he is thought of as being responsible for losing a major artist because of negligence or procrastination.

There are two basic ways by which you will find yourself "signed" to a record label, directly or through an independent producer. In the first instance, the governing contract will be between you and the label. In the second instance, your contract will be with the independent producer, which will in turn enter into a contract with the label whereby it agrees to provide your exclusive services as a recording artist to the label. Let us consider the direct route as the basic situation, become familiar with it, and use it as a point of departure in comprehending the independent-producer situation. In either situation your accountant may recommend for tax purposes that you operate through the vehicle of your own corporation, but for our present purposes we can safely ignore that, and the term "you" as it is used in the following material can be interpreted as you or your corporation—which you will undoubtedly vest with a name of great symbolic or sentimental significance appreciated only by you or your closest confidants. In choosing such a name, please remember that it will stare back at you from your early record albums, made when you were young, impertinent, and improvident; hence try to pick a name that won't embarrass you later on. Back in the early 70s I had the pleasure of representing a group named The Fugs, which was at the time a daring and pioneering group known for the "underground" nature of their lyrics. Their corporation was named G.T.M. Inc. After seeing the name literally hundreds of times, curiosity impelled me to ask what the initials stood for. "Get The Money" was the response.

With that in mind, let's ramble through the first draft (there may be three or four) of your first record contract, which we will assume to be between you and a major record label. Let's presume, lest this be too simple, that "you" are a rock-'n-roll group comprised of four members and that the name of the group is "Us" (which is a lot easier for me to write than "Four Musicians in Search of Fame and Fortune").

Having read Chapter 6 entitled "You've Got A Friend," "Us" found a suitable entertainment lawyer. As you make yourselves comfortable in his office, one member of the group hands the attorney a copy of the contract "Us" has been given by the record company. It is the one with the group's notations. The attorney asks for a clean copy so that his own notes will be clear. This does not present a problem, since the record company has provided you with six copies. A clean copy is found. The attorney lays both your notated copy and the clean copy aside.

"Before getting into these, we have to take care of something that is very important . . ."

"Oh, oh, here it comes; he's gonna want a check."

". . . and that is the relationship between the four of you. Are you equal members of, and participants in, 'Us,' or are some of you 'more equal' than others?"

A hush falls over the lawyer's office as eye contact is sought (and sometimes avoided) between the various members of "Us."

The attorney is trying to get "Us"'s house in order before taking on the record company. He is concerned about two distinct areas, and his experience has taught him that it is best to resolve them at the very inception of the relationship. The first is the division of record royalties among the various members of "Us." The second is the manner in which the income from the songs written by the members of "Us" is to be handled. Let's explore the possibilities.

Usually the members of the group consider themselves equal as recording artists, and the question is disposed of simply by agreeing to split the record royalties equally. Not infrequently, however, an enter-tainment group evolves in a curious fashion. There may be a nucleus of a few members who have starved together for five years and who have been the driving force behind the band, another member who has only starved with the band for one year, and a new drummer who was brought in only two weeks before the offer of a record deal came down and whose performance wasn't even on the demo that led to the deal. The veteran members of the group may well feel that the newer members should participate in royalties on a reduced level, or indeed should not participate in royalties at all but should merely receive a salary.

Of course, the resolution of these questions depends on the dynamics at work within the group. If the new kid on the block is the lead singer rather than the drummer, there are certain realities that can't be overlooked. Often the group has come to grips with this question before contracts are received and the question is quickly, if not always wisely, disposed of. If it is obvious that the question has not been previously thought of, much less resolved, a veteran attorney will suggest that it be the subject of discussion among the group alone and tabled until they can give it the time and consideration it deserves. The lawyer who intrudes in this area is guaranteed to lose the trust and confidence of some members of the group and thus diminish his effectiveness overall. For our purposes, and for the sake of simplicity, let's assume that "Us" decides to split record royalties equally among all members of the group.

Now for the sticky question of the music income! You will recall (if you didn't skip directly to this chapter) that music publishing income is traditionally divided into two parts: the writer's share and the publisher's share, which are roughly equal. Note that when we set up this hypothetical situation, it was stipulated that the recording contract we were to examine was between "Us" and a major record company. We can therefore assume with relative safety that the granting of the music-publishing rights to "Us" songs is not a precondition to the record deal. Thus, all the music-publishing rights, including the copyrights, reside in the writers of the songs. If "Us" is a typical rock-'n-roll group, in all likelihood one or two members of the group will be the writers of all or nearly all of the songs to be recorded by "Us."

"So what?" you ask.

So plenty! By simple subtraction, if two members of "Us" write the songs and own the music-publishing rights, the remaining two members don't own any music-publishing rights. It doesn't pose a problem right now because "Us" hasn't even recorded yet, much less had success. Let's, through the crystal ball of experience, take a peek into the future. "Us"'s first LP has gone gold and is still selling and you can't turn on a radio without hearing its single, which is number five with a bullet on the pop charts, destined for number one. Is everybody happy? Sort of. Well, two members of "Us" are happier than two other members of "Us." Relatively speaking, therefore, two members of "Us" are unhappy. Alas, you just can't avoid human nature! How unhappy are they and why? They are at least $300,000 worth of unhappy, and the reason is that they are not receiving that $300,000—and the two members of "Us" who write the songs *are* receiving it. By now I'm sure you figured it out . . . but just in case:

$$
\begin{array}{rl}
500,000 & \text{albums sold (gold)} \\
\underline{\times\ 10} & \text{songs in the album} \\
5,000,000 & \\
\underline{\times .04¢} & \text{mechanical royalty per song} \\
\$200,000.00 & \text{mechanical income}
\end{array}
$$

In addition to the mechanical income, one can estimate the performance-income value of a number-one single at approximately $100,000 ($50,000 writer share and $50,000 publisher share). There's $300,000 right there. Add to this, ancillary income from print and foreign licenses and residual future income, and you can safely assume $500,000 worth of unhappiness.

Is this apt to create problems for "Us"? If not recognized, confronted, and resolved early on, it most assuredly will. You don't think you'll mind driving a Porsche 928 while the writing members of your group are driving Rolls-Royces? The hell you won't! Not only does this situation lead to friction, dissension, and jealousy, but it also has a more direct and insidious effect on "Us"'s future product and success. When the disparity between the income of the writing and the nonwriting members of a group becomes obvious, and when the long-term value of having a continuously earning catalogue of songs in one's portfolio is realized, there is a natural tendency for nonwriters to try to become writers. In those rare instances when the talent is there, the result is a positive one. In most cases, however, the talent is not there and the result is a fierce competition to have inferior songs included as "B" sides or as "album cuts," thereby diminishing the quality, integrity, and homogeneity of future albums. When such efforts are resisted, as well they should be, the result is predictably quite negative, and ofttimes disastrous. Sure, there are times when there are no ill effects. When the egos of the group members and their maturity permit a realistic appraisal of their relative contributions to the group's success, gratitude can overcome greed and harmony may reign. But often this is not the case. The arguments on both sides can be persuasive.

A nonwriting lead singer argues: "I may not write, but I certainly am an essential element in the songs becoming valuable commercial properties. Our fans in no small part come to see and hear me. I am a very substantial part of the reason they buy our records and a primary source of the group's success. The songs are written if not for me to sing, at least with me in mind. Without me, the songs may not even be created, much less heard and economically valuable. It's not morally correct or economically viable for me not to participate in the tremendous economic benefits they throw off."

A less prominent nonwriting member offers: "The songs are written with all of us in mind. In some indefinable way we all contribute to their creation. The song as recorded by the group is not the same as when we first hear it. As in the case of good wine, something happens in the aging process. Good grapes don't necessarily produce a great wine. The evolution of the song as we play it demonstrates subtle but significant nuances that contribute to its success and value. Even if musicologically it's the same song, it's not commercially the same song. I feel I am entitled to share in the money the song earns."

On the other hand, the writer argues, with some emotion: "I've never considered myself greedy and I certainly don't want to cause pain to the other members of the group, but, frankly, the songs are the key to the group's success. There are lots of bands that can play rock-'n-roll as well as we do who don't even have record deals, much less the economic success we do. The differences between them and us is the songs I write. That is my gift, talent, or whatever that is responsible for our success, and although I am not diminishing anybody else's contribution, I am not about to denigrate my own. I think I am entitled to additional compensation for my unique contribution. The other members are benefiting indirectly but very substantially from my songs through their huge earnings as recording artists. It's not only the money; a part of me would feel outraged at the thought of adding the name of someone who didn't contribute to its creation to one of my songs. The idea offends me and I would feel ripped off economically. I think it would adversely affect my ability to write."

What is the solution to this dilemma? There are many, and they vary with the forces at play within the group, the personalities involved, the closeness of the members, their affection (or lack thereof) for each other, their egos, and their perceptions of each other, themselves, and the group, and of course the role the songs play in the group's success. I have seen resolutions ranging from one in which all members of the group share equally as writers and publishers of all songs recorded by the group regardless of which member or members did the actual writing, to the other extreme, where the writing and publishing are held only by those members who actually write the songs. Both extremes work—and fail—sometimes. Actually, it's a difficult subject for members of a group to discuss candidly and without rancor. I usually try to ease the way by presenting the above arguments in a hypothetical manner, thus making sure the various positions are on the table without any one of the members having to expose his innermost thoughts and risk incurring the displeasure of the co-members. If the situation seems appropriate, I may offer for consideration the following as a possible Solomonlike solution:

The actual writers of songs recorded by the group receive sole writer credit and full writer royalties. The copyrights and the publisher's share of income with respect to the songs recorded by the group are assigned to a publishing company owned equally by the members of the group. How would this work out for our mythical four-man group, "Us"? Assume two members co-write all the songs and a given song earns $10,000. $5,000 would be writers' royalties and $5,000 would be the publisher's share. The members of "Us" would receive the following shares of income derived from the music rights:

| | Writer Income | Publisher Income | Total |
|---|---|---|---|
| Writer Member A | $2,500.00 | $1,250.00 | $ 3,750.00 |
| Writer Member B | 2,500.00 | 1,250.00 | 3,750.00 |
| Nonwriter Member C | - 0 - | 1,250.00 | 1,250.00 |
| Nonwriter Member D | - 0 - | 1,250.00 | 1,250.00 |
| | $5,000.00 | $5,000.00 | $10,000.00 |

TABLE 3.1

Thus the special contributions of the writers are recognized. The contributions of the nonwriters are recognized, albeit to a lesser degree, their jealousy abated, and their inclination to write, perhaps poorly, is stilled. Harmony is maintained, and all members of the group are participating in the creation of a valuable asset which will stand all of them in good stead when their days as performers have passed. Notice that the writers remain total owners of all rights to songs not recorded by the group and are free to develop that aspect of their talent unencumbered and unhindered.

How you ultimately work this problem out depends on facts peculiar to your group, but work it out you should. Good luck!

With that out of the way, you can get back to the business at hand: the recording-artist contract. "Us"'s contract is the latest form of contract being used by one of the major record companies. If "Us" ran true to form, the notes and comments made by the members of the group may not focus on key negotiable areas. By this I mean that the average neophyte recording artist often expresses shock and dismay at the clauses in the contract that are by custom and usage immutable and acceptable. By the same token, there are no notations adjacent to the most outrageous and negotiable paragraphs. The contract received by "Us" consists of thirty-three single-spaced pages. It is a ponderous insomnia fighter, unintelligible to all but experienced entertainment lawyers. It is not "fair." It was created by very competent, well-remunerated lawyers whose job it was to create a document highly favorable to their client, the record company. It was not their job to make it "fair." It is the job of the artist's attorney to cause changes that will render the contract more equitable.

To analyze a thirty-three-page record contract word by word, line by line, even paragraph by paragraph, is beyond the scope of this book and the limits of your patience. It is not, however, beyond your lawyer's ability to perform such an analysis; indeed, it is his obligation. When he does so, as he must, he is exercising professional diligence even though the record company will characterize it to you as "nit-picking." When you hear from the record company's people that your lawyer is a pain in the (expletive deleted), smile pridefully and tell them that's what you pay him for. It means you probably have a good one! When the thirty-three-page contract is dissected, twenty-five of the thirty-three pages consist of boilerplate clauses found in all record contracts, which are not usually the subject of discussions between the artist and his attorney unless specific questions with respect thereto are asked by the artist. Do not lament over this . . . it keeps your fees down. Also, don't be misled. Although the boilerplate clauses are not discussed between you and your attorney, they must be discussed and negotiated between your attorney and the record company's attorney because, although universal in subject matter, boilerplate clauses do vary in their effect on your life and future income, depending upon the malevolence of their creator.

The remaining eight pages of the recording contract cover the "deal points." When the deal is struck between the record company's representative and your representative, whether your manager or your attorney, a transcript of the conversation would probably be less than a page. It is just such a page that the business affairs representative of the record company sends to the record company's lawyer in the form of a deal memo with instructions to prepare your thirty-three-page contract.

So, lest this chapter have the same soporific effect that a full-length record contract has, I shall limit the scope of our discussion to the deal points and to those items that I have learned come as a shock or surprise to artists. Now is a good time to get a cup of coffee and take a deep breath—you will need both.

## Exclusivity

All contracts between record companies and pop artists are exclusive. This means that for the duration of the term of your contract with the record company, you may not record for any other record company. The record company, is not, of course, exclusive to you. It can record and release records by as many artists as it chooses. Unfair? Not really. The record company, with justification, feels that if it invests the time and money to "break" you and if it takes the initial gamble on your talent, it is entitled to enjoy the fruits of its investment and not have you depart with your enhanced stature to a rival label. If you find this intolerable, your only solution is to become a classical musician or an opera singer. These are the only recording artists who enjoy the ability to flit from label to label. This, however, is not a solution available to many.

Remember, exclusive *means* exclusive. No exceptions are apt to be tolerated. If you wish to carve out exceptions, now is the time to do it. Two exceptions to exclusivity that can usually be won in the initial negotiation of a record contract are an exception to permit you to record jingles and an exception to permit you to record as a sideman on other artists' sessions.

Note also that if "you" are a group, your exclusivity extends to you as a group and to each member of the group as individual artists. Therefore, abandon any thought of avoiding your contract by leaving the original group and becoming a single artist or forming a new group.

## The Term

Now that we know that your services are to be exclusive to your record company, the next logical question is: For how long? this is negotiable within limits. I assure you it's not going to be for twenty minutes. For many years the standard term for a record contract was one year, with the record company having the right to extend the term for four additional one-year terms. These are the "options" you have heard about. When your records are successful, the record company "exercises its option" to extend the agreement. When the record company thinks you've had it as an artist, it does not exercise its option for the next year and the contract ends at the end of the year for which the last option was exercised. Democracy does not reign here; the option to continue the relationship belongs to the record company, not to the artist. Don't waste energy fretting about this; accept it. No lawyer can change it—not even yours!

Before this, I explained to you that contracts evolve like insurance policies, in that whenever the insurance company gets burned, a rider to cover the situation is added to the policy. In record-company contracts, the same principle applies although the Band-Aid is applied in the form of a language change or a new paragraph, rather than a rider. A while back, Olivia Newton-John effected a crucial change in the contract you will receive from your record company. I know, you never even met her! Miss Newton-John and her record company, MCA Records, sued each other at a time when she had not completed the number of albums she was obligated to deliver to MCA. Lest she decide to bless a new record company with her not insignificant services, MCA sought a court injunction to prevent her from recording for another record company until such time as she completed the number of albums she was obligated to deliver under her MCA contract. MCA, most experts thought, had been quite correct in its position that Miss Newton-John's contract was suspended each time she failed to deliver an album by the deadline prescribed in the contract, and that therefore she would remain the exclusive recording artist of MCA until such time as she fulfilled her obligations to MCA even if that time went beyond the expiration of the contract's five-year maximum term. The court, however, was of a different mind and expressed its doubt that Miss Newton-John's failure to perform her obligations under the contract could extend the contract beyond its specified five-year maximum term. In other words, a five-year exclusive recording contract could not be converted into a seven-or eight-year exclusive recording contract by virtue of the artist's failing to perform the services required of her (or him) during the term of the contract. Consequently, the record companies were threatened with the loss of their ability to compel the delivery of valuable product and with the loss of their most valued artists.

The court's decision acted to throw the switch on thousands of word processors throughout the entertainment world as record companies and their attorneys rushed to "correct" the court's "mistake," at least with regard to their future signings.

Thus, "Us"'s contract, and no doubt yours, will have a term not defined in numbers of years, but, rather, in numbers of albums delivered with options for additional numbers of albums to be delivered in the future. Accordingly, "contract years" becomes "contract periods" and the exact duration of your exclusive recording artist contract becomes quite conjectural and elusive. At this stage of your career, you are in all likelihood so preoccupied with *getting* a record contract that it is of little concern to you what its duration may be. That is understandable—but short-sighted. So much of the aura of record deals is associated with advances, royalty points, recording costs, and the like that the duration of the contract sometimes takes a back seat. It should not, especially in view of the new duration clauses. A year saved at the end of a record contract can translate into the dollar value of several royalty points over the entire previous term of the contract.

It is in the artist's interest to have the maximum duration of the contract be as short as possible. The record company, on the other hand, strives to have a term of as long duration as possible. Why? The bargaining position of a recording artist is weakest at the beginning of his career, and his initial recording contract will, in all likelihood, be the most favorable for the record company that it will ever be able to negotiate with that artist. Once stardom is reached, the balance of power shifts to the artist, and his next record contract is apt to be a "monster." The record company cannot lose by a long-duration contract. If the artist fails to become successful, the record company bails out of the association by not exercising its option for the next contract period. If the artist becomes successful, the longer the record company enjoys the advantage of the relatively low royalties and advances it was able to negotiate with the "new" artist, and the longer it is able to keep the artist out of its competitors' clutches. Even if a new contract is to be negotiated with the successful artist before the expiration of the full term of the original contract, the remaining years provide the record company with increased leverage during the renegotiation.

A look at the applicable language of the "Us" contract, which is typical of the term language coming into use, will illustrate this point:

1.  *Term*

    1.01

    The term of this agreement will begin on October 20, 1982, and will continue for a first Contract Period ending nine months after the date of completion of the masters to be used in manufacturing the disc Phonograph Record units to be derived from the last Master Recordings made in fulfillment of your Recording Commitment for that Contract Period under paragraph 3.01 below.

    1.02

    You grant Company four separate options to extend that term for additional Contract Periods ("Option Periods") on the same terms and conditions, except as provided herein.

Company may exercise each of those options by sending you a notice at any time before the expiration date of the Contract Period which is then in effect (the "current Contract Period"). If Company exercises such an option, the Option Period concerned will begin immediately after the end of the current Contract Period.

(Paragraph 2 omitted for our purposes.)

3. *Recording Commitment*

3.01

During the Contract Period indicted below, you will perform for the recording of Master Recordings as indicated, cause those Master Recordings to be produced and delivered to Company (the "Minimum Recording Commitment"). During each Contract Period, you will perform for the recording of Master Recordings sufficient to constitute one Album.

3.02

You will fulfill the Minimum Recording Commitment for each Contract Period within the first three months of the Period.

3.03

(a)   During each Contract Period indicated below, Company will have the option to increase the Recording Commitment for that Period as provided below ("Overcall Recordings"). Company may exercise that option by sending you a notice at any time before the end of the Contract Period concerned.

1. With respect to each Contract Period, Company will have the option to increase the Recording Commitment by Master Recordings sufficient to constitute one (1) additional Album.

(b)   Each time Company exercises an option referred to in subparagraph 3.03 (a):

1. You will deliver the Overcall Recordings to Company within three months; and

2. the current Contract Period will continue for nine months after the date of completion of the masters to be used in manufacturing the disc

Phonograph Record units of the Album com-
prising the Overcall Recordings.

I ask you, how would you like to have to read that stuff for a living?

Now for a bit of arithmetic. The term begins on October 20, 1982.
"Us" must complete its first album within three months thereafter (a
somewhat unrealistic time period). Nine months later, the company
exercises its right to receive an additional recording (the company is in
no rush to exercise this option). A full year has now expired! Add three
more months (again highly unrealistic) for delivery of the additional
recording. "Us" is now fifteen months into the first contract period. Add
nine more months for the first contract period to end pursuant to
Paragraph 3.03 (b) (2), and if my addition is correct, the first contract
period will take a full two years.

Using similar arithmetic with respect to each of the option periods,
"Us" is staring at a minimum of ten years with its first record
company—in all likelihood, its entire career. The Olivia Newton-John
case has resulted in a recasting of record contracts in such a way as to
diminish your opportunity to enjoy a second bite of the apple of
success. Incidentally, you might as well add approximately two years to
the total term, because none of the albums is apt to be completed within
the three-month periods provided in the "Us" contract. Remember you
will be on the road touring to promote each album and you will also
have to write the songs for each new album!

Had this book been written a few years ago, one short paragraph
would have sufficed for our discussion of the term. The recent devel-
opments in the industry, including the Newton-John case, the paucity of
record deals, and the increased conservatism of the record companies
have elevated the importance of the term as it is now constituted in
record contracts to a prime subject for negotiation.

An understanding by you of the foregoing is important, because
the term provision as integrated into the "Us" contract is kind of
subtle—it doesn't present a red flag to alert you to its ramifications. So
even if your contract is worded somewhat differently, make sure
someone on your side does the arithmetic. If your record contract is of
modest duration, you may be content to pay your dues and look
forward to your second bite of the apple in your next contract. If it is of
inordinately long duration, you must try to write your second bite into
it in the form of royalties and advances in subsequent contract periods
which are consonant with the success you may assume you will have
attained by virtue of the record company's having exercised its options

for so many successive contract periods and albums.

Okay, enough for the problem. What is the solution? Your attorney will try several gambits. The success of each or all of them will depend, as usual, on your leverage (how anxious the record company is to sign you) and your attorney's ability to read the signals he receives in the course of the negotiation. Obviously, any solution, in order to work, has to be acceptable to both sides. Thus the record company must avoid the Newton-John case and have the right to your services for a long enough period to justify its investment in you. On the other hand, the artist cannot feel he is signing away his entire professional life for a too-modest remuneration.

The basic structure of the "Us" contract term can be maintained and the duration of the term shortened in three ways. First, the total number of albums can and should be reduced. Second, the time period (nine months in this case) between the delivery of the first album in each contract period and the company's exercise of its right to an overcall recording can and should be reduced. Third, the nine-month period between delivery of the overcall recording and the expiration of that particular contract period can and should be reduced. How much can these periods be reduced? It depends upon how long they are to begin with, the record company involved, and the usual intangible factors inherent in your "bargaining position." A reduction from nine months to six months would not deprive the record company of any of the protection it needs (six months being adequate in most cases for them to assess the desirability of exercising their options for overcall recordings and additional contract periods) and would shorten the term by a full two and one-half years, leaving a still too-long term from the artist's point of view. An additional cut in the term can by accomplished only by reducing the maximum number of albums available to the record company. From the artist's point of view, ten albums is too much. A reduction to seven or eight albums, which should be considered reasonable by most record companies, would bring the total term down to a duration that both sides could live with.

There is a much simpler approach which may meet with acceptance by the record companies, especially if negotiated as part of the deal while the deal is still in its "talking" stage. Once a draft contract is received, changes in its structure are harder to make because of the bureaucracy involved in the process. Generally, the larger the record company, the larger the bureaucracy and the more "permissions" are needed to make a change in the company's contract form.

Representing the artist, I would ideally like to see a seven-album deal with one album delivered during each nine-month period. Albums two and three would be elected by the record company on the basis of individual options, whereas the options for albums four and five and albums six and seven would be exercised as two-album "packages."

The total duration under this package comes to sixty-three months, or a little over what was the traditional five-year term, and the two-album "sets" lend some stability to the deal for the artist after the record company has had sufficient experience with him/her to make an intelligent decision as to whether it wants more product.

Perhaps you can do better, perhaps you will do worse; at least you will, I hope, understand what you did and be better able to conduct yourself in a manner that will enable you to make the best of your situation.

## *Product*

Although we pretty much covered this subject in the section covering the term, there are a few additional comments that are in order. During the 60s and early 70s it was more the rule than the exception for a record contract to provide for the initial recording obligation to be in terms of sides rather than albums. The record company would cause the artist to record two or four sides. A single would then be released, and, depending upon how it did, perhaps another single. If the single did well enough to justify a further investment, the record company would cause the artist to record "sufficient additional sides" for an album. Later on in the 70s, when the record industry was booming and money was plentiful and there was little resistance by the consumer to the purchase of albums, it was thought to be more efficient, once the artist was in the studio, just to do the album and pick the singles from the album. Accordingly, virtually all the record deals made during the mid and late 70s were album deals. Now, in the early 80s, with a flagging economy and sagging record sales, we are beginning to experience a reversion to "singles deals" and a relatively new phenomenon, the "EP deal." An EP is an extended-play record, usually consisting of five or six cuts and retailing for considerably less than a conventional LP. The theory behind singles and EP deals is simple. If the record company is to take a shot on a new artist, and if it is to make a mistake, it is better to make a $20,000 or $50,000 mistake than a $100,000 mistake. In addition, perhaps it is better to compete against Pacman for the shrinking teen-age dollar with a $4.98 EP than with a $9.98 LP. If the single or EP looks good, the record company can always exercise its option for sufficient additional sides for an LP.

Although the "Us" contract discussed in the preceding pages calls for albums, your deal may start with a single or an EP. Don't be overly distressed if you don't receive an album deal. There is a theory that the record companies have a tendency to be more generous with future royalties and advances when their initial investment is relatively small.

On the bright side, it seems incontestable that where there is a limited amount of money for investment in new artists, the smaller the initial investment, the more new artists are going to be given an opportunity. One of the artists who may profit as a result could be you!

## Recording Costs

Perhaps after reading this, you will prepare your material and rehearse your songs *before* going into the studio. It is in your interest to do so since all recording costs are ultimately borne by you. Although the record company will pay the recording costs initially, it will charge them to you as advances against your royalties as and when earned. The only exception that comes to mind is in the case of classical artists, who are paid from the first record sold and who are not charged with recording costs. Why? "Tradition" is the best answer I can find. But don't be jealous; the same tradition acts to make their royalty rates significantly lower than those paid pop artists.

The definition of recording costs contained in the Lexicon will suffice for your purposes at this time. The actual language in the "Us" contract is three single-spaced paragraphs long, and its inclusion will serve little purpose other than to confuse you. Your lawyer can chip away at it, but the chips will be little ones at best.

In the basic beginner situation, the record company quite understandably seeks to maintain as much control as possible. Their experience has shown them that too often when they have relinquished control, disaster results. Record-company executives become prematurely gray when the entire recording budget for an album has been expended and all they have to show for it are four or five sides. The best protection the record company has is to sign the producer directly, make him submit a budget for approval, make him live within its limits, and pay the bills itself upon receipt of vouchers. All record-company contracts have a clause whereby the record company has the right to have a representative present at all recording sessions; too rarely do they avail themselves of this right. Too often do record companies abdicate their responsibilities once the contract is signed. Indications are that they have learned (or are learning) this lesson. Most pop artists are young and have not yet attained the maturity that should accompany the responsibility they are so happy to assume. There are two major causes of excessive recording costs. The first is a failure to prepare adequately before going into the studio. Thus, the artist learns his material while paying astronomical studio rates when he could have done so in a loft or a house rented for the purpose at a fraction of the cost. The other is an obsessive quest for unattainable perfection—not knowing when a song is captured well enough to move along to the next number. The result is half an album that is overrefined and half an album that is rushed and inadequately rendered. How does this happen? It's a fact of life that often the producer never acquires, or loses, control over the artist . . . and, unfortunately, the record company usually ain't minding the store. Remember that ultimately it's *your* money that's being wasted and *your* record that's going to suffer from a shortage of money!

Although the foregoing reflects the most common recording-cost structure and illustrates the principles you should be aware of, there are an infinite number of variations on the theme. Sometimes, because of their manager, their attorney, leverage, or other factors, new groups receive more sophisticated and "favorable" deal structures. One of these, much coveted by new artists and their representatives, is the recording-fund structure. Its basic premise is that the record company will set aside a specified sum for each album to be delivered by the artist. Usually the amount of the recording fund escalates from the first album to the last album. That portion of the fund not used for recording costs is to be kept or received by the artist as an advance. Sometimes the record company pays the recording costs as they are incurred and pays the "balance" to the artist upon delivery of the album. Sometimes the artist or its corporate alter ego receives the entire fund and assumes the responsibility for paying recording costs. In the last case, the record company, in order to insure its receipt of an album, will spread the payment of the fund out over the course of the album's production. For example, one-third upon commencement, one-third at the halfway point, and one-third upon completion.

New artists greet this scheme with enthusiasm because they invariably underestimate what the album will cost and therefore anticipate a big "payday" when it is completed. Often, to their dismay, there is nothing "left over."

Beware of inflation. What may seem to be a generous recording fund when you start your first album in 1983 may be grossly inadequate when you start your sixth album in 1985 or 1986. You must try to make sure now that the escalations in the fund are sufficiently large, or that there is a provision for a "cost-of-living multiplier" so that rising recording costs do not all but absorb the "pocketable" portion of the fund that will be available to you in 1986.

## *Advances*

As you have already learned from the foregoing, there are advances and ADVANCES. In this section we shall be concerned with the real advances that you actually can put in your pocket and use as you see fit, as opposed to mythical advances such as recording costs, which, although charged against your future royalties, are not received by you for your own use.

Like most things today, advances ain't what they use to be. In general, they are considerably less in their dollar amount than they were in the past, and are further shrunken by the diminished value of the dollar. So be warned: you are not going to become "instant rich" merely by virtue of landing a record deal. Considering the effect that grotesquely large advances had on some new artists who were ill prepared to receive them and who were misguided or poorly managed, I am not at all sure that this is a totally negative development. Nevertheless, notwithstanding their diminished size, advances are very much on the minds of aspiring recording artists, and upon those who derive their income from serving them.

Advances usually escalate, rising from album to album as the term progresses. Initial advances can be very modest. "None" is very modest indeed, yet not unheard of in today's marketplace. Quite often the initial advance is measured by the artist's needs in order to commence recording. For example, the initial advance may be based on how many dollars are needed to rent a rehearsal loft for a few months, or the costs of essential equipment needed to enable the artist to proceed. After the initial advance, it is really just a question of bargaining. The artist's representative tries to get as much as possible, and the record company tries to give as little as possible. The record company's generosity is usually directly proportional to its estimate of its risk of recoupment. Hence advances are kept low for the early albums, when the artist's success is totally conjectural, and rises dramatically with the artist's longevity. The theory is simple: if the artist doesn't make it after the first few albums, the record company won't pick up its options for future albums and won't have to pay the higher advances called for with respect to those albums. On the other hand, if the options are picked up, it probably means that the artist's success has been established, or is at least predictable and the advances will be recouped out of the artist's earned royalties. The dilemma for the record company arises when after a few albums, the artist is hovering in the gray area between success and failure. If the advance for the next album is too high, it is a deterrent to the record company picking up the option. Most of the haggling over advances therefore takes place with respect to these middle albums. Large advances for albums that occur late in the term are often not as much of a problem; they have a cosmetic effect in making the contract appear attractive, and by the time they must be paid, the artist is established and recoupment of the advance is pretty well assured. In fact, the advances for albums late in the term are often earned when the record is shipped. So, to some extent, the large advances granted late in a contract term are illusory . . . or so argues the attorney for the artist. The record company, of course, argues the other side of the coin: "Why worry about the advance for the albums late in the term, especially if it's an illusion? The artist, at that stage of his career, will be recouping anyway. We'll only be giving him his own money, so why make a fuss?"

Well, it's nice to know that on a certain date, or upon a certain event, a large chunk of money is going to be coming in; it helps in planning. Besides, who knows when a career is going to crest?

Advances vary in amount depending on so many variables that it is impossible to suggest a rule of thumb. Factors that enter into the ultimate result range from the enthusiasm the record company has for the artist (or its fear of losing him to a competitor) to the financial shape of the record company, the manager involved, the chemistry between the negotiators for the respective parties, whether the artist is a singer-songwriter or a multi-member group, astrological signs, the record company's previous bad experience, whether publishing is or is not involved, the royalties payable, who had a good lunch that particular day, and many other factors.

The following schedules of advances are derived from two contracts that were concluded recently. They have been simplified for our purpose. You will see that they vary considerably. Schedule I is derived from a contract between a singer-songwriter with no track record and a newly established record company. This artist also signed a co-publishing agreement with the record company's publishing affiliate. The advances under the co-publishing agreement are listed separately. The two are independent, and the royalties and advances under each are not cross-collateralized against the other. Schedule II is from the "Us" contract, which, you will recall, is between a four-member rock-'n-roll group with no track record and a major record company. The advances in Schedule I are in addition to recording costs. The Schedule II advances are inclusive of recording costs. Hence, to compare the two, you must deduct $75,000 to $100,000 (perhaps even more if the inflationary spiral continues) from the advances in Schedule II in order to compare the two.

TABLE 3.2

## Advances

| | Schedule I | | | Schedule II |
|---|---|---|---|---|
| | Record Advance | | Co-Pub. Advance | Record Advance |
| | Minimum | Maximum (Note 1) | (Note 2) | |
| **Initial Term** | | | | |
| Album 1 | $ 6,000 | $ 6,000 | $ 4,000 | $ 70,000 + 7,500 (Note 3) |
| Album 2 | 6,000 | 15,000 | 4,000 | 70,000 |
| **1st-Option Term** | | | | |
| Album 3 | 10,000 | 25,000 | 6,000 | 100,000 |
| Album 4 | 15,000 | 35,000 | 8,000 | 125,000 |
| **2nd-Option Term** | | | | |
| Album 5 | 20,000 | 40,000 | 10,000 | 125,000 |
| Album 6 | 25,000 | 60,000 | 12,500 | 150,000 |
| **3rd-Option Term** | | | | |
| Album 7 | 30,000 | 80,000 | 12,500 | 150,000 |
| Album 8 | 30,000 | 80,000 | 12,500 | 250,000 |
| **4th-Option Term** | | | | |
| Album 9 | (Note 4) | (Note 4) | (Note 4) | 250,000 |
| Album 10 | (Note 4) | (Note 4) | (Note 4) | 300,000 |

*Notes*

1. In the original draft of this contract, the advances provided were lower than the minimums seen above. In the course of negotiation, they were raised to what you see. When the deal was about to "blow" and the only open point remaining was the advance, a "kicker" was devised whereby the advances set forth would be raised by the difference between 66 2/3% of the artist's royalty earnings on the previous album and the recording costs of that album, not to exceed the total advance set forth in the column labeled "Maximum." When both sides want a deal to "make," they find a way!

2. As a concession for granting co-publishing rights (without which grant the deal would not have been made), the record company agreed to waive an administration fee and agreed to delete the "controlled composition" clause (about which you will learn more shortly).

3. The $7,500 sum represented the cost of some equipment "Us" desperately needed. I don't think "Us" will be able to complete the albums required during the initial term for the $70,000 recording fund provided, much less pocket any real advance. The group thinks it can. The record company merely took the position: "Then you'll ask us for more money and we'll listen to what you did with the $70,000 . . . and we'll see."

4. The original draft provided for another option term. As part of the negotiating process, the fourth option term was traded in exchange for the modest advances and the publishing interest. Thus, after the eighth album, the Schedule I artist is into his second record deal. If he has become a superstar, he is now looking at $1,000,000 plus per album while poor "Us" is looking at $250,000 and $300,000 less recording costs. In addition, if the record company has exercised its option for the fourth option term, you can bet that "Us" will have earned its advance before it receives it. That's what I meant by "illusory."

Which deal is better? You're pretty knowledgeable by now—you figure it out. The answer is not really important. They were the best deals that could be negotiated for the artists with their respective record companies by their respective attorneys.

The important lesson to be learned is that each deal has its own dynamics and tempo. Entire deals can't be compared, much less isolated individual aspects of deals. An artist who is worth X to one record company may be worth much more to a company that has a gap in its roster which that artist fills. How can you tell if the advances in one deal are "better" than the advances in another deal without knowing the royalties being paid? Speaking of which . . .

## *Royalties*

The Scriptures rarely come to mind in the course of negotiating or reading a record contract. Nevertheless, upon the conclusion of the royalty clause, I rarely fail to be reminded of Job 1:21: ". . . the Lord gave, and the Lord hath taken away . . . ."

Every royalty clause starts with the royalty rate the record company will pay the artist with respect to "net sales of albums sold in the form of disc records through normal retail channels in the United States." The royalty rate stated is usually referred to as the "base royalty" or by some similar phrase. The remaining five or six pages of the royalty provision are devoted to debasing the base royalty. It is your attorney's job to resist the encroachments on the base royalty to the extent possible.

The base royalty is invariably a percentage of the record's selling price. Some record companies structure their royalties on the wholesale selling price, some on the retail selling price. The rule of thumb is that a wholesale royalty rate is roughly double that of a retail royalty rate. For example, if RCA, which operates on a retail system, were to offer you a royalty of 8%, CBS, which operates on a wholesale system, would, in order to match RCA's offer, have to pay you 16%. In terms of dollars the two offers would be roughly the same. Why? Because the wholesale price of a record is approximately one-half of its retail price.

What is an adequate royalty rate? Simple. The most you can get. How is it determined? By the law of the marketplace—the law of supply and demand. The smaller the royalty the artist is paid, the larger the record company's profit. Thus the struggle begins. All of the references to "leverage" and "bargaining position" and other variables that I have referred to in connection with advances and elsewhere apply equally to royalties. What is an adequate or acceptable royalty for a new artist? In the last year I have seen contracts proposing base royalties ranging from 5% of retail to 12% of retail (10% of wholesale to 24% of wholesale). What is adequate or acceptable to the artist is usually a function of how often he has felt the sting of rejection and how desperate he is to have his chance. I usually feel that if the initial royalty offered is 7% of retail or more, the record company is serious and wants to do business. I also feel that no offer should be rejected out of hand merely because of a royalty rate that falls short of a preconceived minimum. There are too many ways to play this game.

Before proceeding further, a word of warning. A quick glance at a base royalty may not tell the whole story. Sometimes a deal is structured in such a way that it is the artist's responsibility to procure *and pay* for the services of its producer. Hence the base royalty in such a contract includes the royalty the artist will have to pay the producer, and that royalty (3%-4% of retail) must be deducted from the base royalty to arrive at the actual artist's royalty.

Royalty rates, like advances, are usually subject to escalation or increase. Royalty escalations take two forms. The first is an increase in the base royalty from album to album, or from option period to option period as the deal ages. The second is predicated upon sales, with the royalty rate being increased or "bumped" as sales of an album rise above certain preagreed plateaus. This form of escalation usually works on an album-by-album basis, and the bump only operates with respect to sales that occur after the plateau has been reached that gave birth to the bump. Record companies, when contemplating plateaus, think in terms of the Himalayas or the Rockies. Artists' attorneys think in terms of gentle hills. Finding the right altitude is part of the negotiating game. Record companies like to make the first plateau "gold" and the second "platinum." Artists' attorneys consider these somewhat illusory for any artist who is less than a superstar, and try for 150,000 or 200,000 units as the first plateau. The sales contemplated in calculating these plateaus are usually the combined U.S. and Canadian sales.

Sometimes the artist can obtain the best of all possible worlds and can negotiate escalations combining both methods. The sizes of the increments are subject to negotiation, and logically are to some extent dictated by the initial base royalty. The smaller the base royalty, the more generous are the bumps apt to be. More of this later on when we again compare the royalty provisions of the two deals we compared in the advance section.

You have already learned from the Lexicon and the chapter entitled "Pennies From Heaven" that you can't multiply the base royalty times the selling price times sales and come up with your royalty in pennies.

You've learned that packaging costs, free goods allowances, and the like must be factored in to that calculation. To go beyond those basics I think would be counterproductive and would result in a loss of the forest for the trees. Let's leave the rest of the calculations to the accountants and concentrate for the remainder of this section on how your base royalty can and will be whittled away, and the extent to which the erosion can be, if not prevented, at least diminished. Some record companies have more outrageous form contracts than others. Although custom and usage have, over the years, operated in the artist's favor, many record companies cling to form contracts that do not recognize such custom and usage. Although they will change the offending and outdated provisions if they are asked to, they will not do so voluntarily. Let's assume we are dealing with one of those contracts. Better safe than sorry.

Before the advent of the vinyl disc in 1948, records were pressed from a brittle and breakable composition. To avoid the expense of receiving and crediting returned broken records, the record companies gave their customers an automatic 10% credit and told them to throw out the broken records. This magnanimous gesture was passed on to the artist, who was quite logically paid a royalty on 90% of the records sold. Fair is fair! Although no record has broken in transit since 1948 and the breakage credit soon disappeared from record-company invoices to their customers, payment "on 90% of records sold" curiously still persists in some artists' contracts. If the record company is requested to change this to payment "on 100% of records sold," it will do so. If the request is not made, you will receive payment on 90%. If you have a base royalty of 10%, your failure to catch this has the net result of reducing your base royalty to 9%!

Similarly, when tape cassettes and 8-track cartridges were born, the record companies, perhaps with justification, took the position that because of low sales volume, their high price, their experimental nature, or whatever they could only pay a half royalty rate with respect to sales of "records in the form of tape." Well, today most record companies will pay the same royalty rate with respect to tape as they do with respect to discs. You guessed it: some record companies persist in "trying" and leave the "one-half rate" language in their forms. If you don't ask for the change, you won't get it. With burgeoning tape sales, such a reduced rate would diminish your base royalty by 25% or more (assuming tape and disc sales to be approximately equal).

For many years it was the custom for the royalty rate on sales made outside the U.S. to be one-half the royalty rate on domestic sales.

Artists' representatives started whittling away at this, and it became clear that a better royalty rate than one-half the domestic rate was available. How much better varies with the size of the base royalty rate and the royalty your record company receives from its foreign licensees. It appears that even international record companies adhere to rather rigid licensing arrangements between their domestic and international divisions. The higher the royalty the record company receives and the lower the base royalty it has to pay you, the easier it is for it to pay you a royalty on foreign sales approximating your base royalty on domestic sales. Usually unhappiness should accompany a foreign royalty rate that is less than three-fourths of the domestic rate. Very often, as you will see in the chart at the end of this section, the foreign royalty rate varies from country to country, depending upon the deal your record company has made for itself with respect to each country.

The royalty rate for 45-rpm single records and EP records is usually less than that for LPs. Singles are looked upon primarily as promotional devices with a low profit yield for the record company. It is in the artist's best interest to have the record company promote singles, and hence a reduced royalty to make such promotion practical for the record company is not without justification.

In addition to the aforementioned major areas, your base royalty rate will suffer "shrinkage" with respect to a slew of other "special" areas, including sales through record clubs, sales of budget records, licensed uses of your records, K-Tell-type sales, and premium sales. All of these are grist for your attorney's mill. To pursue them in detail here would be to go beyond the scope of this book and overly burden and confuse you.

Are you still pondering the advances received by our two sample artists? After preparing the chart that follows, I have concluded that it is too detailed and complicated to be "required reading." If you skip it, your comprehension of the chapter will not be adversely affected. Neither will your career. But, on the other hand, for those of you who are "into it," it might be fun to romp through the chart. Consider it reference material that you can refer to as and when you choose. Besides, it required too damn much work to tear up!

It is important to realize that both contracts started off less advantageously for the artist than what you see. Each contract element is the product of give-and-take and compromise. Probing by both sides to find the limits of the other takes a long time, and it is only after this process is completed that the real trading can take place and the contract be concluded. The legal fees charged the artist whose contract is the subject of Schedule I consumed almost all of his initial advances.

## TABLE 3.3
## Royalties

### Schedule I

| | Base Royalty Rate (Retail) | Foreign Royalties (Retail) |
|---|---|---|
| **Initial Term** | | Group A: Japan and Canada - 7% |
| Album 1 | 8% (Note 1) | |
| Album 2 | 8% (Note 2) | Group B: United Kingdom, France, Holland, Belgium, Luxembourg, Australia, New Zealand, Canada, Germany - 6% |
| **1st-Option Term** | | |
| Album 3 | 8% | Group C: Elsewhere - 4.5% |
| Album 4 | 8% | |
| **2nd-Option Term** | | Foreign royalties remain constant throughout the term and do not escalate at all. |
| Album 5 | 9% | |
| Album 6 | 9% | Audiovisual records: |
| **3rd-Option Term** | | The same royalty rates apply to audiovisual records as apply to sound-only recordings. |
| Album 7 | 10% | |
| Album 8 | 10% | |
| **4th-Option Term** | | |
| Album 9 | - | |
| Album 10 | - | |

Notes (Schedule I)

1. In addition to the escalations shown, there are "bumps" of ½% at plateaus of 250,000 units up to 1,000,000 units. For example, if Album 1 sold 780,000 units, the royalty rates payable to the artist would be as follows:

    On sales up to 250,000 units - 8%
    On sales from 250,000 to 500,000 units - 8½%
    On sales from 500,000 to 750,000 units - 9%
    On sales from 750,000 to 780,000 units - 9½%

    The base royalty rate on singles and EPs is a flat 7%

2. This contract also has a feature whereby the highest royalty rate reached on the preceding LP becomes the base royalty rate for the next LP. For example, the starting base royalty rate on Album 2 would be 9½%. The maximum royalty attainable, by agreement is 11%.

### Schedule II

| Base Royalty Rate (Wholesale) | Foreign Royalty Rates (Wholesale) |
|---|---|
| 22% (Note 1) throughout the term inclusive of a royalty to the producer which can be estimated at approximately 6% of wholesale, leaving an artist royalty of 16% of wholesale (roughly 8% of retail) | Group A: United Kingdom and Canada - 16.5% |
| | Group B: European Economic Community, Japan, Australia and New Zealand - 14.7% |
| | Group C: Elsewhere - 11% |
| | These royalty rates remain constant throughout the term (Notes 2 & 3) and include the producer's royalty. |

**Audio-visual records: (Note 4)**

| | U.S. | Foreign |
|---|---|---|
| Videodisc units | 10% | 7.5% |
| Videocassettes and other audio-visual records | 7.5% | 5% |

Notes (Schedule II)

1. The base royalty rate escalates to 24% on sales between 500,000 units (gold) and 1,000,000 units (platinum) and to 26% on sales in excess of 1,000,000 units (platinum).

    The base royalty rate on singles is 16%; on EPs it is 18% with a bump to 20% on sales over 250,000 units.

2. Foreign royalty rates are reduced as follows with respect to singles and EPs:

    Group A: Singles - 12%; EPs - 13.5%
    Group B: Singles - 10.7%. EPs - 12%
    Group C: Singles - 8%; - EPs - 9%

3. Foreign royalty rates are escalated, with respect to albums only, on foreign sales in excess of 1,000,000 units as follows:

    Group A: - 19.5%
    Group B: - 17.3%
    Group C: - 13% plus an egg roll

4. Audio-visual royalty rates are based on wholesale. Please see the discussion in the next section.

If he is successful, the changes won in the negotiation will result in hundreds of thousands, if not millions, of dollars in increased earnings. If he is not successful, he has the satisfaction of having contributed to the college education of two fine young people. (*See table 3.3*)

## Audio-Visual Records

For many years the record industry has been vaguely aware, almost subliminally so, of the potential of audio-visual recordings. Since they had no conception of how the monster might surface, they sought a hedge in their contract definitions of "phonograph record" and "masters." A typical definition reads as follows: ". . . any device, whether now known or unknown, on which sound alone *or sound accompanied by visual images* may be recorded. . . . "

The attorneys for the artists asked, "What does that mean?" The record companies said, "Don't worry about it," whereupon the artists' attorneys started to really worry! Thus the "stand-off" compromise evolved whereby both sides agreed not to exercise audio-visual rights without the consent of the other. Then one day everyone woke up to find that the future was present and that the age of audio-visual recordings had dawned—not yet exploded, but very definitely with us.

You are breaking into the business at the very threshold of the audio-visual revolution. No one yet knows how it will be manifested. Two things are now apparent. First, a stand-off is no longer acceptable to the record companies, which are insisting on a present right to take you into the audio-visual arena. Second, no one is sure of what the appropriate royalty or other compensation for the artist should be. Two solutions to the problem are illustrated in the royalty schedules shown in the chart. Neither of the solutions, payment at the same royalty rate as sound recordings (Schedule I) or at a greatly reduced rate (Schedule II), seems viable in the long run.

A standard will evolve in the not too distant future. For the time being, it is sufficient for you to be cognizant of the problem.

## Controlled Compositions

From 1909 to 1976 the mechanical copyright royalty record companies were required to pay the copyright owners of songs was two cents per record. From 1976 to 1981 that mechanical copyright royalty rose to four cents. Unfortunately, the rise in the mechanical royalty took place at a time when record sales were ebbing and the record companies were beginning to hurt. Consequently, the controlled-composition clause in record-company contracts assumed new importance. A controlled-composition clause provides that with respect to songs owned or controlled by the artist, a mechanical license for the use of such songs will be issued for a royalty less than that required by the Copyright Act. When the statutory mechanical license rate was two cents, the usual controlled-composition clause called for a rate of one and one-half cents. It was really quite academic, because when a knowledgeable entertainment attorney resisted the reduction, the record company invariably folded on the point.

Alas, such is no longer the case. The record companies are now fighting for the retention of their controlled-composition clauses and insisting upon a three-cent rate in lieu of the statutory four-cent rate. Many are making this a "deal point." You are going to need a lot of leverage to win on this one, but obviously it is worth fighting for.

## *Approvals*

A first draft of a recording contract rarely gives the artist much of a voice in the creative decisions attendant upon the production of his records. Indeed, some contracts initially provide that the record company will choose the songs to be recorded. This is especially vexing to a writer-artist, and is in fact more honored in the breach than the observance. Nevertheless, there has evolved through the years a list of factors over which the artist may secure control, or at least a right of approval. Some of these are:

> Producer
> Musical compositions to be recorded
> Times and place of recording
> Pictures and biographical material pertaining to the artist
> Final sound mix
> Album covers, including the artwork
> Liner notes
> Joint recordings
> Use of the artist's recordings in connection with premiums
> Coupling of the artist's recordings with recordings by other
>     artists
> Recording budgets
> Cuts to be used as singles

## *Independent Producers*

Suppose, rather than signing directly with a major label, you are discovered by and signed to an independent producer. Is this better or worse than signing directly with a major label? Well, it's certainly a lot better than not being discovered at all. How much better depends on the independent producer involved. If it's legitimate independent producer with a demonstrable track record who is respected in the industry—congratulations. If it's someone who is unknown, untried, and untalented—good luck and beware . . . he's gonna scare the hell out of the record companies.

If the independent producer who is interested in you is of the first kind, you have to be flattered by his interest and consider any offer he may make very seriously. If the independent producer who exhibits interest in you has no track record, is generally unknown and without clout, I would be inclined to place him on the back burner until all other avenues have been exhausted.

Logic dictates that if you deal with an independent producer, the economics of your deal are not apt to be quite as favorable as they would be if you were dealing directly with a major label (of course, without the clout of the independent producer, you might never attract the interest of a major label). A record company is prepared to pay a certain maximum for each act it records. When the artist is signed through an independent producer, that maximum has to be shared by the artist and the independent producer. In addition, almost universally, the independent producer will seek all, or at least a substantial part, of your publishing. It is the publishing interest that makes the deal viable for, and attractive to, the independent producer. There just isn't enough there to justify the effort, responsibility, and risk without it. To illustrate: suppose the independent production company receives a royalty of 12% of retail from the label. If the artist is a group, it's going to ask for a royalty in the 7% to 10% range. If the power behind the independent production company is also the line producer, he would be entitled to 3% to 4% without the headaches attendant upon operating what amounts to a record company. If the independent production company has to lure an outside line producer, there is very little (if anything) left indeed. Thus you can see why giving some or all of your publishing in a deal such as this is really not optional.

There are a few basic independent-producer deal structures. In the first deal structure, if you didn't know better, you would think you were dealing with CBS, RCA, Capitol, Warner Bros. or some other major record company. It's a contract identical to the thirty-five-page monster we just discussed, and it is negotiated with the same fervor and at the same expense. In turn, after signing you, the independent producer (assuming it's found a deal for your services) negotiates its own thirty-five-page contract with a major label. Wherever the independent producer does better with the label than you did with the independent producer, it benefits. For instance, if the independent producer is paying you a 6% royalty and getting 12%, that's better for the independent producer than if it pays you 8% and it gets 12%. Similarly, if under your contract with the independent producer, you receive a "one-half rate" on foreign sales, and in the independent producer's contract with the record label, it gets a "three-fourths rate," it can pocket the difference as profit. Incidentally, this is a perfectly legitimate way of doing business; it's called free enterprise. It is also very expensive and conducive to dissension. Guess who's paying for recording costs in this situation? Right, you are! So the independent producer starts with that edge— plus, in all likelihood, the publishing.

Well, after a while, some wiser heads concluded that it was to neither the independent producer's nor the artist's benefit to have them beat each other up, especially in view of the fact that they would have to live together for a long time. Thus evolved the short-form "pass-through" independent-production deal. This saves about twenty-eight pages of legal fees and usually has both sides feeling better about each other than the format set forth above. It works like this:

First, the artist's royalty is set. It can be a percentage of either the retail or the wholesale selling price, or a fraction of the royalty the independent producer receives from the record company, or a combination. For instance, the contract may state that ". . . the artist shall receive a royalty rate equal to one-half of the royalty rate received by the independent producer, but *in no event* less than 6% of the retail selling price . . . " Thus, there is a floor to the artist's royalty and a built-in escalation in the event the independent producer has significant "bumps" based on the artist's success.

Next, advance language is provided which could be a fixed number of dollars, or a share of what remains after recording costs are paid. Who bears recording costs? The artist or the independent producer? You can bet that the first draft will have you paying—so may the final draft—but taking recording costs "off the top" has been tried successfully in the past. That's why you have an entertainment lawyer.

Next, the "pass-through" contract earns its name by stating that essentially all of the fiscal provisions of the independent producer's contract with the record label are "passed through" automatically to the artist. By way of example, if the independent producer receives a "three-fourths foreign rate," the benefit is automatically passed on to the artist. Similarly, the artist receives the same free-goods limitation as the independent producer, etc.

The "pass through" is a format that is simpler, cheaper, and a more harmonious way to go . . . and everybody probably ends up the same way in the long run. But don't try to do it on your own just because it looks relatively short and simple. Let's put together a little independent-production-deal checklist so we'll be sure you have an awareness of the major issues:

1.  "Pass through" vs. long form.
2.  Recording costs "off the top"? Worth a try!
3.  Advances. Do the best you can.
4.  Royalties. Do the best you can . . . you need a floor and an escalator for the high end.
5.  Publishing. Try to salvage at least half with a co-publishing deal *and make sure your obligations as a songwriter terminate when the record deal does.*
6.  Make sure the publishing and record deals are not cross-collateralized against each other! Please!
7.  Make sure you have the right to approve the line producer . . . and the right to replace him if success eludes you. Record labels will shy away from deals where they are locked in forever to a certain producer; it scares the hell out of them, for good reason.
8.  Make sure there is a provision—discuss it in front—whereby if a record is not recorded and released by a major label within a certain period of time (six months to one year), the production contract *and* the publishing contract automatically end.

A review of the Lexicon will act as a checklist of other items you may wish to consult your attorney about and ultimately toss into the negotiation hopper.

It is hoped that the foregoing will arm you with the essentials you need to approach your record deal realistically and intelligently. There are myriad other issues over which your attorney will do battle with the record company. With respect to some, he will prevail; with respect to others, he will not. But an informed and interested client will be of inestimable help to him.

# Interview With
# Clive Davis

*Clive Davis is the founder and President of Arista Records, a former President of Columbia Records, and an entertainment attorney. Renowned as a discoverer and molder of talent, he is also a successful songwriter and producer.*

AHS: Of course, we could refer the readers to your autobiography, *Clive*, but, instead, perhaps we could have a brief synopsis of the route one takes from Harvard Law School to the presidencies of two major record companies?

DAVIS: Those things really happen, I think, or at least partly happen, through coincidence. I had been an attorney in a private law firm which happened to represent CBS, an account for which I did no work. One of the lawyers who had previously left the firm to go to Columbia Records as general counsel was being promoted and he was unhappy with his then assistant, who would be in line to succeed him as general counsel. So, about two and a half years out of law school, I got a great offer, unsolicited, purely by luck really, to become assistant counsel at Columbia Records. Then, within six months, when the general counsel's promotion took effect, I became general counsel. Five years later, as is wont to happen in a large company, there was a political reorganization, and Goddard Lieberson, then president of Columbia Records, I think saw in me an underlying enthusiasm for the business, and it just was the right time and the right place to afford me an opportunity to become head of a company without any prior experience. From there it was all really learning the business, plunging in, and out of necessity relying on my creative instincts, which were totally untested. Although there was no indication of any prior creative credentials whatsoever, the existing situation at Columbia Records put me to the test. Columbia Records was steeped in what we call "Middle of the Road" music and classics and Broadway shows, and we had to move into the rock era. I had nobody to do it for me, because all the A & R men had grown up with Doris Day or Mitch Miller or Johnny Mathis or Andy Williams and Streisand, so I had to rely on myself. I did just that at the Monterey Pop Festival by signing Janis Joplin, and, thereafter, Blood Sweat & Tears, Chicago and Santana. Buttressed by the confidence that came out of making the right decisions and fortified with really unexpected good luck and success, I've continued on in the creative arena, so that it's become second nature to me and now I spend probably 75% of my time just doing A & R work.

AHS:    You're very modest. You of course know you are regarded as one of the most talented record executives in the business today. That's talent . . . not intuition and not good luck. Clive, it's very hard to make a record deal today. A lot of young artists appear to be beating their heads against a stone wall. The first look a record company gets at a new artist is usually his demonstration record. I know many of them are done in an absolutely wrong manner. If you could set them, what would your guidelines be for a demo? The number of songs? The duration of the song? The sequence, etc.?

DAVIS:   I think, most often, an artist falls into the category of a singer-songwriter, where his focus is on trying to write a hit song. Let's distinguish that kind of artist from a progressive FM rock-oriented group. You can't have the same rules for every artist, because what is appropriate depends on the category of music. For the singer-songwriter, those that are coming up in the tradition of Paul Simon and Carole King and James Taylor, I think that diversity isn't that significant. I think the important thing is really how many hit songs you're capable of writing! I would limit the tape to no more than six songs. Rather than try to show that you could write a jazz song and a hard-rock song and a soft song, or a ballad and an uptempo, the only criteria should really be the strength of the material and whether or not it qualifies to be a hit record or a hit song in your own mind. That is what we are looking for to break through new artists today in this category . . . not how introspective the artist can be. Occasionally, there is the unusual, the unique artist who stands apart from those who are writing material in the genre of hit material or general singer-songwriter material. The best example of that currently is Rickie Lee Jones. Again, I would not submit more than six or seven songs, but in that category, you would try to demonstrate the uniqueness and originality. Clearly she has, in her phraseology and her words and her imagery, like Springsteen in the early days, made it on the uniqueness of the material. In the singer-songwriter category, I myself can listen to a piano and voice demo because you are listening primarily to the song, and not so much to the artist's voice. If you like the songs and feel they're hits, you're going to see the artist in person after that anyway. Obviously, if you have the money, it is possible to enhance it, perhaps with a rhythm section, in a local recording studio for $15 to $20 an hour, as distinguished from $100 to $150 an hour it costs to record masters. I would say you should keep it simple and keep the number of songs limited to around six.

In the AOR category, where you're talking of a group usually, clearly everything applies that I said before, but you just can't, you cannot, do a piano-and-voice thing. You would have to do the group in a demo studio. Here again, do only the strongest material. Usually it's a good idea to keep in mind the fact that companies are going to look for different criteria in assuming whether or not you can break through. One is whether there is an AOR classic, that kind of cut that cannot be a hit single but which is akin to those classics that broke Bob Dylan and those classics that you look for in a Bruce Springsteen, or if it's harder rock, you're looking for the strength of the material and the playing. Your demos have to be a little bit more carefully planned out. But again, I would do no more than six tunes and just the strongest, strongest material which will show what makes you distinctive; either a unique sound or your ability to create classics or hits.

AHS:    Do you appreciate receiving pictures or lyric sheets with demos?

DAVIS:  I thing lyric sheets are helpful. It takes the strain out of trying to listen for every word. Pictures are useful. Sure, I think it's nice to see what the artist looks like. Not essential.

But certainly useful.

AHS: What is the selection process at Arista? Do you use the committee system? Is it your A & R staff? Ultimately, I'm sure you pass on each act that's signed to Arista, but, ordinarily, does it go through the lower echelons first?

DAVIS: Yes. All demos are reviewed by the A & R staff. If I received a demo in the mail, I would immediately send it to my A & R staff for reviewing. During that process, if anybody is felt to be that talented, the cassettes, as you can see, reach me and I listen. But the early selectivity is at the A & R staff level.

AHS: I would gather from what you've already said that an artist who creates his own songs is looked upon with more favor?

DAVIS: It really is much easier, because if you don't create your own songs, the standard of performance is extraordinarily high for that new Streisand, that new Aretha Franklin. Clearly, in the AOR category, you've got to do your own material. If you're just a performer, you've got to be awesome in talent today, I think, to depend on other people's material and to have a company willing to take on the burden, either itself or through the producer, of finding hit songs for you.

AHS: An instinct question: what's the most common turnoff . . . the most common mistake that makes you think . . . "Ah, that's not for me"?

DAVIS: Usually, when it comes unsolicited from the outside, most of the material is, frankly, not of professional caliber. I think the common mistake of those that have talent is to describe or showcase versatility, rather than strength. So if someone is a great ballad writer, instead of submitting six great ballads, he'll submit two ballads and put all his eggs in those baskets and then do several uptempos and other things.

AHS: What chance does an unsolicited demo have of being listened to, as opposed to demos brought in by various attorneys, accountants, and managers? What is your policy?

DAVIS: At Arista, it is 100%. Everything is listened to. I mean, unsolicited demos take longer to get listened to than a demo submitted by an established attorney or a manager with a track record. Not that I've had any good luck with unsolicited tapes, but there is something about my background or training which requires me to have everything answered. So we answer all mail. I guess I grew up in that tradition. So, not to puff about it, it's just something that we do. We listen to everything.

AHS:        I got the impression that you indicated you've had very little success with unsolicited tapes?

DAVIS:      Yes . . . very little success.

AHS:        Any at all?

DAVIS:      "Unsolicited" means not unsolicited from attorneys and managers, but, rather, through the mails from unknown people. I've recorded through Columbia and Arista maybe two, but I can't recall anything coming from an unsolicited private person that has proven significant.

AHS:        It's a very small percentage considering the number of tapes you've listened to?

DAVIS:      Oh, very. Now on the other hand, obviously, through managers or producers or attorneys, you expect more.

AHS:        You must receive an awesome number of cassettes a year. Do you have any idea of how many?

DAVIS:      No, because I don't know what comes into the A & R Department. They keep track of it; there is a log. I guess I personally get—it varies—somewhere about sixty a week. My A & R staff might get many more.

AHS:        Would you venture a guess as to what percentage of artists that submit themselves to Arista sign deals?

DAVIS:      I could put a percentage, but it is a low percentage, because we have prided ourselves on being a lean company and becoming the alternative to CBS and Warner's. We do not sign ten to get one and throw them up against the wall to see if they stick. We've tried to be very selective. We have only forty-eight to fifty artists on the roster, thirty-five of whose last albums sold in excess of 200,000 units. We have enjoyed great depth and diversity, which stood us in good stead during the previous two flat-growth periods in the record industry. Although I think it's a healthy industry, we are really among the few survivors. Of all the new companies that were started, there are really only two that have survived the last ten years. Among Casablanca, RSO, Arista, and Chrysalis and others, Chrysalis and Arista are the only survivors. The others really have fallen by the wayside because they had only one or two artists, whether it be the BeeGees and Clapton, or whether it be Donna Summer and The Village People. Once those artists peak, the company is dead. Although we had our Manilow at the same time, we broadened into R & B and we broadened into AOR and to jazz progressives, so that we have thirty-five artists whose last albums sold in excess of 200,000 copies. That gives us, with The Kinks and The Grateful Dead and Melissa Manchester and AirSupply— you can just go up and down the line; Aretha Franklin, Dionne Warwick, and just a whole host and variety of artists—good depth. We sign selectively; we focus the spotlight for artists such as Dionne and Gino Vannelli and The Kinks and Aretha. We've been able to bring them back after others had sort of not done their jobs. So we listen carefully, sign selectively.

AHS: Do you prefer a prospective act to be affiliated with a line producer when they come in?

DAVIS: It really depends on the artist, and of course the producer. I mean there is nothing better than to get an artist with a great producer. It makes your life so much easier. That combination is terrific if it's there. If it's with a lousy producer, you sort of cringe because you realize that although the artist might be talented, you know it can't be of long-lasting value because the producer is not that heavy . . . he was just there first. So you've got to be careful. When it's there, where it is a good combination, it's ideal.

AHS: Last question! Do you prefer your artists to come equipped with managers, or do you prefer to mix and match?

DAVIS: Truthfully, there are so few really good managers that it creates a great burden when an artist comes to you and asks you to recommend a manager. It's tough. I prefer the manager to be experienced, whether he is a son of a bitch or a nice guy. The worst thing is to come with an amateur manager who really doesn't know what the hell he or she is doing . . . and it's chaos. They think they're never getting enough, or they're unsure whether or not they are, so they're just totally unrealistic. On the other hand, you don't want someone to be just a lamb. I'm all in favor of a good, strong professional manager that you can relate to and work in harmony with. We all have the same mission, so it makes it that much easier than if we have to pick up all the pieces and fill the void as sometimes we do through product managers or A & R or myself. I certainly prefer an artist to have a strong professional manager, but I have never *not* signed an artist because the manager is inexperienced. . . . It's the artist that you are concerned about. There are times, during everyone's career, where you just have a terrible relationship with a manager or even with an artist, but you can never give the artist up if the talent is there. Even if the artist is a pain in the ass or if the manager is, if the talent is good or extraordinary, you must be willing to put up with a lot of personality extremes and sometime pettiness, sometimes greed, sometimes intolerance. . . . You just have to do it.

AHS:     Any advice or words of wisdom you'd like to pass on to the young people out there who are trying to get started in this industry?

DAVIS:   Well, that it is tough; it is highly competitive; it's got to be in your blood; you've got to live it and breathe it. It's an exciting area to work in. It's not easy to get into, because the points of entry are somewhat specialized. If it is in your blood and you do love it, and that love coincides with a real ability, it's a most challenging field of career endeavor and opportunity. I have found it never dull and always challenging and exciting.

AHS:     Thank you very much.

# Interview With
# Doug Morris

*Formerly a singer, songwriter, producer, and entrepreneur, Doug Morris is now President of Atlantic Records.*

AHS: Doug, first I'm going to ask you for a little bit of your background. I know a *little* bit of it, having been around as long as I have, but I'd appreciate a synopsis of the route you took to where you are at present.

MORRIS: I started as a songwriter and singer.

AHS: I never knew that!

MORRIS: Oh, yes. I spent hours hacking out my own songs on the piano and singing them. I had a record out with ABC and one with Epic—very checkered records, no success. They were basically influenced by the people who were popular then—I think that was the time of Neil Sedaka. My first connection was with a publishing company. I think it was Leeds Music—Lou Levy—but there was another guy there whose name I think was Dave Brown. He was the chief song-plugger then, and he brought me over to Epic Records; that's how I got my contact with Epic. I made a record with Jim Fogelsong & the Jordanaires, and failed, and I did another record with Bert Burns for ABC and failed. I did a bunch of records, went into the Army, and kept writing and recording. When I came back, because of my songs, I got sort of a job with Bert Burns and Bobby Mellon writing. They took the publishing of the songs and gave me $35 a week as an advance. I also did the filing and a lot of other stuff. After the Army, I got a job at about $125 a week working for Bobby Mellon as a "professional man," which means taking songs around to record companies and artists. After about a year and a half there, I got an offer from Laurie Records to be an A & R person. Laurie invited me because they liked the demos that I made of my own stuff. At Laurie I started producing some material I wrote and some other records. I had a little success with "Sweet Talking Guy" by The Chiffons, which I wrote and produced, and a couple of other things, like "Are You a Boy or Are You a Girl?" It was interesting.... I learned promotion because in those days it was different from today—the promotion was more natural. You'd ship a record and the radio stations seemed to *need* the product, and if you had a hit, you found it out quickly. Learning promotion naturally followed producing my own records, because I wanted them promoted. I found I wasn't as good a producer and writer as some other people, so I went into the administrative part of the business, particularly A & R, which is looking for other talent. After about four or five years there, after becoming General Manager and Vice-President, I decided to go into my own business. I realized that the record business is much more simple than people make it out to be. If you have a great piece of product and you get it on the radio, people will come and buy it. I opened Big Tree Records, and after ten years sold it to Warner Communications, whereupon I became the President of Atco Records, and ultimately the President of Atlantic Records.

AHS:     Doug, you mentioned that it was a simple business back then. You were talking in a time frame of about ten years ago. Now, as President of Atlantic Records, do you still find it a simple business?

MORRIS:     It's a simple business in the respect that if you get something people want, they're going to buy it. That's the simple part of it. Getting that piece of product is not that simple.

AHS:     I couldn't have asked for a better lead-in. I've noticed many fine things about your company, but one thing has really impressed me: it's the only major record company whose A & R people periodically call me and my partners to ask: "Hi, how are you? Do you have anything new that we haven't heard?" I noticed that we don't do too many deals; that you're extraordinarily selective, as you must be, which leads me to the core of this interview. There are thousands of artists out there who are aspiring to record deals. What are your prime criteria in selecting talent?

MORRIS:     It's a combination of several things. The musical ability, which comes first, performing ability and magnetism of the artist ... the ability to project a certain image; and third,

AHS:      the management. If you get all three pieces together, you
          have a very good chance of success.

AHS:      When you talk about musicianship . . .

MORRIS:   By musicianship, I really mean talent. Greatness as a
          writer, greatness as a singer . . .

AHS:      You're including the quality of the songs in that. . . .

MORRIS:   Oh, sure! The talent comes first. It's not exactly the songs,
          but it's the combination of the songs, and how the artist
          renders the song. Some people write great songs, but
          they're not artists. Their songs become hits by other artists.
          We prefer, given the choice, an artist who is also a writer,
          because then we know we are always going to get the
          benefit of his best songs. Talent is the first consideration.
          The second most important factor is the artist's—I hate to
          use the word "magic" or "charisma"—ability to offer some-
          thing special onstage. The third consideration is that they
          are well managed by someone who is reasonable, open-
          minded, and intelligent.

AHS:      Do you prefer them to come to you *with* a manager or
          would you like to find the talented artist and perhaps make
          a match?

MORRIS:   Ummm . . .

AHS:      What if you get a wonderful artist and you can't stand the
          manager?

MORRIS:   Well, that's a problem, but if he's a good manager, I'm
          *going* to stand him. I'm not going to not stand him. If he
          doesn't understand the business, then we won't get along,
          because it's a very logical business and most of the real
          professionals understand it. It's pretty common knowledge
          what a deal is for a beginning artist, what a deal is for a
          middle artist, and what a deal is for an established artist,
          so if you get a manager who is knowledgeable, normally
          there is no problem. If you get someone who's nuts, it
          doesn't work.

AHS:      My point is this: if an artist came to you and you were
          enthusiastic about him as an artist . . .

MORRIS:   I would try to suggest someone or make sure that he meets
          a lot of managers and finds someone with whom the
          chemistry is correct.

AHS:      One of the big puzzles and problems for young artists is
          the demo record, which is their calling card to the record

company. If you could set the criteria for a demo, what would your criteria be?

MORRIS: Criteria? Technically? Do you mean state of the art? No, just as long as it's clear and you can get the melody and you can get the lyric of the song. You can make a very good demo on a home tape machine; just playing the guitar or piano, that could be perfectly adequate. If you have the financing and you want to go further, it's very easy to go into a small studio and it's really not that expensive.

AHS: How many songs would like to see on a demo?

MORRIS: I'd like to hear at least three songs by an artist before I get interested, but if someone brought me in one phenomenal thing, I would certainly be very receptive to hearing more.

AHS: What about the kid who sends you in a tape with ten cuts on it or eleven cuts? Does that turn you off?

MORRIS: Ummmm . . . I don't know. I really can't answer that because what I would normally do is give it to one of the A & R people and they would listen. I don't know how they would feel about it. I don't think I would take the time to listen to ten cuts.

AHS: What's the ideal number? If you had your choice . . . three, four, five?

MORRIS: I normally can tell with three cuts if I'm dealing with something that I'm interested in, and if I really like it and we want to go further, then I'd ask them to start preparing more songs. Once artists know that they're on the way to being signed, they suddenly get very creative and it's very interesting to observe that phenomenon.

AHS: I always recommend to artists that they place their best song first on the tape. A lot of artists are inclined to build up to the best song. . . .

MORRIS: I don't believe you should be subtle—best shot first. You're 100% correct.

AHS: What kind of selection process do you use here, Doug? I know, for instance, that Paul Cooper will call me and I'll send him some tapes and then he'll call me back and thank me very much and tell me he passes, but what happens in between the two calls? Do you go through a committee, or . . .

MORRIS: A demo will normally go through our A & R department, which is composed of about seven people. They have listening sessions and they basically decide whether it's in the ball game or not in the ball game. Ultimately, it will come to me or to Ahmet and we'll make the decision. Ahmet Ertegun is the Chairman of the Board of the company.

AHS: You've already told me how important the song is. Are there any particular things that turn you off instantly?

MORRIS: No.

AHS: You're very open-minded. . . .

MORRIS: Oh, yes.

AHS: How important is the source of a demo?

MORRIS: What do you mean "the source of a demo"?

AHS: I know, for instance, that when we entertainment lawyers send in a demo, it's usually listened to. We usually get a response. I imagine it's the same with accountants and managers and other people that you're going to have a long-term relationship with. As a matter of courtesy, I imagine they get listened to. What about all the stuff that comes in over the transom from Oshkosh or Duluth?

MORRIS: We try and listen to it, but, in truth, I would suspect that if someone we know or have a rapport with submits something, it gets a quicker "listen to."

AHS: A more thorough "listen to"?

MORRIS: I'm not sure about "more thorough," but it certainly would get precedence. If you hear something that comes through the mail and it's great, you're going to chase that though, too.

AHS: But is everything that comes in through the mail listened to?

MORRIS: We try to; sometimes it's difficult, but we try to, we try very diligently to.

AHS: Have you ever gotten lucky on something coming through the mail?

MORRIS: Not as a record, but I believe we found songs through the mail which we have used for other artists.

AHS: But never a record?

MORRIS: I really can't think of any at this moment, but I wouldn't want to say no because I'm not sure. . . . It certainly is an advantage if a demo comes from someone we know.

AHS: Do you have any idea, do you keep any track, of how many tapes you get a year?

MORRIS: No. I have no idea, but we get *many*. I have no idea of the numbers.

AHS:      Can you give me an idea of how many signings of new artists you did this year?

MORRIS:      In truth, I don't know. I don't have it at my fingertips, but not many . . . not many. We're signing more than most labels, I believe, because our business hasn't been de- clining— it's been increasing—and when an act comes along that philosophically meshes with what we're doing, we will sign it.

AHS:      Do you have any preference with regard to whether or not an act comes in associated with a line producer? Do you like to pick the producer?

MORRIS:      It doesn't matter to me. If an artist comes in with a line producer and the product is very good, we'll go with it; if the artist comes in without an attachment, we'll try to guide the selection of a producer.

AHS:      Do you have any feelings about independent production companies versus signing the artist directly?

MORRIS:      No. The end result is the only thing I'm interested in.

AHS:      A hit?

MORRIS:      Yes, the music, that it's great, and that they're good in person and that they're well managed.

AHS:      I thank you very much. Is there any word of advice you'd like to give to the stars of the future?

MORRIS:      Well, for people who are truly serious, the only thing I would advise is to be true to what they are as an artist, and not to try to cover a broad spectrum. Don't try and do a disco record and a rock record and a middle-of-the-road record. If you're a rock-'n-roll artist, be a rock-'n-roll artist—that's really the truth. Very often we get demos that are designed to demonstrate diversification. You'll have a couple of good rock cuts, then a jazz cut, and then a ballad, and that really *does* turn me off, because the really great artists *are* what they are, and they can't be anything else.

AHS:      Do you think some of them don't know what they are at that stage of their career?

MORRIS:      No. I really believe that they know what they are. For the ones that are destined to be great rock-'n-roll artists, rock- 'n-roll should be all that they care about. They may *like* other kinds of music, but rock-'n-roll should be what they want to perform. The dance artists are going to end up dance artists and rhythm-and-blues artists are going to be rhythm-and-blues artists. Jazz artists are jazz artists. There can be fusions, but when I hear a potpourri of music by one artist, it's not interesting to me, not interesting at all. I like to know what they are and that *they* know what they are, because that image factor is, second to the music, the most important thing as far as I'm concerned.

AHS:        Do you like lyric sheets with your demos?

MORRIS:     Not particularly.

AHS:        Do you like pictures submitted?

MORRIS:     It doesn't matter. The music is the first thing. If the music interests me, then I or whoever else is involved with it, will search out everything else. It really doesn't matter what people look like in today's idiom. Some of the biggest artists aren't the most handsome people in the world. They're just talented.

AHS:        Some of them can't even sing very well.

MORRIS:     Well, I don't agree with you there. I do think that the ones who are successful have something, although it may not be what we think of as good singing in the classical sense. Bob Dylan certainly wouldn't have been thought of as a good singer, but he had something that touched his audience—in his moment, he had something in his voice, in his performance, that touched people. As a matter of fact, most of the singers that do commercials are fine singers; they're technically excellent and they have great intonation, but very rarely do they make successful records.

AHS:        I didn't want any of my readers to be turned off by the fact that they didn't have classically good voices. . . . I asked the question with that in mind.

MORRIS:     No. It doesn't matter. Just that they can "touch." There are a lot of artists who, though not technically great singers, had the ability to reach an audience. They sold millions of albums. It *is* good that they be distinctive, whether it be a Stevie Nicks, who is identifiable as soon as she comes on the radio, or the Rolling Stones . . . when they come on, you know it's them. Being identifiable, having an identifiable vocal sound, is very, very important.

AHS:        Doug, I thank you very much.

MORRIS:     I enjoyed it very much.

# Interview With
# Rupert Perry

*His background as a musician and music publisher prepared Rupert Perry for his role as President of E.M.I. America/Liberty Records. At the time of this interview Mr. Perry was Vice-President A & R of Capitol Records.*

AHS:    I can honestly say that when you pass on an act, you do it with a certain grace, with an uncommon politeness and sensitivity. Perhaps this is explained by your background. Will you tell me how you started out in the business and where you've been?

PERRY:  Yes. I started out in the business as a musician. I was a drummer in various bands in England. I graduated from being a musician to the music publishing business in England for about four years. Then I got a job working for EMI, and worked for them for about a year and a half. I came to Capitol Records in 1972, and I've worked for Capitol Records ever since.

AHS:    Rupert, if you could set standards and guidelines for demos, what would they be as to number of songs, duration of songs, sequencing . . . what would you advise a young artist to do in the way of demos?

PERRY:  I would advise them to make the simplest demo, showing off the voice as best as possible; to have about four or five songs on the demo; to make sure that the srongest songs are at the front of the demo, because our people, if they don't hear anything in the first two songs, will probably not get to songs three and four. Therefore, it's wise to put the best songs at the front of it. Try to always do original material. If they do a cover song, try to give the cover song a totally different arrangement or feel, not just a pure copy of what it was, because that's of no use to anybody. . . . It has to have a different arrangement. They should also make sure that the tape box or cassette is properly labeled with their name, address, and phone number on it, and that they enclose a stamped, addressed envelope so we can send it back to them. Times are tough and posting things back is getting more and more expensive.

AHS:       Do you also appreciate having a lyric sheet?

PERRY:     Lyric sheets are not imperative.

AHS:       What about pictures? Is it helpful to have a picture of the artist?

PERRY:     Yes, especially if the picture is an attractive one. There are times when a picture can be the kiss of death. . . . If it creates a particularly negative impression, it can affect your attitude with respect to the overall package. It's a gamble.

AHS:       That's a very candid response. What is your selection process? You're certainly not the only person in A & R. How are decisions made?

PERRY:     I think each company has its own way of making decisions. Here at Capitol, a variety of us listen to demos and to demonstration tapes that come in. When we find something that interests us, we generally get five or six cassette copies made of it and we submit it to our other colleagues in the A & R Department to get their feedback. After five or six of us have heard it, if the feedback is positive and we feel it's worth pursuing, that's when we generally go off and start to pursue it.

AHS:       Although it's not called a committee, it is sort of a committee?

PERRY:     It's somewhat of a committee system, yes.

AHS:       How important is it to you that an act be self-contained? Write its own material?

PERRY:     It's important to a degree; however, we're finding more and more that even most of the self-contained acts find it really difficult to come up with ten killer songs every time they go to make an album, and so we're generally searching for outside songs. It's important that an act have the right attitude to outside songs when they're being pursued by a record label, because if they say to any particular A & R man, "Well, I'm not going to do outside material," that could be the one statement that could kill their whole deal. I think they have to have an open mind . . . an open mind to other material. But it is important, obviously.

AHS:       The next question is more difficult. What's the most common turnoff that you come across in demos or in your dealings with artists? . . . What's "instant negative" to you . . . the most common factor?

PERRY:    That's a difficult one. . . . Cassettes with ten or fifteen songs on them. Badly written letters that you can't read, that are illegible. I've always felt that if somebody really is serious about his career, he'll manage to find somebody to type a proper letter for him explaining who and what he is. All of these things . . . Just the very appearance of the package, or the way it's presented to you, starts you making judgments, and you can tell by just looking at the package sometimes that you're not going to have any interest in it because it's not a professional approach.

AHS:     I know when a young lawyer writes to me in search of a job and he misspells my name, his letter instantly goes into the trash can.

PERRY:    That's right. Absolutely . . . And it's the same thing for people calling up. When I return people's phone calls and I say I'm Rupert Perry and I'm returning your phone call, and they say, "Oh, yeah, um, which company are you with?" . . . well, I know at that point that he's the last person I want to be in business with, because he's not a professional. What one has to remember is that the business is a *real* business, and the people in it are business-orientated people.

AHS:     I gather from what you just said that you do listen to unsolicited material?

PERRY:    We do; we listen to it very roughly. It gets put into a pile. . . . My own habits are that about once a month I go through the pile, and I flick through it very, very quickly because 99.9% of it is of no interest whatsoever. The tapes that are given more attention are obviously the tapes that are submitted by professional people and people that we're already in business with, or people we've done business with, i.e., managers, agents, attorneys, or accountants, those types of people.

AHS:     Boy, I'm glad of that. [Laughter] How many submissions of artists' tapes do you receive a year? It's a very important question, to give the readers some sense of scale, an idea of what their odds are.

PERRY:    Probably in the whole department, the whole A & R De-

|   |   |
|---|---|
| | partment, we're probably getting in anywhere from a hundred and fifty to two hundred tapes a week. |
| AHS: | That's a lot of tapes. |
| PERRY: | A lot of tapes that are just sent to Capitol Records we'll return and we don't even listen to. Here again, it gets back to that professional approach to the business. If you're really serious about your music, and you're really serious about your career, we would have expected you to have found out who, in Capitol Records, or CBS, or Warner Brothers, is the person to send the tapes to. I know that's very difficult for a lot of people starting out, but just sending it in blindly to Capitol Records, it's not going to get anywhere, and we get a lot of that. |
| AHS: | That's very interesting. Are those included in the two hundred a week? |
| PERRY: | Yes. They're probably included in the two hundred a week. |
| AHS: | A little tougher question . . . what percentage of the two hundred a week are seriously considered at one time or another? In other words, how many of the two hundred a week are liked enough to be passed from you to your colleagues or from your colleagues to you? |
| PERRY: | About 5%, maybe. |
| AHS: | And out of that 5%, what percent are offered deals? |
| PERRY: | A quarter? |
| AHS: | That's close enough. 1.25% . . . is what it comes down to? |
| PERRY: | Yes. That's about it. |
| AHS: | Do you prefer a prospective act to already be affiliated with a line producer? Or would you prefer that they come to you open to various suggestions and possibilities? |
| PERRY: | I would prefer that they come open. There's nothing wrong with already being affiliated with a producer, and that can be a bonus. |
| AHS: | Depending on the producer, I guess? |
| PERRY: | Depending on the producer, and also it can be a bonus to the artist, because that would be a way for him to get his foot in the door of the record company. The problem comes when, if you get to the point of signing the act, it has to be signed through the producer's production company. Down the line, the second, third, or fourth album, you may want to change producers and that may prove tricky if the producer insists that he continue to produce the act. |

That's the problem with the producer bringing the act in the door. I must say that I have had that situation arise, and producers have been pretty open . . . and others have not been . . . "No, I've . . . I've got to produce this," and here again, the statement "I've got to produce this" can kill the deal.

AHS: My next question is similar, and it applies to managers. In general, do you prefer an infant act to have a manager, or would you rather have the ability to suggest a manager that you think is suitable for them and who is compatible with you?

PERRY: It's basically the same answer; it really kind of depends on the manager, and in some instances, you know, it's really helpful to have a manager, because trying to find a good manager for an act is one of the impossibilities of all of our lives.

AHS: But young acts don't usually have good managers . . . that's the problem.

PERRY: That's the problem, yes. It's a real catch here, you know, because sometimes you can introduce them to people and sometimes it's very difficult. It's certainly very important that they have a manager if you get to the point of starting to release product, because you need somebody to be sort of a liaison between the record company and the artist.

AHS: The next question is really sort of ephemeral. Would you be less hospitable to a demo of a genre of music that your company does not specialize in or is not known for? Does Capitol have any proscriptions?

PERRY: Yes. I think every record company, in its own funny way, has certain things that it tends to be a little better at than other companies. If you submitted a jazz act to us . . . we've not been in the jazz business, which we think is a specialized business and needs the specialized marketing and promotion approach. . . . We've tended not to be in that side of the business, where CBS and Warner Brothers have been. So if somebody submitted a jazz act, we would probably say, "We're really not in that part of the business. Try Warner Brothers or try CBS."

AHS: Is there any particular area that you're soliciting right now, or would be more favorably disposed to?

PERRY: No. I try to keep as open a mind as possible. My own

philosophy about A & R is very open. I don't agree in saying, "Well, we're not signing anything for three months," or "We're only looking for this type of thing or that type of thing," because I think that you tend to miss out on something. The exciting thing about the business is that each tape that you listen to, or each person that walks in the office to play you something, could be something totally alien to what you might be looking for, but you might become very interested in it, and if you sort of set certain restrictions on yourself, you're going to miss something.

AHS:  Thank you, Rupert.

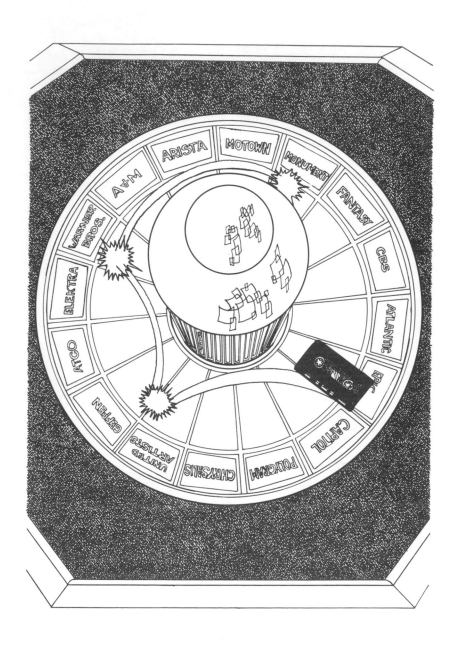

*Cassette Roulette*

# 4

# *Get It Right The First Time*

**A**lthough I have forgotten all I ever knew about navigation, gunnery, Morse code, and the like, one of my officer candidate school lectures remains vividly in mind. It was a class in naval etiquette, and most of the time was devoted to the proper form in which to have our calling cards printed and the appropriate manner in which to disseminate them. I'll bet you didn't know that in the entry hall of every commanding officer's residence there is a little silver tray upon which an officer paying his respects is expected to leave a calling card. Well, I never had the cards printed, never left one, and never suffered any dire consequence. In fact, I never again thought of that lecture until this morning while psyching myself to write this chapter.

This chapter is about your calling card—your demo record. The difference is that if you don't follow the rules, the consequences for you will be much more serious.

This is to be a short chapter because it is a redundant one. Each of the music-publishing executives and each of the record executives whose interviews appear following the chapters on songwriting and recording have answered searching questions about demo records. Their answers are fuller and much more interesting than the distillation that follows. I urge you to read them in their entirety. For those of you who have your amps plugged in and are overrehearsed, here is the short course:

How many songs should be on a demo?

In general, a minimum of three and maximum of six. The rule is not rigid, but fewer than three leaves the listener without a sense of what you are about, and a large number of songs is a definite turnoff to people who spend their days listening to demos. If they haven't heard "it" after six songs, you can bet the eject button will be pressed. Of course, if you are a songwriter submitting particular songs to a publisher or an artist, there is no minimum.

In what sequence should my songs appear?

Best song first, second-best song second, third-best song third, etc. This is an absolute, unbreakable rule. To do otherwise is the height of folly. Many inexperienced writers and artists think of "building" a demo as one would an album. Wrong! Don't be subtle. If you think you are going to build your listener up gradually and knock him out with the fourth song, you're in for a surprise—he's never going to hear the fourth song.

What is a sure way to diminish my chances of impressing a publisher or a record-company A & R person?

Submit a demo that illustrates how diversified and varied your talent is. Include a ballad, a rocker, perhaps a jazz number, and top it off with a novelty tune. Buy a box of Kleenex for the tears as the "passes" pour in. Although I didn't realize it until I started interviewing music and record executives for the preparation of this book, a varied demo seems to be the universal kiss of death. The publishers and record companies, especially the latter, want to know who you really are, and want to know that you know who you are. If you are a rock-'n-roll writer or artist, do a rock-'n-roll demo. If you are inherently a MOR writer or artist, do a MOR demo. Be yourself, not what you think "they" may be looking for.

Must a demo be made in a recording studio or can it be made at "home"?

The answer really depends on who is making the demo, the intended purpose of the demo, and how well equipped the "home" is.

If you are a songwriter and are "demoing" a song for submission to a publisher or an artist, in all likelihood you can do the demo without resort to a studio. A simple piano or guitar vocal should be adequate as long as the equipment you use is capable of producing a cassette that is clear and pleasant to listen to. Most modern equipment found in the homes of music-oriented people is equal to the task. The publisher is listening for the song, not your talent as a singer, nor for your ability as a producer. In the back of his mind he is going to consider whether your demo can be used as his demo, so keep that in the back of *your* mind.

If you are a singer-songwriter preparing a demo for record companies, pretty much the same standards apply as for the songwriter. Record companies, when listening to singer-songwriter demos, listen at least initially for the hit song. Competition for record deals is so fierce, however, that one can't help but feel that the better the demo the better the chance. If you can embellish your performance with a rhythm section in an inexpensive demo studio, it probably wouldn't hurt. But, good Lord, don't throw up your hands and quit because you can't do this. It is not an essential.

If you are a group depending for recognition upon your "sound," it would seem that the closer your demo approaches master quality, the better are your chances. Thus, unless "home" is a very well-equipped loft, a demo studio is indicated.

Can I sing my songs on my demo or must I procure a "professional" singer?

Well, obviously, if you are a recording artist, you damn well better sing your songs. If, however, you are a songwriter, the question is well worth asking. The answer depends on how bad a singer you are. You don't have to be a good singer, but if you are so bad that the song can't come across, you would do well to use a friend who can sing or a professional demo singer to sing the lyric. If you sing passably well, your interpretation of the song may more than make up for your vocal deficiencies. Even if you can sing well, it would not be best for you to sing one of your songs that is clearly intended for a singer of the opposite sex with a clearly different vocal style. If you have a torch song clearly written for a sultry, sexy female voice and you happen to be a male baritone, you might well profit by having the song demoed by a female with a sultry, sexy voice.

How can I make sure that my demo lands on the little silver dish and not on the floor where it will go unnoticed?

By doing your homework. Record companies are turned off by amateurism. Even if you are not yet a professional in the technical sense, a professional attitude is appreciated and helps create a receptive attitude. Have the letter accompanying your demo typed neatly, so that it is legible. Include only relevant and pertinent information that will aid the listener. Two pages on how badly you want to become a star will, I assure you, be counterproductive.

Be professional enough to learn the name of the particular person in the record company or the music publisher who is the appropriate listener for your music and address your demo to him or her personally. Sending a MOR cassette to the head of the Black Music Division doesn't inspire respect for your professionalism. As you have learned from Rupert Perry of Capitol Records, addressing a demo to Capitol Records, Hollywood, California, is akin to consigning it to oblivion.

And, for God's sake, don't forget to put your name, address, and phone number directly on the cassette. Cassettes and boxes are soon separated.

What is the one thing every writer and artist can do to better his demos?

Be incredibly selective about the songs. If you have any doubt about the quality of a song, don't use it.

Have you seen any of the old World War II aviation movies on TV? They all had an obligatory scene in which, after clobbering the ball-bearing factory in Schweinfurt, the pilot reaches for the radio: "This is Blue Leader . . . . We left our calling cards. . . ."

Make sure your calling card isn't a "bomb."

# 5

# *Show Me The Way*

**A**s an aspiring recording artist, sooner or later you are going to be faced with the most important decision of your career: the choice of a manager. Note well that the decision is not whether or not to have a manager. You will have a manager. You must have a manager!

How important is it that wisdom accompany this decision? Well, if the statistics follow the current trend, they show that your relationship with your manager will probably endure for a longer period than will your relationship with your spouse! At least during the early years of your career (and probably during the not so early years too), you may well spend more time with your manager than with your spouse, and your emotional reliance on him may even be greater. One would hope, therefore, that the choice of a manager is made with less impetuosity than ofttimes accompanies that other choice. Rather than incur the wrath of Ann Landers, Dear Abby, or Dr. Brothers, we had best abandon this track and leave the spousal considerations to them.

Although the Lexicon offers a definition of the manager's role, it is very difficult to portray the essence of the manager-artist relationship. One could analogize a manager to a football coach or a manager of a baseball team, and in certain areas, such as strategy planning, it might be valid. Further use of this analogy fails because the nature of the relationship between the coach or baseball manager and their players is really one of the employer-employee rather than the very personal and symbiotic relationship that should exist between the recording artist and his manager. Not only does the manager mastermind your career,

*The Artist/Manager relationship
(as perceived by the manager's mother)*

whip your record company to have product in the cities you are touring, and coordinate the myriad people, trades, and skills involved in the pursuit of your success, but he's also the guy holding your forehead when you retch from "nerves" before going on.

Sufficiently impressed with the importance of the decision you must make? Okay, let's try to go about it wisely, for, as in the choice of a spouse, it is very expensive to correct a mistake.

I know I said "sooner or later" you would need a manager. If you run true to form, you're wondering which it is: "sooner" or "later"? *When* to acquire a manager is probably the most frequently asked question concerning the subject of management. In the abstract, the question is susceptible to a simple answer. Ideally, you should have a manager the moment you decide to pursue a career as a performing artist. Before you run off in search of the "yellow pages," it is my unhappy task to remind you that we live in a less than ideal world, and that the world of entertainment, though probably no less ideal than the real world, certainly isn't any more so. If you are to choose a life in the fast lane, be assured that the road to perdition is well paved. With reality in mind, let's revise our answer to "when." You should acquire a manager as soon as you find a good one who wants to manage you. There are two key words in this statement: "good" and "wants." Let's discuss the latter first. There is little sense in having reluctant management. To hound and badger a prospective manager into signing you, even if you are able to do so (which is unlikely) is counterproductive. You will remain a contract in a file cabinet until you accomplish something on your own. In the meantime, you will be without the guidance you need and, in all likelihood, you will have signed, out of misguided gratitude or anxiety, a less favorable management contract than you could have negotiated had you been sought after. When a manager wants to manage you, you will know it—he'll come a courtin'. This is not to say that you should not initiate the contact. Once he is aware of your existence, he must believe that with his guidance you (and he) can become successful, rich, and famous. If you are less than positive that any prospective manager fervently believes this, I would suggest that you not engage his services.

How do you know a manager is good?

There are three general categories of managers. The first, and smallest in number, are the supermanagers. They are the "heavy hitters" of their profession. They manage the superstars and are to no small extent responsible for their success. Record-company presidents take their telephone calls.

The second, and by far the most numerous, are those who work at their profession, gather experience and knowledge, work hard to develop their artists, but who, for one reason or another, have not yet broken a "monster" act. As the trades put it, they are "bubbling under." It is from their ranks that the supermanagers of tomorrow and, in all likelihood, your first manager will emerge.

The third general category, the soft underbelly of the management profession, is that of the would-be managers. They call themselves "managers" (anyone can do that, you know; there are no educational or licensing prerequisites) but know little or nothing about the entertainment industry other than a few buzz words they use to turn on unsuspecting and inexperienced artists. They make little effort to learn, or are perhaps incapable of learning. They usually carry with them dog-eared Xerox copies of other managers' form contracts with the original names blanked out. If, in spite of them, something should happen with regard to an artist they "represent," they run to an entertainment attorney, and the artist finds that he is being managed by a manager being managed by a lawyer. Ultimately, you will buy him out or sue him—both expensive. Such would-be managers are a blight on an honorable profession, are shunned by legitimate managers, and should be shunned by you.

Artists, especially those who have tasted of success, are very demanding of their managers, both emotionally and with respect to their time. Being all too well aware of this, supermanagers are reluctant to overextend themselves and consequently represent but a few artists at any given time. Simply stated, there just aren't enough supermanagers to go around. The demand for their services from artists who already have a "name" is so great that your chances of affiliating with one of them early in your career are remote.

Thus, if you are to enter into a management relationship sooner, rather than later, it will probably (having been warned of the third group) be with a manager in the second group. You can hope that you will be the "monster" act that will propel him into the ranks of the supermanagers.

Whether or not a prospective manager is good enough to be entrusted with your career is a question not susceptible of scientific determination. Sometimes it's easy, as in those instances where a supermanager perceives you to be a prospective David Bowie. It's easier too when a prospective record company endorses a manager and indicates that if he managed you, it would feel secure enough to close a deal. Most of the time, however, life conspires to make things more difficult, and the mating of an artist with a manager is somewhat more of a crap shoot for both. But even in that ancient game, the knowledgeable player exercises some control by knowing the odds. The best way to narrow the odds in your favor is to spend as much time as possible with a prospective manager. Spend that time listening and asking questions. Talk to the other artists he manages. Take a reading of their barometers of satisfaction. Does he have a game plan for your career? Does he understand what you are about? Does he have a "handle" on you? Check him out with your attorney and with other people in the business that you have come to know, and then make a value judgment. Unfortunately, there is no litmus paper that tests compatibility, or I'd tell you to buy some and use it.

I will now give you Siegel's Rule (modesty forbids "Law") for eliminating prospective managers (note this is not a rule for choosing managers; I am neither sufficiently stupid nor sufficiently courageous to propound that rule):

IF YOU HARBOR A SUSPICION THAT YOU ARE SMARTER, BRIGHTER, OR MORE INTELLIGENT THAN HE IS, LOOK ELSEWHERE.

Of course, this leaves some of you with a wider field to choose from than others. You must realize that your perception, as well as its accuracy, is important.

Elitism? No. Pragmatism. If the rule is ignored, the manager will be unable to manage effectively because you will be unmanageable. He will not be able to lead because you will not be able to follow. As is said in the Scriptures, "And if the blind lead the blind, both shall fall in the ditch." If the above seems a bit philosophical to you, let me leaven it by making a flat and unequivocal (albeit personal) statement. Every supermanager I have had occasion to deal with has been, if not brilliant, extraordinarily bright. There is an old adage known to all familiar with aviation lore: "There are old pilots and there are bold pilots, but there are no old bold pilots." Similarly, there are dumb managers and great managers, but there are no dumb great managers.

One other thing, there are no dumb record-company presidents. Who do you think your manager is going to spend most of his time working with, over, or on, during the most critical period of your career? You guessed it. There are few things more stimulating than witnessing a heated "discussion" between a really knowedgeable manager and a record-company president—or few things more depressing when the manager is overmatched.

Suppose you were very careful in selecting a manager who you believed was perfect for you; suppose you waited patiently till you found the one who believed in you and who you believed was good enough to manage you (this could be after your very first gig, or not until you have landed a record deal); and suppose, just suppose, you were wrong and it was a mistake. It could have been a mistake for many reasons. Conceivably you were conned by one of those so-called managers in the third group we discussed above. Perhaps the manager you chose would have been terrific for someone else but the chemistry between the two of you just wasn't right. Just possibly your nature is such that you demand inordinately much of a manager and will never be satisfied—a Flying Dutchman doomed to sail for eternity through an endless sea of managers. Maybe one of the manager's other acts made it big at the wrong time (for you), and you feel you're not getting enough of the manager's time. Could be you realize he's just a lousy manager.

In any case, the question remains: If you've made a mistake, how do you cut your losses, and how do you minimize the effect of a wrong choice in the future? The first part of the question is easy to answer. You run—do not walk—to a competent entertainment attorney (see Chapter 6). The answer to the second part is less expensive. You study the remainder of this chapter so that you understand the consequences of the contractual relationship you are contemplating.

The nature of the relationship between the manager and the artist is a unique one. It is perceived differently, of course, by managers and artists, and even by one manager and another and by one artist and another. At one end of the spectrum you have the position that it is strictly an employer-employee relationship, with the manager being merely the artist's hired hand. At the other end of the spectrum, you have the manager who acts as if his artists work for him. Somewhere in the middle, you have those who conceive of the relationship as a partnership, through which each makes a valid and valuable contribution to the success of the artist's career.

Although I have seen management contracts reflecting each variation stated above, the key word in the preceding paragraph is "perceived," because regardless of how the contract reads, the attitude of the people involved in the relationship will govern what is really important—how they treat and act toward each other.

The vast majority of management contracts are structured in a manner whereby the artist retains the services of the manager to advise the artist in connection with his career. For these services the artist pays the manager a share of the artist's gross income. Although the relationship is not in the technical sense one of "employment" (with its many legal ramifications), but, rather, one between "independent contractors," the artist is hiring the manager and is, in everyday language if not in the legal sense, the employer. The manager works for the artist—usually.

At this point I think it is appropriate to share a grotesquerie with you that is illustrative of all that a management contract and a manager-artist relationship should not be. As they used to say at the beginning of the old radio dramas: "This story is true; only the names have been changed to protect the innocent". . . and unfortunately, in this instance, the guilty too!

Several years ago, I was approached by a manager who indicated that he had just presented a new management contract to a group he represented, and that he thought they ought to have independent counsel represent them. A friend of his had heard me lecture on management contracts while attending an entertainment-law course and had recommended me. I thought the manager was being quite noble and prudent. I met with the group and was presented with a thirty-page agreement (the average management contract runs from two to five pages) and was told that their manager had instructed them to have me read it in their presence, advise them on the spot, and not to permit me to make or retain a copy of the agreement. I refused to represent them on this basis. They called the manager and received "permission" to have me make a copy and to review it in the normal course and provide them with a letter of comment setting forth the major points in contention. Another meeting with the artists was scheduled. The review of the agreement was revelatory. It was a pastiche of the most onerous clauses that could be culled from a variety of contracts, including many that were not of management origin. It was clearly unconscionable (so onerous and one-sided as to be unenforceable by a court) and to a great extent unintelligible. By its terms, the manager all but owned the artists. It was as close to being a "slave" contract as one is apt to come across. It had annexed to it promissory notes and confessions of judgment for many, many thousands of dollars, representing sums the manager had purportedly loaned or advanced to the artists.

At the subsequent meeting with the artists, they were advised of the nature of the agreement, and the fact that it was not susceptible of "fixing." They were also advised that the agreement was such that a letter of comment would be of no purpose and would be so long and expensive as to be impractical. I advised them that the agreement was so out of tune with industry norms that I could only recommend that an entirely new agreement be drafted. It was at this point that they forlornly advised me that other copies of the agreement and the notes as well as the confessions of judgment had been signed by them before the manager had approached me. What was going on? Perhaps belatedly, I got the message. I was being used to legitimize what amounted to a charade. My letter of comment was to be used solely for the purpose of demonstrating at some future time, if and when the agreement was challenged by the artists, that they had had counsel, indeed an "authority," advise them and that they had ratified the existing contract with full knowledge of its contents. Fade out.

Several years later I received a call from the artists. They had "fired" the manager and had, at great expense, won a lawsuit he had brought to enforce the confessions of judgment. Some record companies were now interested in them and they wished me to represent them. I indicated that I would do so, but warned them that if they had any success, the manager would surface and claim rights under the old management contract. Why, I asked them, had they gone along with the manager's scheme three years before? They thought at the time that they were on the verge of success and were threatened with abandonment and lawsuits for the monies the manager had advanced. They were concerned that either of these threats, if carried out, would have destroyed all they had striven for over the years. Well, they had modest success, and, as predicted, the manager sued them under the so-called management agreement. At great additional expense to the artists, the manager's action was defeated and the abominable agreement finally laid to rest. A happy ending? Not really. The artists' prime years were spent fending off their manager rather than building a career, and monies better spent on that career were dissipated on legal expenses that could have been avoided.

"Combination plates," though tasty and tempting when served in Chinese restaurants, lose their piquancy when they appear as part of an entertainment package. All too often a management contract appears as the fried rice! When this happens, the sauce covering the "egg foo publishing" is usually cold and congealed and the crust on the "production roll" is a bit soggy.

"What the hell is he talking about?" you ask. Very often new artists, when "discovered," are presented with a set of papers consisting of an exclusive recording-artist contract, an exclusive songwriting contract, and a management contract. Usually, when the combination plate is served, the waiter is an independent producer. In this event, the management contract is the dish from Column B. Sometimes the waiter is a manager and the songwriter and recording contracts are Column B dishes.

How and why do these situations evolve? Usually they are a function of paranoia, sometimes of greed, and sometimes the result of the best business judgment of the waiter serving the lunch.

The songwriting and recording-artist courses have already been served (see Chapters 2 and 3), and you are presumably a gourmet with respect to those dishes, so, for a moment, let's devote ourselves to the management contract in the context of the combination plate.

The independent producer who signs a recording artist does so in the belief that the artist can be, indeed will be, a huge success, a real megabucks machine. He also perceives of this potentially huge success as being his creation, a product of his knowledge, prescience, guts—and money. Is it not understandable for him to be concerned that some stranger, whose natural role tends to be antagonistic to and competitive with his, will arrive upon the scene and interfere with his game plan or intrude in his dream? What better way to avoid that threat than by "throwing in" a management contract too?

On the other hand, managers are not immune to the failings of human nature. Often when about to invest heavily of themselves and their treasure in what they perceive as *their* creation or dream, they dwell on the frailties of the manager-artist relationship, the absence of security, the absence of an equity or ownership position, and all the zillions of dollars they are about to make for some strange music publisher, record company, or producer. The result is often an order to their attorney to ". . . sign him as a writer and artist too!"

Sometimes these combination plates work out. The lawyers prepare the contracts so that the apparent conflicts of interest are resolved (the manager waives management commissions on the artist's income from the related songwriting contract and recording-artist contract). Sometimes the producer-turned-manager demonstrates a talent for his adopted role, and the manager expanding into the production and publishing areas proves competent.

If partaking of a combination plate is the way to get your career launched, reach for the soy sauce, but be aware of where the Rolaids are, because indigestion may follow.

There are two major weaknesses in the combination-plates situation. They are equal in importance and you should understand them. One of the main functions of a manager is to drive, wrestle, and cajole others involved in your career—the record company and music publisher, among others—to act more in your interest and less in their own. If "their interests" are his interests, the checks and balances are gone, and the entire system tends to lose its equilibrium. Can your manager renegotiate your deals with his own companies? Few are sufficiently objective or saintly. The other inherent weakness should be clear. If a producer-publisher launches his management career with you, you are obviously not getting the best and most experienced manager. If a manager decides to launch a production and publishing empire with you as its nucleus, you are obviously not getting the best and most experienced production and publishing support. The dishes on a combination plate are never all from Column A. Ordering your manager a la carte is usually more satisfying.

Enough of this food analogy! Let's look over a typical management menu—oops, I mean contract. In general, management contracts are the shortest of the entertainment contracts dealt with in this book. Are they also the simplest? I think that depends on how much you know, or perhaps on how much you are disposed to fret over all the possibilities their seemingly simple clauses engender. An honest answer is "Yes—and no."

The brevity of the average management contract is perhaps what makes it the most insidious of the agreements to be thrust upon an inexperienced artist. When handed a twenty- or thirty-page exclusive songwriter or exclusive recording-artist contract, there is built in an early warning device that triggers the brain to think: "Whoa! Maybe I'm not prepared to handle this. It looks 'heavy.' Help may be needed." The management contract, often printed on the front and back of a single page, is less apt to trigger the same response. In addition, its language is beguilingly straightforward and simple. This is a function, unfortunately, of its all-encompassing nature rather than the benevolent attitude of the manager or its creator, the manager's attorney. It is much simpler to say that the manager is to receive commission on "all gross income" rather than to dissect "gross income" and deal with its constituents. It is not until you have an inkling of what "all gross income" means that you wish you had sought help before signing the damn thing. In all fairness, many managers are as unaware of the Machiavellian nature of some of the clauses in their own contracts as you are.

You should be aware of certain universal features of management contracts and the issues that should be raised, discussed, and resolved in the course of their negotiation.

Let's start at the beginning, the very beginning. In the first few lines of the contract, you will find your name as "Artist" and next to it you may well find the name of a strange corporation as "Manager." For months now, you have been hanging out with, been romanced by, and have decided to place your trust and confidence in John Doe. Doe's name is no place in the agreement. When you ask him about it, he explains that he works through a corporation for tax reasons, that it is quite common and you don't have to worry about it. Worry about it! . . . if you don't want to find yourself managed by strangers sometime in the future! Whether Doe or his corporation is named as the manager, insist on language that states that you may terminate the agreement if, at any time during the term, Doe ceases to be in charge of and to have the primary responsibility for the day-to-day supervision of your career. This protects you in the event Doe sells the corporation, retires, or seeks to assign your contract.

The word "exclusive" is invariably prominent in a management contract. As in the other entertainment contracts we have explored, it is a one-way street. You are exclusive to the manager; he is not exclusive to you. He can manage other artists but you cannot have another manager while he is managing you. You cannot change this clause, nor should you wish to do so. You can always fire your manager; the nature of the relationship is considered one of trust and so personal that a court will not force you to "live with" a manager you abhor. But—and it's a big BUT!—if you fire him without legal cause, you will be required to continue paying him, *and* his successor, compensation. A very heavy burden indeed.

Few would argue that a manager who was instrumental in the creation of a successful career was not entitled to a contract of sufficient duration to enable him to enjoy the fruits of his labor. What happens, however, if you made one of the mistakes alluded to above? In general, a performer's career is relatively short, and to be tied to what proves to be an ineffectual managerial relationship for a long term is disastrous. When you read the first draft of your management contract, it will in all likelihood provide for a term of five years. Perfectly fair and fine if the relationship works. If it doesn't, it's the precursor of a lot of trouble. Except for those rare instances in which the relationship is severed by mutual agreement, you may look forward either to buying your way out of the contract or to an expensive lawsuit (which will probably end in a negotiated settlement anyway). The solution to this dilemma, which is usually acceptable to both the artist and the manager, is to provide language in the contract whereby if certain criteria of success are not met within prescribed time frames, the artist will have the right to terminate the contract. The criteria are usually couched in terms of gross income earned during a specific period of time. The one exception to a dollar criterion is the one for the first step up the term-duration ladder. It is the thing in the forefront of each artist's mind—a record deal.

If drafted by the artist's attorney, and assuming a five-year term, the clause will probably read more or less as follows:

> Artist shall have the right to terminate this agreement by notice in writing to the manager at the following times, upon the happening of the following events:
>
> a. At the end of the first year of the term hereof in the event the Artist has not entered into an exclusive recording artist agreement with a major record company.
>
> b. At the end of the second year of the term hereof in the event the Artist has not earned gross income during the preceding year of ($X$) dollars.
>
> c. At the end of the third year of the term hereof in the event the Artist has not earned gross income during the preceding year of ($Y$) dollars.

Assuming that your manager is willing to accept such an arrangement (and some won't, feeling it can take two or three years to bring the artist to the point where he is ready for a record deal or to earn significant gross income), his attorney will attempt, quite properly, to dilute the burden of the success criteria. How? Watch. Take "a" above. First, he'll try to change "entered into" to "received an offer for" and, finally, he'll probably try to delete "major" or at least insist on a very broad definition of "major." Dastardly? Reprehensible? Not at all. How could it be? These changes are exactly what I would try for if I represented the manager. Both sides can make, and will make, moving and convincing arguments for their respective positions. The result? Usually a compromise that approximates "fairness." Of course, if the record deal already existed, there would be a dollar criterion in "a."

Interested in how to dilute "b" and "c"? I'll redraft as I would if I were the manager's attorney:

> c. At the end of the third year of the term hereof in the event that the Artist has not *received offers for employment which, if accepted,* would have resulted in gross earnings during the preceding *two years totaling (Y)* dollars.

What did this little revision accomplish?

1. Although Y remained the same, it now includes dollars for gigs that should not be accepted, because to do so would be counterproductive in the building of your career—gigs that the manager would not want you to accept!

2. Y now also includes dollars for gigs that you could not accept because of a conflicting engagement.

3. Even if raised to a higher amount, say, to Z dollars, it now

covers two years. If you had a great year in the second year of the contract and earned Z dollars or more but your manager neglected you entirely during the third year and as a result your career was plummeting, you could not terminate because the criterion had already been met in the second year. Thus, the very purpose of the clause is frustrated.

4. It convinced you that you ought to have an entertainment lawyer negotiate your management contract.

Management contracts invariably contain a disclaimer, usually in boldface type, to the effect that the manager will not act as an agent to procure employment for the artist. This disclaimer is twofold in purpose. It prevents a termination of the agreement by the artist based on a claim that the manager falsely represented that he would procure employment for the artist. In addition, most jurisdictions require employment agents to be licensed as such. Managers as a rule are not licensed agents and hence may not function in that capacity. If a manager procures employment for the artist, it may in certain jurisdictions constitute sufficient grounds for the artist to terminate the management contract. Note that in certain jurisdictions agents are referred to as "Artist's Managers" as opposed to "Personal Managers." Don't confuse the two.

I put it off for as long as I could, but now it is time to deal with the manager's compensation. I procrastinated because it presents some very complex issues which are not easily explained. I have, for many years, argued the issues about to be presented from both sides of the bargaining table, and always manage to feel I am absolutely right. If this section sounds a bit schizoid, it is because it is. Alas, there are a few rights or wrongs in connection with the issues that arise with respect to a manager's compensation.

Simply put, the traditional compensation for managers is a share of the artist's gross income from any and all sources in the entertainment field. The share varies, but anything between 15% and 25% is within the "ball park." It is negotiable in some circumstances and not negotiable in others. I determined not to include sample form contracts in this book because I was confident that they would be misleading and misused. There is no definitive contract on any entertainment subject, and the one chosen for inclusion in a book intended for laymen would attain an undeservedly exalted status and implied endorsement. Contracts thus included would be misused by do-it-yourself types, who could not appreciate the subtleties wrought by clever professionals with hash marks covering their sleeves and battle stars adorning their breasts. I also felt that their inclusion would interfere with the readability (such as it may be) of the book and would act as a deterrent, rather than an aid, to comprehension. Although I am not going to break my own rule, I am going to bend it to the extent of including below the compensation language I drafted some time ago for my manager clients. It has stood the test of time and will serve to highlight the major problems we are confronted with in all management-compensation provisions. In this excerpt, "I" is the artist, and "You" is the manager:

> Instead of payment to you of a fixed compensation or fee, I agree to pay to you a commission equal to twenty (20%) percent of my "gross earnings" (as hereinafter defined) from any and all sources in the entertainment or allied fields including but not limited to, television, motion picture, radio, stage, personal appearances, the production of and performances contained on phonograph records and mechanical or electrical transcriptions, music publishing, songwriting, commercial endorsements, and from the sale, lease, license or other disposition of literary, dramatic and musical material or productions, for use in any medium of communication or entertainment, whether now known or hereafter invented, and from any and all allied, kindred or other fields of entertainment or endeavor (including but not limited to cable television, pay television, audiovisual devices, etc.) in which I may be professionally engaged.
>
> You shall be entitled to the above compensation from all gross earnings *received by me during or after the term* hereof to the extent such gross earnings result from any and all agreements and arrangements *now existing, as well as those entered into or substantially negotiated during the term hereof, and in addition, from all renewals, extensions, amendments, modifications and substitutions of any such agreements and arrangements,* notwithstanding the fact that such gross earnings may be received by me after the expiration of the term hereof.
>
> *"Gross earnings"* shall mean all monies, properties and considerations of any kind or character, including, but not limited to earnings, fees, advances, royalties, re-use payments, bonuses, gifts, profits, proceeds, allowances, shares of stock and stock options, without deductions of any kind, whether payable directly or indirectly to me, or to any person, firm or corporation in my behalf, if such are related to my professional activities and career.

The first problem arises with regard to what items of gross earnings (note, I used gross "earnings" as opposed to gross "income," because for technical reasons I felt it was broader and more inclusive) the manager is to receive commission on. The language above is quite comprehensive (I hope) and is designed to include everything the artist receives, whether he keeps and has the use of it or not. From the artist's point of view it would appear patently unfair for the manager to receive commissions on monies the artist does not enjoy. Some examples? Okay.

Suppose your record contract is in the nature of an independent production contract and by its terms the record company pays to your independent production company $100,000 per LP. It is your obligation to produce and deliver a finished album. The recording costs are

$78,000. Under the above language, assuming your manager's commission is 20%, he is entitled to $20,000. Let's see, $78,000 for recording costs, $20,000 for the manager, and $2,000 for you—but only temporarily because the entire $100,000 was an advance to you which you must pay back out of your royalties.

A similar situation arises when a record company gives you money for tour support. Suppose you receive $100,000 from your record company for tour support. Assume the tour costs you $110,000 and your gross earnings from the tour are $90,000. The manager is entitled to 20% of $100,000 plus 20% of $90,000, a total of $38,000. Not bad? What did you end up with?

| | |
|---|---|
| $100,000.00 | tour support |
| + 90,000.00 | gross earnings |
| $190,000.00 | total |
| -110,000.00 | costs |
| $ 80,000.00 | |
| - 60,000.00 | manager's commission |
| $ 20,000.00 | your net? |

Not quite. In all likelihood, there is a 10% agent's fee, another $20,000 off, reducing your "end" to zip. Want to add insult to injury? The $100,000 (or at least half of it) that you received from the record company was probably an advance against your future royalties.

One last example. You have presumably become successful and a TV network offers you a special, for which they will pay you $1,000,000. You hire all the talent and pay all production costs. What's left over, you keep:

| | |
|---|---|
| $1,000,000.00 | received from network |
| - 670,000.00 | talent and production costs |
| $ 330,000.00 | |
| - 200,000.00 | manager's commission |
| $ 130,000.00 | |
| - 100,000.00 | agent's commission |
| $ 30,000.00 | your net |

Well, you didn't lose money!

Are the three situations set forth above possible? Yes. Were my numbers manipulated for dramatic effect? A little. Are they likely to happen? It depends on the manager and the situation. If the contract language were not modified to exclude recording costs, tour costs, and packaging costs, I would venture to say that in the early stages of your career, when money is tight, most reputable (and wise) managers who are in for the long haul would waive or at least defer commissions on

those costs. How do managers respond if requested during the negotiation of the management contract to exclude such costs from commissionable gross income?

There are a relatively small number of managers who will make no
concession whatsoever, feeling that they would prefer to handle each
situation as it arises on an ad hoc basis. They feel they will make a
proper judgment based on the relationship and the financial situation
at the time in question.

Some will yield on all.

Most managers will yield on recording and packaging costs.

It appears the toughest of the three for a manager to swallow are
the tour costs. From the manager's point of view, I have heard the
following arguments:

1.  "Tours, early in a career, are the toughest part of the manager's
    job; this is where I really earn my keep and it's one of the few
    sources of income for me at this stage of an artist's career. I
    need it to cover my nut."

2.  "The primary purpose of a tour is not to make money for the
    artist. The primary purpose is to promote the then current
    album. The artist's payday is down the pike—from record
    sales. He's the one who will be the superstar with heavy
    earnings for many years. I may not be around next month,
    much less five years from now. What about my contract?
    Today it's a contract; tomorrow it may just be an expensive
    lawsuit."

It's easy to see where reasonable men may differ.

The next portion of the compensation language to be discussed is
probably the most difficult to resolve to the artist's and the manager's
satisfaction. The issue is the extent to which the manager is entitled to
commissions after the end of his contract with the artist, with respect
to both events during the term of his contract and certain income
sources occurring after the term has expired. Study the second paragraph of the quoted compensation language. Now let's consider the
following situations:

A.  Your management contract expires when you have recorded
    three albums of a six-album record deal. You enter into a
    management agreement with a new manager before recording
    albums four, five, and six.

B.  After completion of the sixth album in A above, your new
    manager renegotiates your record deal and you sign a new
    contract with the same record company for four more albums.

C. Your record deal and your management contract expire at about the same time. Your records recorded during the term of the record deal will continue to earn substantial sums for many years.

The question is, of course, to what extent is the original manager entitled to commissions.

In situation A, it is clear that he is entitled to receive commissions on the earnings from albums one, two, and three. It is also clear from the contract language that he is also entitled to commissions on albums four, five, and six. The new manager is also entitled to commissions on albums four, five, and six. Therein lies the dilemma. You are going to have to pay a double management commission—unless something was done to change the above language before you signed the contract containing it, or you have made an appropriate modification in the new manager's contract.

In situation B, given the quoted language, you will also pay double commission on the four additional albums under the new deal. To avoid this, you would have to give up a lucrative deal with your present record company, with which you feel at home, for a deal with another record company.

In situation C, it is clear, and in my opinion properly so, that the manager must continue to receive commission on those earnings for as long as you do.

There are more questions and problems in the above situations than I have raised here, but these will suffice to familiarize you with the kinds of problems that can arise. Obviously, it is in the artist's interest to negotiate language that preserves his economic integrity and ability to pursue his career in a positive manner rather than being motivated by a need to avoid double compensation. It is equally obvious that it is in a manager's best interest to preserve the language in his contract as his lawyer drafted it.

This is one of the few situations where I can feel equally comfortable on either side of the bargaining table. Managers make cogent arguments for their side of the question. If they are intrumental in creating an artist's career, why, they argue, should they be cast aside just when their labors are about to bear the ripest fruit? Why should not the subsequent manager, who is inheriting an already created situation, not waive his commissions or at least accept a diminished commission? To some extent, the justice of whatever resolution is arrived at depends on how "wonderful" the original manager was, and what part of the artist's success is rightfully attributable to the manager's skill and effort. Unfortunately, management contracts do not come with crystal balls, hence each side must negotiate the best deal possible in the blind, so to speak.

From an artist's point of view, the most felicitous resolution is for the manager to receive commission with respect to all services performed by the artist, including recordings, that are rendered during his tenure as manager, but not those that occur after he is no longer manager. The commission with respect to such events should be applicable to all income from such commissionable events so long as they earn income.

Curiously, some very fine managers also subscribe to this philosophy, as you will learn from the interviews accompanying this chapter. You will also perceive that there is little unanimity of opinion among the managers interviewed. By nature, they are a rather independent lot.

One last observation. There is a language in certain management forms whereby if the artist forms a corporation for certain purposes during the term (to do packaging, for instance), the manager is to receive a share of the stock in such corporation. Be very wary. You are contracting for advice and guidance—not a "partner."

All management contracts have a paragraph devoted to the powers the artist grants to the manager to act on the artist's behalf. Invariably they are so broad and so all-encompassing as to be tantamount to a general power of attorney. I defined and commented on powers of attorney in the Lexicon. Take a minute and look it up again. Under the usual management contract as presented to the artist, the manager can sign *any* contract (including a long-term recording contract) on the artist's behalf without so much as asking the artist's opinion, much less permission. Few managers would, or do, utilize these broad powers. Then why have them in? The answer is that they shouldn't be in, and therefore it is incumbent upon you to take them out. The only power of attorney appropriate in a management contract is the limited power to sign contracts for short-term personal appearances. Often, buried in a powers clause, you will find the right granted to the the manager to receive all of the artist's gross income, to deduct therefrom his commissions and other sums owed him by the artist, and then to remit the balance to the artist. One might well understand a manager's reluctance to have all income payable to a young artist inexperienced in financial matters. Artists, too, experience qualms, whether justified or not, in losing dominion over their monies. A satisfactory compromise is for the artist and the manager to agree upon a mutually satisfactory business manager or accountant to handle all income and to account to both the artist and the manager, as dictated by the management contract.

Although we have explored the major and most troubling issues in the traditional management contract, we have not discussed—nor can we—some of the more aberrant or unusual provisions that come along. The negotiation of a management contract is not for do-it-yourselfers. You're in lawyer country and you had better know the terrain. Hire a guide.

# Interview With
# Shep Gordon

*Shep Gordon is the founder of Alive Enterprises, Inc. He has been instrumental in the careers of Alice Cooper, Debbie Harry, Anne Murray, Teddy Pendergrass, and other artists.*

AHS: Shep, one of the classic problems with young artists is the question of the chicken or the egg. Young artists can't get a really good manager because the really good managers aren't interested. How does a young artist get to meet a manager or get a manager interested in him?

GORDON: I'm sure there are a lot of different paths. I'm sure that given twenty different artists, there will be twenty different ways that they meet their manager, but all the paths are just ... hard work ... banging your head against the wall until it opens up.

AHS: How would you advise someone to go about doing that?

GORDON: Just to believe in what they are doing and find out how much they are willing to give up. What sacrifices they are willing to make. I used to always tell Alice that it was only a couple of guys who started Christianity, because they believed in it. I think if anybody believes in what they're doing, they have a chance of doing it. It's just dedication.

AHS: What are the key considerations in determining whether you or your organization will take on a new act? Do you take on new acts?

GORDON: Acts that are new to our office, yes, but rarely acts that are new to the public. My main consideration most of the time is whether an act is one of a kind. I love to deal with "one-of-a-kinds" and have the opportunity to make a history book. When I say "one of a kind," I mean unique talent, something unique within them, either in the way they look or the way they sing, some kind of unique gift that's singularly them. Usually, I would say the greatest deterrent to making it for any artist has nothing to do with their art; it has to do with their understanding of what it takes to make it. So I tend to gravitate towards artists who have been out there for a long time knocking their heads against the wall so that they know when it's better. New artists don't really know when it's better because they're just starting. So fantasy and reality become mixed. This is really a business. And a lot of new artists, when they get their first successes, expect it to be some kind of a luxurious ride through the world, and that's really not what it is about. You burn out much too fast. For me, the long haul is really important, so I usually become interested in tested people—people who have persisted.

AHS:        You really didn't hit exactly what it is that they should be looking for. You indicated that new artists really don't know where it's at, but what kind of things don't they know?

GORDON:     No, no, I'm not saying they don't know where it's at. In order to be a successful, commercial star, one part of the puzzle, but only one part, is talent, another part of the puzzle is personality, another part of the puzzle is being able to allow people to do things for you, another part of the puzzle is presence when you walk into a room. There's a lot of pieces to a puzzle that makes someone a star, a talent being only one. So when someone has been out there in the wars for years, usually . . . most of the pieces of the puzzle are developed. Whereas, with a new artist, his art may be as valid as anyone else's, but perhaps he may not be the kind of person who can show up for dates on time. It's not within his character. He may be the kind of person who, when asked the wrong kind of a question, gets offensive and explosive. He may be the type of person who needs a lot of time in the country and would rather dedicate himself to his personal life rather than to his career. He may be the kind of an artist who, when he has reached a certain plateau of economic reward, loses all incentive to grow professionally. He may be the kind of artist who has problems in his relationships with women and, because of it, constantly suffers depression which adversely affects his work. There are a million different possiblilties, and it's not limited just to the music field . . . it's present in every other area. I'm sure in professional sports there are great quarterbacks who just couldn't adjust to the system. I like things that are straight, clean, and simple, and someone who works for his career and does it for the right reasons. I don't mean it to degrade their art at all; it's just that the art is a very small portion of it. An artist is on stage an hour and ten minutes out of twenty-four hours and works only a couple of days a week and only a couple of months a year. What he does for the rest of his time, how he conducts his other life . . . that other stuff is really important, really important.

AHS:      Do you consider it a positive or negative factor if an act has a record deal, or would you rather take an act and put together your own deal?

GORDON:   Ummm! Each case is different. It depends on their record company and the deal.

AHS:      This is one of the dumb questions.

GORDON:   No. It's valid, I have no preference.

AHS:      The next question you may not want to answer, but I think most young artists are interested in managers' fee structures. I know they do vary considerably.

GORDON:   I'd say they vary between 15 and 20%. That's a reasonable range, considering what a manager does for an artist.

AHS:      I remember in the old days when certain managers were getting 50%.

GORDON:   Yes. Well, I guess, I'm sure there are relationships where maybe it's deserved. I would say in the normal course of business, 15 to 25% is reasonable.

AHS:      Shep, do you generally try to participate in the publishing or production of an act you manage on an equity basis?

GORDON:   I try to participate in everything involved with the artist's career. I won't get involved with an artist unless I'm rewarded economically in every phase. If someone wants to eliminate a portion of income, then I would have to eliminate part of the day. . . . That would be absurd.

AHS:      I want to clarify my question. I think I didn't articulate it clearly enough. I certainly understand that you expect to be commissioned on publishing, for instance, but do you require an equity interest in the publishing? For instance, ownership of a copyright?

GORDON:   I don't require it. I'd like it, but I don't require it.

AHS:   Do you have a fixed-fee structure or does it vary from act to act?

GORDON:   It varies.

AHS:   I would imagine it would.

GORDON:   It varies on what their nets are. How expensive it is for them to operate. It's really all about, for me, the long haul and everybody making what they want to make out of it. It does me no good if I make a lot and they make nothing.

AHS:   What is the minimum term of years for which you'll get involved?

GORDON:   I don't sign acts. I still have no contracts.

AHS:   You don't have any contracts with your artists?

GORDON:   I still don't. [Laughs]

AHS:   It's a handshake and when they get fed up they walk, or if you get fed up, you walk, and that's it? But not too many people walk.

GORDON:   Yes, I've had some. Everybody has been really honorable. It's been really nice. No one's ever given me cause to regret not having a written contract. All of them, all of my ex-clients are really amazing.

AHS:   It is a tribute to you.

GORDON:   And to them.

AHS:   Well, you pick your acts.

GORDON:   [Laughs.]

AHS:   You find each other. . . . The next question becomes moot because I was going to ask you whether you would agree to terminate a contract under certain circumstances if various criteria weren't met. Since you have no contracts and your acts are free to walk at all times. . .

GORDON:   At all times.

AHS:   . . . the question becomes moot. . . . Do you feel that the new audio-visual aspects of the industry are affecting the careers of aspiring artists?

GORDON:   I don't think they're affecting young artists. I think it's the future of the industry. I think it's the way that in the future musical artists will get their art to the public and be paid for it. I think it's all within that audio-visual world. But I don't see the artist having to change now because of it necessarily.

AHS:   Do you invest your own money in acts?

GORDON:     I would if I had to, but I don't start with any new ones, so I really don't come up against that situation.

AHS:        You haven't started with any new ones, but if somebody came in who had that particular charisma . . .

GORDON:     It's possible, but it would not be a condition. You know what I mean . . . in the course of the artist's career, if investment was called for I would do it. Plenty of times I've put a fortune into artists even when they were established . . . as you well know. I do whatever it takes.

AHS:        I assume your compensation is based on a percentage of gross income.

GORDON:     Yes.

AHS:        Do you normally commission gross income that the artist doesn't actually receive, such as recording costs?

GORDON:     No.

AHS:        Or cost of touring?

GORDON:     Yes.

AHS:        You take commission on gross on touring but not on recording?

GORDON:     No, on recording; yes, on touring. I work on a percentage of gross on touring.

AHS:        You work very hard on tours, don't you?

GORDON:     Yes.

AHS:        Do most of your acts make money on tours?

GORDON:     All my acts.

AHS:        With new acts, that very often isn't the case.

GORDON:     Difficult . . .

AHS:        So it's a different situation?

GORDON:     Really difficult, and it's a large part of my business too. I have been doing a lot of other acts. We're really honing it to a science now. I did Kansas' last show. We produce the show, package it, and put it out so it makes money.

AHS:        I find your handshake deals so refreshing because I hate drafting and negotiating management contracts. There are certain areas that are never properly resolved. There is just no simple resolution for some of the problems. One of the things that comes up most often is the question of the duration for which the manager is to be commissionable on something that took place while he was managing, and the problems of double compensation. Suppose the artist signs a record contract during the fourth year of a manager's five-year deal. The record deal is for five years; if you pay that manager for the full five years and you don't renew with him, where do you get the money to pay the commission to the subsequent manager? You work on a handshake, so I guess you don't come to grips with this as a practical matter.

GORDON:    No. I came to grips with the problem, at least in my own mind. I want to be paid on the records I worked on for their life.

AHS:    Just the records you worked on?

GORDON:    And that's what we shake hands on. But if I negotiate a five-year record deal, and after the first year of the deal we separate, they can keep the next four years, but I want to be paid on the records they put out in the first year . . . for their life.

AHS:    I always think of that as the equitable and proper solution.

GORDON:    I think it is. I think the concept that it's the manager who gets the record deal is a little bit silly. It's the artist. The record company doesn't give up a lot, or anything more than they want to give up.

AHS:    It's very tough, especially for a new artist to walk into a record company and get a deal.

GORDON:    He needs a manager.

AHS:    But if a Shep Gordon walks him in, at least he's going to be listened to.

GORDON:    That's it.

AHS:    They won't make the deal because of you . . . maybe . . .

GORDON:    Exactly, so I don't know if just because you're the one who gets them to listen, you really deserve to own a piece of the artist's life.

AHS:    I think you're going to be drummed out of the managers' union if you persist.

GORDON:    I'm not in it. They don't even invite me. I'm not very popular.

AHS:    Shep, how did you get into the business? What is your background?

GORDON:    I was a sociologist. I went to the University of Buffalo, and got my master's at the New School.

AHS:    Then you became a manager?

GORDON:    No. I just floated around and didn't do anything. Then I ran into the Chambers Brothers one day. They were living next door to me; they came in one day and they said, "You're Jewish, aren't you? . . . You should be a manager." I said okay.

AHS: That's the way it started?

GORDON: That was it.

AHS: It's funny. I thank you very much. Any pearls of wisdom that you would pass on to an aspiring writer or artist today?

GORDON: Just not to be discouraged by anybody about anything, ever. . . . If they really believe in what they are doing, all things are possible.

# Interview With
# Miles Lourie

*Miles Lourie, former entertainment attorney, is the manager of Barry Manilow and the head of the management organization Miles Lourie, Inc.*

AHS: The first question that novice artists usually ask is, "When do I need a manager, when should I seek out a manager?"

LOURIE: Well, in an ideal world, I would certainly recommend that an artist have management from the very beginning, before agents, before a record company, before publishers. If I'm correct in my belief that managers are the people who, more than anyone else, help to orchestrate a career, the sooner in the career the orchestration occurs, the more chance there is that the career will flourish. In fact, our business is a crap shoot! The odds against success are terribly high, but if you succeed, the rewards are obscenely great. So the real consideration in trying to handle a career is to do it in such a way as to reduce the odds against failure and increase the probability of success. I think the chances for success are enhanced if an astute, caring manager is in the career earlier, rather than later.

AHS: I was setting a trap for you.

LOURIE: I know you were; I'm working into it. If the relationship of the artist and the manager is good, the manager is the intermediary between all other people and the artist. It's important that the manager be involved in the choosing of those other people in the artist's career, the publisher, the record company, the agent and so forth, even the lawyer, to some extent. Because the manager will be on the front line of representing the artist with these people, the manager should be involved in creating the team. If you were to come to me as an artist and say you want me to manage you, I would say there are certain agents, for example, that

I can work with better than others. There are certain record companies with which I have a better rapport. If you come to me signed to a record company that I might not work as well with, it affects my effectiveness for you. So it's good for the manager to be able to be involved in such things.

AHS: Can an inexperienced act find a good manager willing to work with him? Will an astute manager get involved with an artist who is two, three, or four years away from signing a record deal, and who will therefore require a tremendous investment of time and effort by the manager?

LOURIE: That is a real problem both for the young artist and for a conscientious manager. I find that very often, in the early stages of the career, an artist will tend to accept management from a friend, a bartender at a club that they play in a lot, someone who's not really a manager, who hasn't got the background. It's a sad truth that very often at the early stages of a career, the more successful and astute and knowledgeable managers will not be willing to make the investment of time necessary . . . and the artist will probably sign with a manager who he'll have to get rid of later on when he is in need of a more astute manager. In simple terms, he'll have to pay him off, make him his road manager, or do something when the time comes to make room for a manager who's been in the business a long time, who knows better what to do. Sometimes those inexperienced managers, acquired by artists in the early stages of their careers, will develop into really fine managers, but it's rare, and I think it is a major problem for a young artist. I'm a firm believer that artists should do as much for themselves as possible in developing their art and their product to the point where an adept manager will want to get involved. In any event, the manager tends to be willing to commit to a career earlier than an agent, record company, or anybody else. Managers, because they're on a percentage, and because they have longevity, a term— three-, four-, five-year contracts—should be more than willing to spend a year, a year and a half, two years of that time involved with an act before they are ready to score for a record deal. I believe most really astute managers will do that. I rarely hear professional managers saying, "Well, I'm too busy to sign a new act, I don't want a start-up situation," as you used to hear. I think really good managers realize that the best place to start with an act is fairly early in the development of the act. . . . Am I rambling too much?

AHS:        No, keep going; you're making my life very easy.

LOURIE:        However, on the other hand, the more that the act has had going for it before it approaches me for management, clearly the more likely is it that I'll sign the act. Thus, it's a balancing process. On balance, I would rather start with an act that is new and is maybe six months to a year away from being ready for a record deal.

AHS:        But will you?

LOURIE:        Yes. I have two of them now that I'm working with; absolutely!

AHS:        How many acts do you represent?

LOURIE:        I'm expanding at this point. My son just came to work with me, as you may know, but at this point I manage three acts; there are two unknown, unsigned acts that I'm working on right now. I have been approached by another act which has a record deal and is changing management, but it's been my experience that those situations have as many disadvantages as an unsigned act has, from a manager's point of view. They're just different kinds of disadvantages. Usually they have an old manager who's continuing to take a percentage. As you know, Alan, the first thing a lawyer for such an act will say is, "Well, listen, he's got a manager; he's paying X% to his old manager, so you have to adjust. . . ." That's the kind of problem you have to get through with a previously signed act. An act may have a bad record deal, or they may be with an agency that isn't working too well for them; there are all these kinds of things you have to start going in there to clean up. Obviously, the situation probably is not perfect or else they would stay with the old manager. Right?

AHS:        Sometimes that's an insoluble problem.

LOURIE:        I agree. I do think that it is a very serious problem.

AHS:        All right, a really tough question. I happen to be of the mind that a bad manager's worse than no manager at all. Does it pay for a young act to affiliate himself with an inept manager, rather than go it alone until he reaches the stage

|          | where he would be of interest to an established manager? |
|----------|----------|
| LOURIE: | I agree completely that a bad manager, like any bad partner, is worse than no manager at all. I would recommend that, on balance, they not sign with a manager, but try and do it themselves in the early stages. Can I talk about an example? . . . I managed Orleans, a rock-'n-roll band, about two or three years ago. |
| AHS: | We represented them at one time. |
| LOURIE: | Right! Of course. In effect, they had booked themselves, put together the band, and created their own publicity kits. . . . They were very astute. I've always respected them. When they asked me to manage them, they, in effect, brought to me a package that they had created, but they needed me to improve it and help it along. I don't think it's as much of a voodoo dance as many young acts think it is, because the primary job, early in the career, is finding a place to play, and working up your art, getting your art together, and that's where the act is best able to do it for itself. The business is less important at that stage. I can go even one step further. My biggest problem with young acts is that they are unable to keep themselves financially alive while they're going through that process. I don't believe in management that supports acts. I don't support acts, I will not. . . . |
| AHS: | I can cross that question off. |
| LOURIE: | Well, I knew you'd get into that and obviously it's an important question. The main problem for young acts is to find a way to keep food in their mouths, a roof over their heads, and clothes on their backs while they're creating their new product. A manager who does that for an act is ultimately hurting the act, I think. I think it is counterproductive to do it. So obviously the only kind of acts I would want to work with are acts that are together enough, as human beings, to wait on tables three days a week, to have some kind of straight job that will allow them to develop their talent. In the old days, in the 50s and 60s when I was in the business, artists used to be really contemptuous of the need to do that—"Oh, man, I'm an artist, I can't be expected to wait on tables or deliver mail or drive a truck or a cab while I'm working on my art." . . . Well, I think today artists have gotten more sophisticated. |

I think most of the people in this business realize more and more that we are not in a *fine* art, we are in a popular art field, and there's nothing inconsistent with a good artist being personally together enough to have gotten that part of his life straight, so that he can develop his art. As a matter of fact, one of the reasons why most artists make mistakes in the early part of their careers is the pressure of having to make a decision fast because they don't know how they're going to eat. Consequently, they jump at the first opportunity, they accept the first manager, they accept the first record deal, they accept the first publishing deal, when in fact if they could only get their lives straight as human beings (even if it took them twice as long to get to the point of a record deal), they could avoid imposing that incredible pressure on themselves.

AHS: Very often I find a conflict between the attorney and the manager in certain areas. Who negotiates the record deal? Who finds the record deal? It's clear from your original answers that you consider the manager to be the orchestrator and the leader of all these projects, but you are a very successful manager and you also have a legal background. Very often the managers aren't that well equipped and you get into some fuzzy areas.

LOURIE: I think one of the hallmarks of the inept manager is not knowing how to use lawyers well. That's part of the business acumen that a manager should bring to an act. I believe the manager and the artist are partners in the career. I mean the artist doesn't employ the manager and the manager doesn't employ the artist; there's a species of partnership between the two where the manager brings certain talents and the artist brings certain talents to bear, and they come together and produce an enormous pot of gold, bigger than either one of them could produce without the other . . . if it works!

AHS: Synergism.

LOURIE: Right. If that's true, one of the talents that the manager should bring is the ability to motivate and choose and control lawyers who will work well for the partnership. There should be direct contact at all times between the artist-client and the lawyer. At no time should the manager not support and induce contact between the lawyer and the act. But between the manager and the artist on one hand, and the lawyer on the other hand, the manager and the artist are a team. They jointly hire the lawyer, who is being paid for by the artist, but the manager is the first line of communication with the lawyer for the artist. That should be one of the manager's talents. I think the manager should find the record deal in the first instance, negotiate the major points of the deal, because the lawyer who is being paid on an hourly rate should not have the responsibility of finding the deal. The difference between a manager and a lawyer is that percentage. That percentage is the hallmark of a manager and the absence of a percentage, to me, is the hallmark of an attorney. An attorney should not be on a percentage; I've always been against that. I think it deprives the attorney of the objectivity and professionalism that an attorney is required to have.

AHS: I'm going to get to some more mundane things now. Would you mind indicating what your general deal would be for a new artist? I assume it's different for a new artist than an established artist.

LOURIE: Yes, it would be, although I must say that I have never signed an established artist. I really live by what I said before about the difficulties of signing an established artist as opposed to signing a new artist. I would prefer to sign a new artist.

AHS: Were you with Barry Manilow from the beginning?

LOURIE: I was his lawyer for three years and then *we* decided to become manager-client. That was just at the time he stopped being Bette Midler's music director. I prepared and negotiated his deal with Bell Records at the time. Yes, we've been together from the beginning. In the deals I suggest to clients, the percentage is between 15 and 20%, starting at 15% and going to 20% at some level of income that we negotiate and agree upon.

AHS: Very modest for a manager of your stature.

LOURIE: I know, and also I do not take publishing; I do not take production. . . . I am solely and exclusively a manager. I will not do the other because of the obvious conflict involved in doing so. Before, we were talking about managers investing in acts. Well, this is where the act gets screwed, forgive my French, because if a manager goes in

and puts an act on salary for a couple of years, that
investment has to be secured from the manager's point of
view. How they secure that investment of dollars is by
taking publishing and by taking production, and that
hurts the act, and it puts the manager in a position of
conflict with the act. If the manager is also the publisher,
how can the manager yell at the publisher when he's also
the publisher? That's the most expensive money an act can
get . . . that kind of support. As you know, there is
expensive money and less expensive money. That money is
the most expensive money that an act can get. It's much
better for the act to get it by going out and driving a cab. So
the commissions are between 15% and 20%. The level at
which it will go to 20% is negotiable. I will not sign an act
for less than three years, with an option for a future if a
negotiated level of success is reached during the third year.
I must have a workable power of attorney; that's an act of
trust from the act—if the act is not willing to trust my
judgment and my honesty, we shouldn't be together.

AHS:    That's something every lawyer fights to take out of a
management contract.

LOURIE:    I know. I think it's incredibly important from a manager's
point of view as a practical, operating necessity in the
partnership venture. Of course, whatever controls the act
wants in terms of checking bank accounts, separating and
segregating funds, etc., etc., is agreeable.

AHS:    Miles, as a practical matter, what would you need a power
of attorney for, except possibly for one-nighters? You're
certainly not going to use your power of attorney to sign a
long-term record deal or a long-term . . .

LOURIE:    I would exclude from the power of attorney film deals,
record deals, signing with an agency, all the deals with
respect to which the other party would not accept my
signature in any event. But there are other kinds of deals
where once the client is satisfied the deal should be signed,
I should be able to sign his name for it. I sign deals like
mechanical licenses for the client's publishing company,
synchronization licenses, contracts with sound companies,
light companies, travel agencies . . . things in connection
with tours.

AHS:    We're really not that far apart. . . .

LOURIE:     No, I certainly wouldn't insist upon signing a record con-
            tract; it's a fruitless thing anyway; the record company
            would not accept any signature other than the artist's.

AHS:        Do you exclude anything from gross income in computing
            your commissions? Would you exclude recording costs,
            things like that?

LOURIE:     Yes, I exclude recording costs and television production
            costs.

AHS:        Miles, is there any advice you would care to give to artists
            who are starting out? You know the problems that they're
            up against.

LOURIE:     Yes, the advice I would give to young artists is on a more
            emotional, nonbusiness level. I think it's one of the most
            emotionally difficult, most searing, isolating occupations
            one could pursue. It will enlarge on any psychic crack in
            your emotional armor. The most destructive and corrosive
            thing that you can go through is success! Success will
            destroy you unless you are really stable emotionally. I've
            represented a lot of artists as a lawyer and a couple of
            artists as a manager. The minute they start believing their
            own publicity that they walk on water, which the whole
            industry tells them they can do, the minute they believe it,
            they're dead. Dead professionally; dead as human beings.
            There is a loss of capacity for fallibility that comes with
            that success—an arrogant insistence that they are perfect.
            And we, the business people, induce it, feed on it, and
            destroy them with it. The more aware young artists are
            that they've got to fight *daily* against the feeling that they're
            superstars, even when they are being told that they are
            superstars, the more chance there is they will have a good
            home life and have good relationships with human beings,
            and won't be destroyed by that success.

AHS:        That's where I would talk . . .

LOURIE:     And the manager can help there. That's where a manager
            can help more than anywhere else, if the relationship is
            good. The most important part of management is longev-
            ity. Once you've managed an act into success, the problem
            is to manage it into continued success. The manager-artist
            relationship is one of the most contentious, painful, diffi-
            cult there is, even more so than husband and wife. The
            manager has to be incredibly sensitive to the needs of the

artist and yet never fawn over him. He has to be incredibly sensitive to what the artist can and cannot hear, and yet never refuse to give negative feedback when it's necessary. A client will often say to a manager, "How come I get a heartburn every time I talk to you? Why are you the only person I have to steel myself to call, because every time I talk to you, I . . ." and the manager should say, "Because I'm doing my job, because you've got the rest of the world telling you how great you are, and that there are no problems." It's an incredibly difficult and exciting role to play in an artist's career, but the artist has to support the manager's willingness to be a pariah! If the artist at any time says to the manager, "If you continue to ruffle my feathers, I'm going to fire you," the manager will stop ruffling his feathers, and the minute the manager stops ruffling the artist's feathers, the manager's not doing his most important job.

AHS: Let me go back for one second, out of context, back to the basic deal. Do you commission income that accrues after the termination of a relationship?

LOURIE: Absolutely. I must. If this is a partnership, a species of a partnership between a manager and an act, then, as in any partnership, there will be a flow of activities that you contributed to for that partnership that you should continue to share in as an ex-partner.

AHS: Let me give you an example of what I mean. Say a record deal is in its third year, three years of a five-year deal, when your management contract expires. I don't think there's any question but that you would commission income which emanates from things done before the expiration of your contract. Most management contracts, before they're negotiated, certainly provide that if the contract were entered into during your tenure as manager, you would continue to commission income from it, even with regard to those records that were recorded after the termination of your management.

LOURIE: As does mine.

AHS: Okay. That's what I wanted to know.

LOURIE: I would fight for that. There are arguments in favor of my continuing to commission, and there are arguments in favor of the artist saying you should at least reduce those commissions. Where between those two opposite points of view agreement is reached depends upon how much is conceded by either party in other areas of the contract. If I start out seeking 15% to 20% commission, then I think the important place for me to fight in a negotiation is in other areas such as this. I cannot tell you the pain of feeling that an artist can fire a manager and say, "Okay, you've helped make me a star; now you're done; it's totally over." It would be terrible, wrong and unjust.

AHS: You've never had that experience, from what I gather; you. . .

LOURIE: The truth is, Alan, that the better the manager does his job and the more successful the act becomes because of the combination of the manager and the act working together, the more the power shifts to the artist. As a manager, the feeling grows that the better the job you do for the partnership, the more you're doing yourself out of a job and out of the power to keep the job! Thereafter, the only power the manager has, as a practical matter, is trust and credibility. In the final analysis, that's what really counts.

AHS: Thanks, Miles.

# Interview With
# George Schiffer

*George Schiffer has been involved in all aspects of the entertainment field, as an attorney, a record executive, and, most recently, founder of Corporate Affairs, Ltd., which has the privilege of managing Ashford and Simpson and other entertainment acts.*

AHS:   The neophyte artist very often comes to an attorney and says, "Do I need a manager?" A typical response might be, "You can't get a decent manager at this stage of your career, and a bad manager is worse that valueless." How do you suggest they overcome that problem, or what do you think the correct answer is?

SCHIFFER:   I don't think there is a correct answer. In certain classic situations, the artist and the manager learn the business together. Brian Epstein and the Beatles are an example. In other situations, the artist had to find somebody pretty good at an early stage. . . . Elvis Presley and Tom Parker come to mind. The basic problem for newcomers in the business is that they require a huge investment, which is a very high-risk investment, which most professionals in the business simply don't want to make, nor should they. In other words, I think basically an artist is on his own until he has demonstrated something. After that, they can probably get the kind of professionals involved with them that they need. Up to that point, it's often more a matter of friendship. I think that the best manager/client relationships are formed between people who know each other extremely well. With lawyers and agents, that's really not necessary. I don't think that the management function is really possible unless the people really know each other. . . . You may know somebody for years before you take them on. Otherwise, it's one of those things that lasts for a while and then breaks up. At least that's been my experience.

AHS:    What would be the key considerations in determining whether or not you would undertake the management of an inexperienced act or an unknown act? What would you have to hear, or see, or feel, before you would undertake that economic risk that you alluded to before?

SCHIFFER:    I have to be very, very thoroughly convinced as to the person's talent, commitment, personality. . . . It's a very tough, demanding kind of business, and unless you felt that the person had the kind of stability and was the kind of person that you could really depend on, it's fruitless to start with them. Those are major considerations quite aside from talent. There's an awful lot of talent around that's going nowhere.

AHS:    Would you consider it a positive or negative factor that the act had a record deal with a particular record company, or would you feel it important that you be able to place the act at a company you felt comfortable with?

SCHIFFER:    Well, I think the question kind of answers itself. If the record company is a company that is a good place for that act to be, then it's a plus. If it's a company where the act is not very well served, then it's a minus. Obviously, the plus is a very big plus if it's there, because it means that you've got somebody who has already taken a big step. The artist is not really new anymore. The record company, under those conditions, has made a commitment of a lot of money and is desperately trying to find the act some management, and is obviously going to lean over backward to get a qualified manager to take it on. That's not a bad way to start.

AHS:    Most young artists are concerned with the fees charged by a manager. How does your fee structure work?

SCHIFFER:    Ah, basically we deal with a 15% commission. Some other people deal with a 20% commission structure, some people even go as high as 25%. It depends. There are situations where I would probably insist on 20%; there are also variations where you don't necessarily take the percentage on everything. It depends on what the situation is.

AHS:    I think you answered my next question, which was whether or not your fees vary from act to act. Apparently they do. Do you have any desire, George, to participate in publishing or production on an equity basis with your acts?

SCHIFFER: Oh sure, depending on the situation.

AHS: You would co-publish with them?

SCHIFFER: I would if it were appropriate, sure. When it comes to new people, I've kind of made a rule that, from here on out, I'm never going to take on anybody new unless it's on an equity basis. It just doesn't make any sense. With established people it's different, but with new people, unless you're involved with the equity side, you might as well not bother.

AHS: Okay. Assuming you can forge an equity participation, will you then invest in a new act? Will you advance living expenses? Will you advance money for demos? Will you do those types of things?

SCHIFFER: In general, with any act, you end up coming up with certain amounts of money. There are some managers who come up with a lot of cash money. Our position is generally that we won't do it. What ends up happening is that we end up coming up with money that we can't raise elsewhere, under certain kinds of conditions, where we think it makes sense.

AHS: As we discussed before, a manager's compensation is usually based on a percentage of gross income. You indicated a moment ago that sometimes you exclude certain items from gross income. Would you exclude recording costs?

SCHIFFER: Yes. Generally we would exclude recording costs. We try to deal with it realistically. . . . It becomes kind of a wash if you start commissioning recording costs, then there's going to be a deficit that has to be made up some other place; so it's easier and it makes everybody more comfortable simply not to commission recording costs.

AHS: I assume tour expenses would fall in the same category, or packaging costs in a package deal?

SCHIFFER: Generally speaking, if there is a expense allowance from, let's say, a record company, in terms of tour support, then we would not commission that, but we would commission the tour income. But to the extent that those tour expenses are going to be recoupable against royalties, you are going to create a mild accounting problem somewhere down the line. So you tend to deal with those things flexibly. Whatever's fair. Again, right at that moment, the tour support money is needed to pay expenses, so there's really no point in taking a commission and then lending it back. But there are other managers who would do it that way. I don't think there's any rule that says it ought to be done one way or the other.

AHS: There's a classic problem that I've never been able to resolve to everybody's satisfaction. What happens after the term of the contract ends? If there's a carryover from a deal that was entered into during the manager's term or negotiated during the manager's term, what is your attitude with regard to commissioning that income? As you know, the usual manager's contract provides for the manager to receive commissions for the duration of a deal, even if it goes beyond the term of the manager's contract. It creates the problem of double commissions for the artist. How do you resolve that in your mind?

SCHIFFER: I think the manager's entitled to that commission and the new incoming manager should be the one who makes whatever concession is necessary. I have deviated from that . . . really, again, it depends on the circumstances. I remember one specific case where I was the incoming manager and I simply waived the commission. It's a matter to me of practicalities, also a question of how much is involved really; if the ongoing commissions were, you know, hundreds of thousands of dollars, I would probably look at it differently than if it were a matter of a few thousand dollars one way or another.

AHS: What is the minimum term of years for which you would undertake the management of a career?

SCHIFFER: Well, I have a kind of a peculiar attitude with respect to that. It really doesn't make any sense to take on anybody for less than five years; on the other hand, the relationship is of such a nature that if it doesn't work, it doesn't work. The deal ought to be for five years, because, especially with a new artist, you have to figure that it's going to take three years to get them off the ground, unless somebody gets very, very lucky. On the other hand, it's equally clear that if the relationship breaks up, it doesn't make any difference how long the contract is; it can break up after a year, or two years, or whatever.

AHS:      Would you be receptive to the idea of having success criteria built into a contract? For instance, if after two years the act hasn't earned X dollars, it would then have the right to terminate?

SCHIFFER:      It wouldn't bother me, because if it's not a successful situation, it's costing me more than it's costing the act.

AHS:      George, would you give me a little of your background?

SCHIFFER:      I went to Harvard College and I went to Harvard Law School; then I went to work for the legal department of Warner Brothers Pictures for five years. Then I was in practice with a small firm specializing in the music business, and then on my own for quite a while. Then I was Vice-President in charge of Corporate Planning for Motown Records for three years, and then I went into the management business. I've been in the management business for about five years.

AHS:      Thank you. George, what do you think young artists should be particularly sensitive to or aware of in the 1980s as opposed to the artist of, say, five years ago?

SCHIFFER:      Well, I think an artist today has got to look at the total performance, not merely at the musical performance. They're in show biz, and to succeed, they're going to have to be very show conscious. They're going to need to know a little bit about acting; they're going to need to know how to talk . . . to succeed, they're going to have to be audio/visual. That places a lot of extra demands on the new artist. You're always going to have bar bands, people making some kind of a living out of performing music. But for the people who want to be stars, to be a star is going to take far more work and far more awareness. . . . It's already happening. Audiences really are looking for much more and an artist's income in the future is going to be related not merely to records and concerts and things like that, but also to audio/visual media of all kinds, and if the artist is not prepared for that, then he'll be in trouble.

AHS:      The corollary of what you've just said is that it's going to require a lot more of a manager.

SCHIFFER:      Sure.

AHS:      There are very few managers who are equipped to take an artist into this new area.

SCHIFFER:      Right. Well, I think that generally you're going to find managers becoming much more professional. There are more and more really qualified, intelligent people rather than backslappers of the old type who have gone into management as a business and as a professional service. I think somewhere along the line here traditional concepts of the relationships have to be reexamined. For example, a record company, years ago, did a whole bunch of things that they don't do anymore; record companies today are essentially marketing and financing organizations. It's easy enough to foresee that over the next twenty years the coupling of the computer's library and home-taping of satellite transmissions are going to eliminate the need for record inventory, and, at that point, so-called traditional record company function may become even more limited than it is today. The record companies are most unhappy with this development, and a great deal of the conflict between artists and record companies relates to the simple fact that, in reality, very often record companies don't make the product and don't know how to promote it, but they still demand the bulk of the income to cover enormous overheads that are not justified anymore. All those people that are running around those companies are not necessarily producing anything of economic value. So, when you go to a record company and say, "I need money to pay for independent promotion . . . and I need it because your guys cannot do the job," what you're really saying is "You're taking a large share of the money produced by the record because you are supposed to perform certain functions . . . but you're not doing the job, so give me some of that money and let me hire somebody else to do it." It makes everybody uncomfortable. Now that's only one area, but it's true all the way across the board. Conceptually, it really is not clear whether an artist works for a manager or a manager works for an artist. Sometimes it's one way, and sometimes it's the other, and sometimes it's kind of confused, because, as a practical matter, the manager is required to do a great many things . . . and pay for a great many things which are inconsistent with the artist being the boss. Some artists get very uncomfortable with that situation. But the artist on his own is not going to be able to do what the artist would like to do. So all these relationships have to be constantly reexamined because otherwise people get very confused, and what they're getting confused about is their perception of who they think they are as against what they really are doing. That's probably clear as mud.

AHS: I think it's very clear. I think it's also going to make you very unpopular with a lot of record companies.

SCHIFFER: Well, you know, the fact of the matter is that the good record people fully understand that they're in a kind of partnership. Not like in the old days when they were in command and they could call all the shots. It does make a great many of the older executives uncomfortable, very uncomfortable, when a manager comes in and takes a position which, in effect, says: "Look, you do your job, and we'll do ours." They really don't like it. But they can't do what was traditionally their job anymore. They're not even equipped to do it anymore.

AHS: Thank you, George.

# *Interview With Jerry Weintraub*

*Jerry Weintraub is the founder of Management III and the manager of such performers as John Denver, Bob Dylan, and Neil Diamond, among others.*

AHS: The first question is one that seems to come up a great deal: what comes first, Jerry, the chicken or the egg, insofar as managers for unproven artists go? Usually they can't attract a good manager, because good managers aren't interested in people who haven't accomplished something.

WEINTRAUB: I don't think that that's necessarily true.

AHS: Do you think it's imperative that a young artist start off with management? And, if so, how does he go about attracting a good manager?

WEINTRAUB: I don't think it's imperative that a young artist start off with management at all. I think it's imperative that a young artist finds a . . . if he's a singer, finds his way to a record company . . . somehow, that believes in him. All the record companies are interested in new talent, and they do listen to music. The major companies have hundreds of employees, and they have people that are always listening to new tapes. I don't think it's imperative they have a manager. I think it's great for a young artist if he has a manager with a reputation who can help him, who could pick up a telephone and get him a record deal or at least have people listen to him and take notice of him early on in his career. How do they get a manager? You know, we're the biggest management company in the world and we have some new artists here, and they found their way here.

AHS: That's my next question.

WEINTRAUB: How? I don't know how.

AHS: How do they find their way to you? What attracted you to the new artists you represent?

WEINTRAUB: To be honest, initially they're attracted to me, personally. Very few new artists can attract my attention unless they attract somebody's attention in my company first. We have a couple of new artists that we're working on right now, and they attracted somebody's attention around here. And somebody attracted my attention. They said, "Come down and listen to this."

AHS: What are some of the key considerations that would turn you on to a new act?

WEINTRAUB: Me, personally?

AHS: From a business point of view.

WEINTRAUB: The only thing that turns me on to an act is how many seats they sell, how many records they sell. I'm a businessman, you know.

AHS: Is it important to you that an act also be a writer, for instance, a singer who writes his own material?

WEINTRAUB: No.

AHS: It doesn't matter to you?

WEINTRAUB: Not necessarily. I mean I have a history of working with those people. . . . Diamond and Dylan and Denver, you know. I work with such artists, but it isn't a necessity.
[Jerry declined to address a series of questions relative to his fee structure, indicating that he considered the subject to be confidential.]

AHS: What is the minimum term of years for which you would get involved with an act?

WEINTRAUB: A new act? It takes years to get a new act launched. Over the years, I've noticed that two things accompany the success of an act. First, a certain fickleness develops, and, there seem to be a diminished appreciation of what the manager accomplished in aiding the artist to attain his success. In addition, a lot of people, who are not by profession managers, feel that once an artist is established they are then capable of handling his career from that point forward. Thus, a manager has to contend with a natural tendency on the part of the successful artist to experiment with change and a growing pool of "experts" who are not reluctant to take advantage of that tendency. Thus far, because of my success and reputation, I have been the beneficiary of that tendency towards fickleness. Nevertheless, I would not enjoy having the fruits of my labors, in connection with an artist's career, enjoyed by another manager, or would-be manager, who comes upon the scene after the initial gamble in time and effort has been taken by me. I think the only protection that a manager has, in that situation, is his contract with the artist, and I would therefore like that to be for as long a period of time as possible . . . at least five years.

AHS:          One last question because I can see you're very busy. Have you contemplated the effect that the new technology and the audio/visual exploitation are going to have on the industry, and how it will affect new artists?

WEINTRAUB: New artists? It doesn't affect new artists initially. It will affect them later on, depending on how their lawyers negotiate their contract with the record company, television company, and so on.

AHS:          With the audio/visual thing being so important, will acts have to have more than just good voices . . . and good songs to attract a record deal?

WEINTRAUB: I don't think the record companies are too concerned yet. I think they're still selling a lot of records, so if a guy can write and sing songs . . . a deal can be made. I know that there are a number of artists that I don't think will be worth anything in the audio/visual field, but still sell a lot of records. Look, the audio/visual field is the coming thing, there's no question about it, and so is cable. I am very, very cognizant of this and I have been for years, and I have been very, very careful in all my contract negotiations with everybody, to protect those areas for my artists. I can say that my artists are protected in those areas. I don't think everybody has done that. I think a lot of people are going to wake up one morning and find out that they don't own and control a lot of stuff they thought they owned and controlled. We have protected these things and I think they're going to be the most valuable things that we have.

AHS:          Give me a little of your personal background. I think the readers would be interested in that.

WEINTRAUB: Ah, I don't know how I got into show business, you know, I found my way into it somehow. I came from New York, and you either became a doctor or a lawyer or a CPA or went into the garment center or show business. I found my way into show business. I started as a pageboy at NBC, went from there to the mailroom at William Morris, and from there to MCA. From MCA I went into my own business. And the rest is pretty much history. I was in the right place at the right time.

AHS: And had a great deal of talent.

WEINTRAUB: No. . . . I've been involved with a lot of artists with a great deal of talent. . . . I have a talent for what I do, sure, but I've been lucky with the artists I've represented . . . they have been great for me.

AHS: And they have been very lucky to have you.

WEINTRAUB: Well, I appreciate it.

AHS: And I thank you.

WEINTRAUB: Thank you, Alan.

*The execution of a contract*

# 6

# *You've Got A Friend*

Music and lyrics by Carole King
© 1971, Colgems-EMI Music, Inc.

**G**etting a little bored reading about you? Okay, let's talk about entertainment lawyers for a while.

Whether or not you greet the idea with enthusiasm, I must advise you that an essential part of your success kit will be the services of a *qualified entertainment lawyer*. Note that the italics are not an accident: no, a lawyer will not do; he really should be a *qualified entertainment lawyer*.

To become a lawyer today is very difficult. Once that goal is attained, however, it is easy to become an entertainment lawyer. All it requires is the declaration, "I'm an entertainment lawyer." It's kind of like the old joke: "Make me a malted," and the genie responds, "Okay, pfft, you're a malted!" Well, pfft, you're an entertainment lawyer. "Just like that?" you ask. Yes . . . and no. Puzzled?

A person aspiring to become a lawyer, not unlike the person aspiring to become a singer or a songwriter, must also pay dues. After graduating from college, he must succeed in being accepted into a law school. Once accepted into a law school, he will spend the next three years studying, among other things, contracts, torts, evidence, civil procedure, federal practice, international law, constitutional law, conflicts of laws, trusts and estates, commercial law, criminal law, taxes, labor law, corporate law, family law, comparative law . . . and squash. Notice anything missing?

Graduation day finally arrives. Does our hero emerge as a lawyer? No. To be a lawyer and practice law, he must first pass the bar exam of the state in which he hopes to practice. After three years of law school, shouldn't the bar exam be a snap? Perhaps it should be . . . but it ain't. The law school graduate has no idea of what the law is in his state. In law school he learned that with respect to each issue in each course he took, there were four points of view—"the best one" and three others— none of which was wrong. What will our would-be lawyer do? He does the same as every other law school graduate does. He enrolls in a cram course, where for six or eight weeks he attends classes for eight hours a day, absorbs fifty-five pounds of photo-offset material, and learns the real "best view"—the view he had better learn if he is to pass the bar exam.

So, he studies all the questions and answers of the last twenty-three state bar exams and passes, and ultimately is granted his license to practice law.

Just think, a sovereign state has just licensed our friend to defend you on a murder-one rap, co-op your apartment house, merge your father's railroads, represent you in your divorce, and negotiate your record and songwriting contracts (if you beat the murder-one rap). While at law school he took a course in criminal law and a course in evidence, and the fifty-five pounds of material that came with the cram course contained three pounds of criminal law. You're right; you didn't see entertainment law listed in the law school curriculum, and there wasn't an ounce of it in the entire fifty-five pounds of cram material. Obviously, it makes more sense to hire our graduate for your murder problems than for your entertainment problems.

Why no training in entertainment law? Of the four hundred students entering a particular law school in any given year, only 2.3 of them are going to practice entertainment law. Forty-seven of the fifty states do not boast a New York City, L.A., or Nashville; hence no body of law relative to entertainment ever evolved. Even in New York, California, and Tennessee, where the entertainment industry thrives, there are few laws directly pertaining to it, and relatively few lawyers practicing it.

Inspired by his part in his high-school production of *Guys and Dolls*, or by his experience as a member of the teen-age rock band, or by his thirst for the glamour of "the business," our neophyte subscribes to *Billboard*, and, pfft . . . you guessed it . . . declares himself to be an entertainment lawyer.

I don't know if it would be legal for a newly licensed physician to perform a triple bypass operation on you, but he would sure have a hell of a time finding a hospital in which to do it. All a self-proclaimed entertainment lawyer needs is a yellow pad! Sunglasses are optional equipment. If there are no special degrees for entertainment lawyers, no uniforms with insignia, no certificate to hang on a wall, how does an artist or songwriter distinguish an entertainment lawyer from all the other breeds?

An entertainment lawyer is a lawyer who, by design or accident, has evolved a practice consisting primarily of clients whose business interests are in the ambit of the entertainment industry. There are various subspecialties within this category—for example, motion pictures, television, music and records, and theatre. They have, through mistakes made at the expense of your predecessors, garnered the experience necessary to guide you through the business and legal maze associated with your profession. In choosing one, it behooves you to make sure you're not a "predecessor."

Ah, but you're a cynic. "He's drumming up business. My family lawyer has been practicing for thirty years; he can handle any contract." Wrong! If he deserves your faith in him, he'll do one of two things: he'll find a good entertainment lawyer to act as his "colleague" on your matters or he'll find a good entertainment lawyer and refer you to him. If your faith is misplaced, he'll represent you himself. He's licensed to do it. But regardless of what the bar examiners said thirty years ago, he's *not* qualified. It's a test of character. After all, if a local boy is going to be another Elvis, is it not human nature to want to board the glory train? If you read the papers, you will note that the "top" murderers, the real professionals, are always represented by well-known criminal lawyers. This is probably the only instance where using the "family" attorney is appropriate. Your life is on the line, too, at least your professional life. If someone accused of murder were to hire an entertainment lawyer to represent him, he would deserve "the chair," and would probably be so rewarded. If you intend to be a professional in the entertainment industry, treat yourself no less kindly than a murderer does.

The Anglo-American system of jurisprudence is known as the "adversary system." Every attorney practicing under it is trained and obligated to act as an advocate of his client's cause—"a hired gun," if you will. It is not his function to be "fair" or "impartial"; it is his obligation to do as well for his client as is possible within the bounds of professional ethics. Your "adversaries," the record companies and music publishers, retain some of the best entertainment lawyers in the business. It is incumbent upon you to do no less.

When is the appropriate time to engage an entertainment attorney? The facile answer is, "Before it's too late." Actually, that answer is not very helpful, for two reasons: first, the uninitiated don't really know when "too late" is approaching, and, second, it varies from situation to situation.

If you are a songwriter but not an artist, you can in most instances wait until there is some "action"—until some publisher indicates a desire to contract with you with respect to your exclusive services as a songwriter or with respect to one or more of your songs. At that point it is incumbent upon you to demonstrate enthusiasm without committing yourself to any specifics. The easiest way is to be honest: "Sounds great, but I just stick to the music part; my lawyer handles the business end." Then, find "my lawyer" damn quick.

As an artist or singer-songwriter, you may profit more from an early association with an attorney than would the "naked" songwriter. There is more diffusion in the songwriter's career—he will enjoy relationships with and have his songs published by many publishers. The songwriter's dealings with publishers reflect more of a nurturing or evolutionary process. Exclusivity is not endemic to the songwriter-publisher relationship. It *is* to the artist-record company relationship. A writer can "place" a song with one publisher in the morning and another with that publisher's competitor in the afternoon. The artist-record company relationship is more of a "big bang" relationship. The monetary and career stakes are high. The record company has a large investment at risk, and the artist has failure at risk. The industry knows only of a writer's successes. Have a flop record as an artist, and the whole world knows and remembers it. The record industry is more frenetic, and access to it is more elusive.

One way to acquire access to the record companies is through an attorney who has some clout. While a songwriter can make the rounds, a neophyte artist finds it much more difficult to be heard. An entertainment lawyer usually can get you heard. So, as an artist or singer-songwriter, it is wise to seek a relationship with an entertainment lawyer when you have a demo you consider representative of your talent and upon which you are willing to stake your career.

When you make a major investment or purchase, it is usually after much rumination, soul-searching, comparison, and "shopping." The search for the attorney who will guide you through the most important decisions of your professional life should be made with no less care than you would exercise in purchasing an amp. The process is really not mysterious; in fact, it's quite simple. As you make your way through the industry, you will meet other artists and writers as well as producers, publishers, managers, and the myriad people associated with them. When you deem the time is right to seek the services of an attorney, ask the people you've met whom they use, whom they recommend, whom they have heard about. Amass a list of several who seem promising and call them. Explain who you are and that you would like to meet with them to discuss possible representation. Entertainment attorneys come in all sizes, shapes, and forms. Some look like bankers and some look like "freaks." In Los Angeles, entertainment lawyers are not permitted to purchase or wear neckties. In New York, ties are permitted but not mandatory. You will visit posh offices with general practices spanning all specialties, of which entertainment will be only one. You will visit smaller offices housing only a few attorneys whose practice is devoted entirely to entertainment law. Each has advantages and disadvantages, and the trappings are not dispositive of the issue. You can find warmth, understanding, and compassion on Park Avenue, and, conversely, an elegance of manner and style at less pricey addresses.

There are only two elements upon which your choice should be based: competence and compatibility. The only way you will be able to secure a handle on these qualities is by meeting and talking with several prospective counselors, and asking a lot of questions—tough questions. The dynamics of a first meeting between a prospective attorney and a prospective client are interesting. You should realize that while you are appraising him, he is also trying to determine whether or not you are a good gamble upon which he should bet his time. If you have nothing going for you *yet*, no record company offers, no songs on the charts, in short, no "track record," the established entertaiment attorney has to assess the likelihood of your developing into a profitable, fee-producing client. Once your success is secured, you can be sure of being treated in princely fashion. The trick is to find the entertainment attorney who will treat you that way before your coronation.

"Lawyer stories" circulate among artists and writers much the same way as "client stories" circulate among members of the entertainment bar. The concerns shown in these stories are evident in the following questions asked by your brethren, all of which found their genesis in the experiences (mostly bad) of others, and deserve to be asked—and answered:

"Will you take my telephone calls, and will you get back to me promptly if you can't?"

This is one of the greatest sources of frustration and dissatisfaction among artists and writers who are not yet established. Stars always have their calls responded to rapidly—for obvious reasons. This question, even if not answered honestly at the time it is asked, may have a salutory effect when you call in the future.

"Will you [assuming you are talking to a prominent attorney with a large supporting cast] actually work on my matters or will they be delegated to someone else?"

An honest answer should be, "Yes and yes." Where his prestige and experience are needed, he should be personally involved. For example, he should "talk" your deal with a record company. But for him to fill out your copyright registration certificates would be a waste of his time and your money and that chore should be delegated to a less senior attorney with a less senior billing rate.

"Who are some of your clients?"

A good question if you are trying to establish whether you have truly found a bona-fide entertainment lawyer. Ethical considerations aside, he will probably supply you with a litany of names that will knock your socks off. Don't ask for their phone numbers—he won't give them to you. In most instances he'll probably "drop" enough names and "war stories" so that you won't have to ask the question. What the hell, lawyers are human, too.

"How much will you charge me? I don't have much money, you know."

You won't surprise him with this question. He has been evaluating the economics of representing you all the time you have been sitting in his office. Everybody seems to feel uncomfortable when it comes to discussing fees, especially young lawyers and inexperienced clients. The young lawyer's discomfort stems from an innate insecurity over his worth (often well founded) and a fear of scaring off a real, live client. The inexperienced client's discomfort stems from a fear that he won't be able to pay the bill (also often well founded). An old wardog of a lawyer and an experienced businessman have no such problems; they deal with it openly, like any other business factor, and both fare better for it.

To leave the question of fees undiscussed, especially with an inexperienced client, can only lead to bitterness and unhappiness. Lawyer's fees have, of necessity, kept pace with the soaring inflation and concomitant increases in overhead. An unprepared client is apt to need mouth-to-mouth resuscitation and heart massage when he opens his first bill. His lawyer should feel chagrined and sheepish if the client's faltering words "I . . . I . . . I had no idea . . ." are spoken with justification. If your lawyer does not raise the issue of fees, you should. It will be the only time till you attain stardom that you will have him on the defensive—and it may convince him that you intend to pay your bills.

There are many ways to skin a cat, but only three basic fee structures utilized by entertainment attorneys. There are, however, an almost infinite number of variations and combinations of the three. In looking at them let's keep your present stature and status (or relative absence thereof) in mind.

The annual retainer is a neat and most satisfactory fee arrangement, and one that you should be cognizant of for the future, though not one that you should consider at this stage of your career. It entails a fixed annual fee, usually divided into twelve equal monthly payments. After it is agreed upon, the client is presumably entitled to call upon the services of the attorney in more or less unlimited fashion without the payment of additional sums, with certain exceptions. For an annual retainer to work, it must be fair to both sides. To arrive at a fair annual retainer, there has to be a history between the attorney and the client and a degree of stability in the client's career. As in most areas of commerce, the annual retainer involves a trade off. The attorney receives the security of knowing that he has a fixed source of income that he can rely upon for the duration of the retainer term. In exchange for his obligation to make the fixed payments, the client should receive a financial reward; thus the annual retainer should be significantly (but not excessively) less than his straight-time charges would have been. Hence the need for a history, or track record, in the relationship before a fair and mutually satisfactory annual retainer can be arrived at. If things get out of balance, one party or the other will feel "ripped off," and the relationship will break down. Annual retainers only work when there is mutual trust and respect and an understanding that the retainer is subject to review and reevaluation by both parties at regular intervals. Most new attorney-client relationships involve fervid activity by the attorney in the initial stages, when he must review and sort out existing contracts and relationships, unscrew things previously screwed up, and, in general, get the client's house in order. This period is usually followed by a period of general calm. You can't have it both ways—have the benefit of the retainer while the attorney is battling a hurricane of paper and then switch to time charges when the storm has passed and your legal affairs are drifting through the horse latitudes. You would be surprised at how often this is suggested, with insouciance, by clients.

There are three items that are never included in a retainer and for which you will be billed separately and additionally. They are litigation, services rendered at your behest in a distant geographic location ("travel"), and disbursements. These should be mentioned and discussed. If your attorney fails to mention these, it is not because he is laying a snare for you. He just presumes (incorrectly) that you couldn't possibly think otherwise. Although I do not subscribe to the practice of reducing retainer agreements to writing, other attorneys may do so. There is no right or wrong on this point. I have just never found it necessary; nor do I feel the practice compatible with the kind of relationship I hope to nurture with a client.

The most usual fee arrangement, and the one that in all likelihood will be suggested to you, is that of paying for services on a time basis. Under this arrangement you pay your attorney (as you would a plumber) for the time he spends on your matters. All attorneys do, or at least should, keep preceise records of their time. It is their "inventory control." It is their only way of knowing the economic viability of their various client relationships. Therefore, time is kept even in a retainer relationship, and it is the tool used by the attorney in reevaluating a retainer from time to time. You can be sure that whenever you leave your attorney's office, the first thing he does is make a notation in his diary of the time spent with you. He also does this when he finishes a phone conversation with you. It matters little to him whether his time is expended in meetings or over the phone. You might also find it useful to know that there are usually minimum time units. There are no three-minute diary entries. Minimum units vary from "tenths" to "quarters of hours." So, if you wish to minimize your legal bills, call only with respect to matters of substance and call (except in emergencies) when you have collected enough queries to make the most economical use of a minimum unit.

Hourly rates vary from location to location, from law firm to law firm, and, within a particular firm, from lawyer to lawyer, depending on seniority. You will enjoy the dubious distinction of paying fees that are well into the high end of the spectrum. The industry the entertainment bar serves requires that its practitioners maintain offices in the highest-rent districts of the most expensive cities in the country. The nature of the clientele requires surroundings and trappings consonant with its attainments, status, and, alas, sometimes only dreams. And this elitist bar faces competition for the "best and brightest" of the current law school graduates, who are now being offered about $45,000 per annum "to start" by the "Wall Street" firms. You're going to pay for a lot of overhead. But take comfort in the fact that your legal fees are tax deductible. The trick is to earn the income from which to deduct them.

Hourly rates vary from about $75.00 per hour for the "new associate" to about $300.00 per hour for the firm's senior partner. Invariably your time charges are a blend of various rates. No new associate is permitted to work without supervision and review of his work by a more senior lawyer. The disparity in hourly billing rates has been rationalized by the observation that the more experienced lawyer works faster and hence it "all evens out." To some extent this is true, but in fact, when you are dealing with the more stratospheric hourly rates, there is no doubt that there is a prestige or "clout" factor built in. It would be absurd to use a $300.00-an-hour senior partner to plug names and titles into a form songwriter agreement, and few clients would countenance it. The clout factor has real economic significance in those instances where, because of it, a record company's first draft incorporates what its lawyers know will be demanded by an experienced attorney with whom they have previously dealt. If five or six billable hours of negotiation can thus be avoided, the economic benefits accruing from the judicious use of a more senior attorney can easily be realized. Often an experienced attorney can predicate a new deal upon a contract he negotiated with that same company for another client. Thus the weeks that were spent forging the original deal, which were paid for by another client, are reduced to a few brief meetings. A not inconsiderable savings to you! Besides, when you become a star, you will expect your "price" to rise. So does the entertainment attorney.

There are two more factors that should be discussed between you and your lawyer, whether you are on a retainer or time basis. Both will be reflected in your bills and should be talked about either in your initial meeting or when they are likely to occur. Woe to the lawyer who doesn't at least mention them.

An entertainment lawyer is likely to do a certain amount of "agenting" or hustling of tapes in an effort to obtain a record or publishing deal for his clients. He does this, and indeed is sought after to do this, because over many years he has acquired access to the industry's deal makers. It is unrealistic to think that he will charge you only for the tenth or quarter of an hour it took him to make the contact that resulted in the deal. He fully expects, and is entitled to, a reward consonant with his accomplishment. It is incumbent upon him, however, to warn you of this up front.

Occasionally an event arises in an artist's career that is so important and time-consuming for his attorney that an extraordinary fee arrangement is dictated by circumstances. Once again this is justified and perfectly acceptable if discussed openly and thoroughly before the work is undertaken. To present an unsuspecting client with a whopping bill without first setting a proper predicate is uncomfortable for both the attorney and the client. Even if the bill is paid without a hassle, the relationship invariably suffers.

Another form of fee structure that is sometimes (though not often) agreed upon between lawyers and novice artists is a percentage of the artist's gross income. In theory, it seems fine. While the artist is earning little, he is not saddled with disproportionately large legal fees. On the other hand, if the artist "makes it," the attorney is rewarded for his faith, loyalty, and willingness to gamble on the artist's talent. "Fair," you say? In theory, perhaps. But human nature, unfortunately, has a way of interfering. On the one occasion when my firm tried this, all went well up to a point. That point was reached when the artist, after several years of being "carried" by the firm, finally made it. His success was sudden and big. As the artist's accountant related the story, when he presented a six-figure check to our order for the artist's signature, it was promptly torn up with the observation that "no [expletive deleted] lawyer deserves that much!" You might want to try this fee structure if you can find someone with a great deal of faith in your talent and honor.

There is a good possibility that, regardless of the fee structure arrived at, your attorney will ask you for a "retainer in advance." This is a payment in anticipation of the services to be rendered, and it will be applied against your bill. It is not a negative reflection on you, or on him. It is merely a reflection of his experience and the number of times he has gotten "burned" in the past. There is an uncanny correlation between unfulfilled dreams and unpaid bills. If a deal doesn't reach completion, regardless of how hard the attorney has worked, and notwithstanding the prodigious hours he has poured into it, he knows the likelihood of receiving compensation for his time is relatively small. Groups are particularly prone to such conduct. The members seem to draw upon and reinforce each other's baser instincts. So, if you're serious, bite the bullet; it hurts for only a minute. Besides, the modest advance will probably buy thousands in credit.

Every successful entertainment attorney works at 150% of capacity. No matter how clean the top of his desk may be, in it, or near it, is a pile of work that is overdue for completion. Each pile has a top and a bottom. The guaranteed method of having your work occupy the bottom is to not pay your bill. Even if you can't pay it all at once, part payments are welcome and will assure a continuing interest in your matters. Ignoring bills courts disaster on another level. Eventually, you will become too embarrassed to call for advice or for an appointment. You will either seek another attorney, in which case you will pay again for his education with respect to your matters, or act without the aid of an attorney, in which case you will pay dearly to have your self-inflicted disasters rectified. Attorneys, contrary to popular belief, are human, and will respond to a demonstration of a sincere effort to honor an obligation.

Using your attorney to say "no" for you or otherwise take care of unpleasantness is not an act of cowardice. It is an invaluable use of his time. No attorney worth his salt will shrink from the role of "heavy." One of the most useful functions attorneys can serve is as an insulator between their respective clients. While they are "leveling," their clients can be having a pleasant lunch and their future creative endeavors can proceed unmarred by all the exchanges that begin with "Frankly . . ."

Some artists and songwriters fear that the introduction of an attorney into their relationship with a record company or music publisher will "poison the relationship," demonstrate a lack of trust, or otherwise jeopardize their chances of closing a deal. Quite to the contrary, most legitimate record companies and music publishers welcome the introduction of an experienced entertainment attorney into a negotiation. (Of course, they may welcome some more than others.) Their reasons have nothing to do with altruism. They have all had contracts challenged, after an artist or writer has attained success, on the grounds that the artist or writer was not represented by counsel at the time the contract was signed and that the contract was "unconscionable" and lacked "mutuality." Translated, this means that the contract was so one-sided or unfair that the artist or writer couldn't have understood it, and hence the court should not enforce it. The presence of an experienced entertainment attorney on the artist's or writer's behalf effectively nullifies such a challenge. In addition, the presence of an entertainment lawyer expedites the conclusion of the negotiation in that endless hours are not wasted discussing points that the nature of the business dictates can't be changed. The entertainment attorney has a perception of which points these are. As a result, a reservoir of acrimony is avoided that might otherwise carry forward into the relationship.

Sometimes instinct or some factor other than logic determines the pairing of entertainment lawyers and their clients. As a young lawyer, I was very flattered to be chosen by a prestigious client of our firm to accompany him and his staff to an industry convention in the south of France. The purpose of the trip was to negotiate foreign publishing and record deals with substantial advances. I had heard that the client had a strong belief in astrology. During a lull in our rounds of meetings, I casually asked him whether he really believed in "that stuff." His reply was simple. "You're here, aren't you?" He had had his astrologer work up charts on all of the attorneys in the office. He chose the best chart to accompany him. Well, who is to say? We came home with a lot of money!

Sooner or later, you're going to need a good entertainment lawyer, and sooner is probably better.

*Home taping — when it's YOUR royalty!*

# 7

# I've Heard That Song Before

Music and lyrics by Sammy Cahn and Julie Styne
© 1942 by Cahn Music Company
and Morley Music Company

With perhaps the exception of sex, few subjects hold more mystery or engender more unfounded anxiety for the uninitiated than the subject of copyright. Both abound in misconceptions (no pun intended), misinformation, and misapprehensions.

I was shocked to learn recently of a group that declined a wonderful opportunity to do a showcase performance simply because they had not yet registered their songs for copyright. What foolishness! What motivated them to act this way, I wondered. Was it fear that they would lose the copyrights in their songs? Was it fear that their songs could be ripped off with impunity if they were not registered?

In any case, read the following, accept it blindly, casting all old misconceptions and superstitions aside, heave a sigh of relief, and relax.

You *automatically* acquire a copyright in your song the *instant* you create it.

In general, copyright registration does not provide you with copyright protection. You acquired that when you created your song. Copyright registration merely bestows upon copyright owners certain advantages in the enforcement of the rights they already possess. Although copyright registration is desirable and to be encouraged, it is not invested with the urgency you may have previously attributed to it.

You may perform your songs to your heart's content, even on network television, without fear of losing your copyrights—whether or not they are registered.

Similarly, you may record your songs, without registering them, without fear of losing your copyrights.

You need not worry about a copyright notice on your songs or recordings till they are "published," and even then the Copyright Act permits you to correct an omission or mistake should you have failed to provide a copyright notice or perhaps used an erroneous one. As a practical matter, in most instances "publication" will not take place until there is a commercially released recording of your song. There is little chance of printed "published" copies until after a successful record, because no print market will exist. You can also be fairly well assured that neither a record company nor a music publisher will permit "publication" of your songs without the requisite copyright notice.

The general subject of copyright basics has been so well handled by the United States Copyright Office in its Circular R1 that, rather than rewrite it, as learned as that may have me appear, I have asked the publisher to reprint it in its entirety in this chapter—thereby saving you a 20¢ stamp. Read it. It will clarify many things that may have puzzled you up until now. It may also convince some of you skeptics that what I wrote above is true. You may think I have dealt cavalierly with copyright, and in fact I may have, but I did so because I have perceived an untoward proccupation with the subject by inexperienced artists and songwriters. An acceptance and comprehension of what is contained in this chapter and in R1 is all you really need in your arsenal at this stage of your career. Later on you will have "experts" to handle such mundane matters for you.

Your concern should not be about copyright, but, rather, about creating copyrights worth worrying about.

Considering the number of copyrighted songs that are recorded and broadcast each year, the number of infringement claims of any substance at all is infinitesimally small. Of that small number, I would venture that most of them involve unconscious or unintentional copying. Most arise because a writer's subconscious has captured a musical phrase, stored it, and reprocessed it as its own. Considering that both you and Beethoven had only seven notes to play with, it is truly amazing that infringement isn't rife. But it isn't. Oh, well, Shakespeare and I fooled around with the same twenty-six letters, and we haven't run afoul of each other either.

There are two Ripleyesque facets of copyright I want to pass on to you before moving on. Believe it or not, if two writers independently create the same song, they each enjoy independent and separate copyrights in that song. And, believe it or not, it doesn't matter who wrote the song first. Unlike patents, where the first to register wins all, there is no seniority or priority accorded the first to create a copyright. No infringement can take place without a copying.

If you read R1, you will perceive that before you can bring an infringement action you will have to register your copyright. You will also realize that certain other advantages (such as establishing prima facie validity of your copyright) will follow early, rather than later, registration.

Should you fret about the possibility of someone stealing your song? Hardly. Most writers share your belief that the songs that *they write* are the best; therefore, why steal an inferior song? Besides, if an infringer makes your song a hit, it's a way of breakin' in!

Incidentally, the Copyright Act provides that copyright protection is not available for any work of the United States Government, so here for your pleasure and enlightenment, is Circular R1.

Circular **R1**

**Copyright Basics**

# Copyright Basics

On January 1, 1978, the Copyright Act of 1976 (title 17 of the United States Code) came into effect. This general revision of the copyright law of the United States, the first such revision since 1909, makes important changes in our copyright system and generally, but not entirely, supersedes the previous Federal copyright statute. For highlights of the overall changes in the copyright law, request Circular R99 from the Copyright Office.

### What Copyright Is

Copyright is a form of protection provided by the laws of the United States (title 17, U.S. Code) to the authors of "original works of authorship" including literary, dramatic, musical, artistic, and certain other intellectual works. This protection is available to both published and unpublished works. Section 106 of the Copyright Act generally gives the owner of copyright the exclusive right to do and to authorize others to do the following:
- *To reproduce* the copyrighted work in copies or phonorecords;
- *To prepare derivative works* based upon the copyrighted work;
- *To distribute copies or phonorecords* of the copyrighted work to the public by sale or other transfer of ownership, or by rental, lease, or lending;
- *To perform the copyrighted work publicly,* in the case of literary, musical, dramatic, and choreographic works, pantomimes, and motion pictures and other audiovisual works; and
- *To display the copyrighted work publicly* in the case of literary, musical, dramatic, and choreographic works, pantomimes, and pictorial, graphic, or sculptural works, including the individual images of a motion picture or other audiovisual work.

It is illegal for anyone to violate any of the rights provided to the owner of copyright by the Act. These rights, however, are not unlimited in scope. Sections 107 through 118 of the Copyright Act establish limitations on these rights. In some cases, these limitations are specified exemptions from copyright liability. One major limitation is the doctrine of "fair use," which is now given a statutory basis by section 107 of the Act. In other instances, the limitation takes the form of a "compulsory license" under which certain limited uses of copyrighted works are permitted upon payment of specified royalties and compliance with statutory conditions. For further information about the limitations of any of these rights, consult the Copyright Act or write to the Copyright Office.

### Who Can Claim Copyright

Copyright protection subsists from the time the work is created in fixed form; that is, it is an incident of the process of authorship. The copyright in the work of authorship *immediately* becomes the property of the author who created it. Only the author or those deriving their rights through the author can rightfully claim copyright.

In the case of works made for hire, the employer and not the employee is presumptively considered the author. Section 101 of the copyright statute defines a "work made for hire" as:

(1) a work prepared by an employee within the scope of his or her employment; or

(2) a work specially ordered or commissioned for use as a contribution to a collective work, as a part of a motion picture or other audiovisual work, as a translation, as a supplementary work, as a compilation, as an instructional text, as a test, as answer material for a test, or as an atlas, if the parties expressly agree in a written instrument signed by them that the work shall be considered a work made for hire. . . .

The authors of a joint work are co-owners of the copyright in the work, unless there is an agreement to the contrary.

Copyright in each separate contribution to a periodical or other collective work is distinct from copyright in the collective work as a whole and vests initially with the author of the contribution.

### Two General Principles

- Mere ownership of a book, manuscript, painting, or any other copy or phonorecord does not give the possessor the copyright. The law provides that transfer of ownership of any material object that embodies a protected work does not of itself convey any rights in the copyright.
- Minors may claim copyright, but state laws may regulate the business dealings involving copyrights owned by minors. For information on relevant state laws, it would be well to consult an attorney.

### Copyright And National Origin Of The Work

Copyright protection is available for all unpublished works, regardless of the nationality or domicile of the author.

Published works are eligible for copyright protection in the United States if any one of the following conditions is met:

- On the date of first publication, one or more of the authors is a national or domiciliary of the United States or is a national, domiciliary, or soverign authority of a foreign nation that is a party to a copyright treaty to which the United States is also a party, or is a stateless person wherever that person may be domiciled; or

• The work is first published in the United States or in a foreign nation that, on the date of first publication, is a party to the Universal Copyright Convention; or the work comes within the scope of a Presidential proclamation.

### What Works Are Protected

Copyright protection exists for "original works of authorship" when they become fixed in a tangible form of expression. The fixation does not need to be directly perceptible, so long as it may be communicated with the aid of a machine or device. Copyrightable works include the following categories:

(1) literary works;
(2) musical works, including any accompanying words;
(3) dramatic works, including any accompanying music;
(4) pantomimes and choreographic works;
(5) pictorial, graphic, and sculptural works;
(6) motion pictures and other audiovisual works; and
(7) sound recordings.

This list is illustrative and is not meant to exhaust the categories of copyrightable works. These categories should be viewed quite broadly so that, for example, computer programs and most "compilations" are registrable as "literary works"; maps and architectural blueprints are registrable as "pictorial, graphic, and sculptural works."

### What Is Not Protected By Copyright

Several categories of material are generally not eligible for statutory copyright protection. These include among others:

• Works that have *not* been fixed in a tangible form of expression. For example: choreographic works which have not been notated or recorded, or improvisational speeches or performances that have not been written or recorded.

• Titles, names, short phrases, and slogans; familiar symbols or designs; mere variations of typographic ornamentation, lettering, or coloring; mere listings of ingredients or contents.

• Ideas, procedures, methods, systems, processes, concepts, principles, discoveries, or devices, as distinguished from a description, explanation, or illustration.

• Works consisting *entirely* of information that is common property and containing no original authorship. For example: standard calendars, height and weight charts, tape measures and rules, and lists or tables taken from public documents or other common sources.

## How To Secure A Copyright

### Copyright Secured Automatically Upon Creation

The way in which copyright protection is secured under the present law is frequently misunderstood. No publication or registration or other action in the Copyright Office is required to secure copyright under the new law, unlike the old law, which required either publication with the copyright notice or registration in the Copyright Office (see NOTE below). There are, however, certain definite advantages to registration. (See page 221.)

Under the new law, copyright is secured *automatically* when the work is created, and a work is "created" when it is fixed in a copy or phonorecord for the first time. In general, "copies" are material objects from which a work can be read or visually perceived either directly or with the aid of a machine or device, such as books, manuscripts, sheet music, film, videotape, or microfilm. "Phonorecords" are material objects embodying fixations of sounds (excluding, by statutory definition, motion picture sound tracks), such as audio tapes and phonograph disks. Thus, for example, a song (the "work") can be fixed in sheet music ("copies") or in phonograph disks ("phonorecords"), or both.

If a work is prepared over a period of time, the part of the work existing in fixed form on a particular date constitutes the created work as of that date.

*Note:Before 1978, statutory copyright was generally secured by the act of publication with notice of copyright, assuming compliance with all other relevant statutory conditions. Works in the public domain on January 1, 1978 (for example, works published without satsifying all conditions for securing statutory copyright under the Copyright Act of 1909) remain in the public domain under the current Act.*

*Statutory copyright could also be secured before 1978 by the act of registration in the case of certain unpublished works and works eligible for ad interim copyright. The current Act automatically extends to full term copyright (section 304 sets the term) for all works in which ad interim copyright was subsisting or was capable of being secured on December 31, 1977.*

### Publication

Publication is no longer the key to obtaining statutory copyright as it was under the Copyright Act of 1909. However, publication remains important to copyright owners.

The Copyright Act defines publication as follows:

"Publication" is the distribution of copies or phonorecords of a work to the public by sale or other transfer of ownership, or by rental, lease, or lending. The offering to distribute copies or phonorecords to a group of persons for purposes of further distribution, public performance, or public display, constitutes publication. A public performance or display of a work does not of itself constitute publication.

A further discussion of the definition of "publication" can be found in the legislative history of the Act. The legislative reports define "to the public" as distribution to persons under no explicit or implicit restrictions with respect to disclosure of the contents. The reports state that the definition makes it clear that the sale of phonorecords constitutes publication of the underlying work, for example, the musical, dramatic, or literary work embodied in a phonorecord. The reports also state that it is clear that any form or dissemination in which the material object does not change hands, for example, performances or displays on television, is *not* a publication no matter how many people are exposed to the work. However, when copies or phonorecords are offered for sale or lease to a group of wholesalers, broadcasters, or motion picture theaters, publication does take place if the purpose is further distribution, public performance, or public display.

Publication is an important concept in the copyright law because upon publication, several significant consequences follow. Among these are:

- When a work is published, all published copies should bear a notice of copyright. (See discussion below of "notice of copyright.")
- Works that are published with notice of copyright in the United States are subject to mandatory deposit with the Library of Congress. (See discussion on page 224 on "mandatory deposit.")
- Publication of a work can affect the limitations on the exclusive rights of the copyright owner that are set forth in sections 107 through 118 of the law.
- The year of publication is used in determining the duration of copyright protection for anonymous and pseudonymous works

(when the author's identity is not revealed in the records of the Copyright Office) and for works made for hire.

- Deposit requirements for registration of published works differ from those for registration of unpublished works. (See discussion on page 222 of "copyright registration" procedures.)

### Notice Of Copyright

When a work is published under the authority of the copyright owner, a notice of copyright should be placed on all publicly distributed copies and on all publicly distributed phonorecords of sound recordings. This notice is required even on works published outside of the United States. Failure to comply with the notice requirement can result in the loss of certain additional rights otherwise available to the copyright owner.

The use of the copyright notice is the responsibility of the copyright owner and does not require advance permission from, or registration with, the Copyright Office.

### Form of Notice for Visually Perceptible Copies

The notice for visually perceptible copies should contain the following three elements:

- *The symbol* © (the letter C in a circle), or the word "Copyright," or the abbreviation "Copr."; and
- *The year of first publication* of the work. In the case of compilations or derivative works incorporating previously published material, the year date of first publication of the compilation or derivative work is sufficient. The year date may be omitted where a pictorial, graphic, or sculptural work, with accompanying textual matter, if any, is reproduced in or on greeting cards, postcards, stationery, jewelry, dolls, toys, or any useful articles; and
- *The name of the owner of copyright* in the work, or an abbreviation by which the name can be recognized, or a generally known alternative designation of the owner.

Example: © 1981 John Doe

The "C in a circle" notice is required only on "visually perceptible copies." Certain kinds of works, for example, musical, dramatic, and literary works, may be fixed not in "copies" but by means of sound in an audio recording. Since audio recordings such as audio tapes and phonograph disks are "phonorecords" and not "copies," there is no requirement that the phonorecord bear a "C in a circle" notice to protect the underlying musical, dramatic, or literary work that is recorded.

## Form of Notice for Phonorecords of Sound Recordings

The copyright notice for phonorecords of sound recordings* has somewhat different requirements. The notice appearing on phonorecords should contain the following three elements:

- *The symbol* ℗ (the letter P in a circle); and
- *The year of first publication* of the sound recording; and
- *The name of the owner of copyright* in the sound recording, or an abbreviation by which the name can be recognized, or a generally known alternative designation of the owner. If the producer of the sound recording is named on the phonorecord labels or containers, and if no other name appears in conjunction with the notice, the producer's name shall be considered a part of the notice.

Example: ℗ 1981 John Doe

*Note: Because of problems that might result in some cases from the use of variant forms of the notice, any form of the notice other than these given here should not be used without first seeking legal advice.*

## Position of Notice

The notice should be affixed to copies or phonorecords of the work in such a manner and location as to "give reasonable notice of the claim of copyright." The notice on phonorecords may appear on the surface of the phonorecord or on the phonorecord label or container, provided the manner of placement and location gives reasonable notice of the claim. The three elements of the notice should ordinarily appear together on the copies or phonorecords. For further information about methods of affixation of the notice, write to the Copyright Office.

## Publications Incorporating United States Government Works

Whenever a work is published in copies or phonorecords consisting preponderantly of one or more works of the United States Government, the notice of copyright shall also include a statement identifying, either affirmatively or negatively, those portions of the copies or phonorecords embodying any work or works protected by title 17 of the United States Code.

## Unpublished Works

The copyright notice is not required on unpublished works. To avoid an inadvertent publication without notice, however, it may be advisable for the author or other owner of the copyright to affix notices to any copies or phonorecords which leave his or her control.

* Sound recordings are defined as "works that result from the fixation of a series of musical, spoken, or other sounds, but not including the sounds accompanying a motion picture or other audiovisual work, regardless of the nature of the material objects, such as disks, tapes, or other phonorecords, in which they are embodied."

**Effect of Omission of the Notice or of Error in the Name or Date**

Unlike the law in effect before 1978, the new Copyright Act, in sections 405 and 406, provides procedures for correcting errors and omissions of the copyright notice on works published on or after January 1, 1978.

In general, the omission or error does not automatically invalidate the copyright in a work if registration for the work has been made before or is made within 5 years after the publication without notice, and a reasonable effort is made to add the notice to all copies or phonorecords that are distributed to the public in the United States after the omission has been discovered.

*Note: Before 1978, the copyright law required, as a condition for copyright protection, that all copies published with the authorization of the copyright owner bear a proper notice. If a work was published under the copyright owner's authority before January 1, 1978, without a proper copyright notice, all copyright protection for that work was permanently lost in the United States. The new copyright law does not provide retroactive protection for those works.*

## Copyright Registration

In general, copyright registration is a legal formality intended to make a public record of the basic facts of a particular copyright. However, except in one specific situation*, registration is not a condition of copyright protection. Even though registration is not generally a requirement for protection, the copyright law provides several inducements or advantages to encourage copyright owners to make registration. Among these advantages are the following:

- Registration establishes a public record of the copyright claim;
- Registration is ordinarily necessary before any infringement suits may be filed in court;
- If made before or within 5 years of publication, registration will establish prima facie evidence in court of the validity of the copyright and of the facts stated in the certificate; and
- If registration is made within 3 months after publication of the work or prior to an infringement of the work, statutory damages and attorney's fees will be available to the copyright owner in court actions. Otherwise, only an award of actual damages and profits is available to the copyright owner.

Registration may be made at any time within the life of the copyright. Unlike the law before 1978, when a work has been registered in unpublished form, it is not necessary to make another registration when the work becomes published (although the copyright owner may register the published edition, if desired).

\* Under sections 405 and 406 of the Copyright Act, copyright registration may be required to preserve a copyright that would otherwise be invalidated because of the omission of the copyright notice from the published copies or phonorecords, or omission of the name or date, or a certain error in the year date.

### Registration Procedures

### In General

If you choose to register your work, send the following three elements to the Copyright Office *in the same envelope or package:* (see page 229 for what happens if the elements are sent separately).

(1) A properly completed application form;

(2) A fee of $10 for each application;

(3) A deposit of the work being registered. The deposit requirements will vary in particular situations. The general requirements are as follows:

- If the work is unpublished, one complete copy or phonorecord.
- If the work was first published in the United States on or after January 1, 1978, two complete copies or phonorecords of the best edition.
- If the work was first published in the United States before January 1, 1978, two complete copies or phonorecords of the work as first published.
- If the work was first published outside the United States, whenever published, one complete copy or phonorecord of the work as first published.
- If the work is a contribution to a collective work, and published after January 1, 1978, one complete copy or phonorecord of the best edition of the collective work.

*Note: COMPLETE THE APPLICATION FORM USING INK PEN OR TYPEWRITER. After registration is completed, the application form becomes a part of the official permanent records of the Copyright Office so the application forms must meet archival standards. Therefore, applications must be submitted only on forms printed and issued by the Copyright Office and should be completed legibly in dark ink or typewritten.*

**Unpublished Collections**

A work may be registered in unpublished form as a "collection," with one application and one fee, under the following conditions:

- The elements of the collection are assembled in an orderly form;
- The combined elements bear a single title identifying the collection as a whole;
- The copyright claimant in all the elements and in the collection as a whole is the same; and
- All of the elements are by the same author, or, if they are by different authors, at least one of the authors has contributed copyrightable authorship to each element.

Unpublished collections are indexed in the *Catalog of Copyright Entries* only under the collective titles.

**Special Deposit Requirements**

The Copyright Act gives the Register of Copyrights authority to issue regulations making adjustments in the statutory deposit requirements. These regulations as now issued require or permit, for particular classes, the deposit of identifying material instead of copies or phonorecords, the deposit of only one copy or phonorecord where two would normally be required, and in some cases material other than complete copies of the best edition. For example, the regulations ordinarily require deposit of identifying material, such as photographs or drawings, when the work being registered has been reproduced in three-dimensional copies.

If you are unsure of the proper deposit required for your work, write to the Copyright Office for that information and describe the work you wish to register.

*Note: CATALOGING IN PUBLICATION DIVISION. The Copyright Office is operationally separate from the Cataloging in Publication (CIP) Division. Correspondence concerning registration and the required deposit copies of books must be addressed to the Register of Copyrights, Copyright Office, Washington, D.C. 20559. A book may be copyrighted but not necessarily cataloged and added to the Library's collections. For information concerning the CIP program or for obtaining a catalog card number, contact the CIP Division, Library of Congress, Washington, D.C. 20540.*

## Corrections And Amplifications of Existing Registrations

To deal with cases in which information in the basic registration later turns out to be incorrect or incomplete, the law provides for "the filing of an application for supplementary registration, to correct an error in a copyright registration or to amplify the information given in a registration." The information in a supplementary registration augments but does not supersede that contained in the earlier registration. Note also that a supplementary registration is not a substitute for an original registration or for a renewal registration. Form CA is available from the Copyright Office for making a supplementary registration. For further information about supplementary registrations, write for Circular R8.

### Mandatory Deposit For Works Published In The United States With Notice Of Copyright.

Although a copyright registration is not required, the Copyright Act establishes a mandatory deposit requirement for works published with notice of copyright in the United States (see definition of "publication" on page 218). In general, the owner of copyright, or the owner of the right of first publication in the work, has a legal obligation to deposit in the Copyright Office, within 3 months of publication in the United States, 2 copies (or, in the case of sound recordings, 2 phonorecords) for the use of the Library of Congress. Failure to make the deposit can give rise to fines and other penalties, but does not affect copyright protection.

The Copyright Office has issued regulations *exempting* certain categories of works *entirely* from the mandatory deposit requirements, and reducing the obligation for certain other categories.

### Use Of Mandatory Deposit To Satisfy Registration Requirements

With respect to works published in the United States the Copyright Act contains a special provision under which a single deposit can be made to satisfy both the deposit requirements for the Library and the registration requirements. The provision requires that, in order to have this dual effect, the copies or phonorecords must be "accompanied by the prescribed application and fee" for registration.

### How Long Copyright Protection Endures

#### Works Originally Copyrighted on or After January 1, 1978

A work that is created (fixed in tangible form for the first time) on or after January 1, 1978, is automatically protected from the moment of its creation, and is ordinarily given a term enduring for the author's life, plus an additional 50 years after the author's death. In the case of "a joint work prepared by two or more authors who did not work for hire," the term lasts for 50 years after the last surviving author's death. For works made for hire, and for anonymous and pseudonymous works (unless the author's identity is revealed in Copyright Office records), the duration of copyright will be 75 years from publication or 100 years from creation, whichever is shorter.

Works that were created before the new law came into effect, but had neither been published nor registered for copyright before January 1, 1978, have been automatically brought under the statute and are now given Federal copyright protection. The duration of copyright in these works will generally be computed in the same way as for new works: the life-plus-50 or 75/100-year terms will apply to them as well. However, all works in this category are guaranteed at least 25 years of statutory protection.

## Works Copyrighted Before January 1, 1978

Under the law in effect before 1978, copyright was secured either on the date a work was published, or on the date of registration if the work was registered in unpublished form. In either case, the copyright endured for a first term of 28 years from the date it was secured. During the last (28th) year of the first term, the copyright was eligible for renewal. The new copyright law has extended the renewal term from 28 to 47 years for copyrights that were subsisting on January 1, 1978. However, the copyright *must* be timely renewed to receive the 47-year period of added protection. For more detailed information on the copyright term, write to the Copyright Office and request Circulars R15a and R15t. For information on how to search the Copyright Office records concerning the copyright status of a work, ask for Circular R22.

## *Transfer Of Copyright*

Any or all of the exclusive rights, or any subdivision of those rights, of the copyright owner may be transferred, but the transfer of *exclusive* rights is not valid unless that transfer is in writing and signed by the owner of the rights conveyed (or such owner's duly authorized agent). Transfer of a right on a nonexclusive basis does not require a writing.

A copyright may also be conveyed by operation of law and may be bequeathed by will or pass as personal property by the applicable laws of intestate succession.

Copyright is a personal property right, and is subject to the various state laws and regulations that govern the ownership, inheritance, or transfer of personal property as well as terms of contracts or conduct of business. For information about relevant state laws, consult an attorney.

Transfers of copyright are normally made by contract. The Copyright Office does not have or supply any forms for such transfers. However, the law does provide for the recordation in the Copyright Office of transfers of copyright. Although recordation is not required to make a valid transfer as between the parties, it does provide certain legal advantages and may be required to validate the transfer as against third parties. For information on recordation of transfers and other documents related to copyright, write to the Copyright Office.

### Termination Of Transfers

Under the old law, the copyright in a work generally reverted to the author, if living, or if the author was not living, to other specified beneficiaries, provided a renewal claim was registered in the 28th year of the original term. The new law drops the renewal feature except for works already in their first term of statutory protection when the new law took effect. Instead, the new law generally permits termination of the grant of rights after 35 years under certain conditions by serving written notice on the transferee within specified time limits.

For works already under statutory copyright protection, the new law provides a similar right of termination covering the newly added years that extended the former maximum term of the copyright from 56 to 75 years. For further information, write to the Copyright Office.

### International Copyright Protection

There is no such thing as an "international copyright" that will automatically protect an author's writings throughout the entire world. Protection against unauthorized use in a particular country depends, basically, on the national laws of that country. However, most countries do offer protection to foreign works under certain conditions, and these conditions have been greatly simplified by international copyright treaties and conventions. For a list of countries which maintain copyright relations with the United States, write to the Copyright Office and ask for Circular R38a.

The United States is a member of the Universal Copyright Convention (the UCC), which came into force on September 16, 1955. Generally, a work by a national or domiciliary of a country that is a member of the UCC or a work first published in a UCC country may claim protection under the UCC. If the work bears the notice of copyright in the form and position specified by the UCC, this notice will satisfy and substitute for any other formal conditions a UCC member country would otherwise impose to secure copyright. A UCC notice should consist of the symbol © accompanied by the name of the copyright proprietor and the year of first publication of the work.

An author who wishes protection for his or her work in a particular country should first find out the extent of protection of foreign works in that country. If possible, this should be done before the work is published anywhere, since protection may often depend on the facts existing at the time of **first** publication.

If the country in which protection is sought is a party to one of the internatinal copyright conventions, the work may generally be protected by complying with the conditions of the convention. Even if the work cannot be brought under an international convention, protection under the specific provisions of the country's national laws may still be possible. Some countries, however, offer little or no copyright protection for foreign works.

### *Who May File An Application Form*

The following persons are legally entitled to submit an application form:

- The author. This is either the person who actually created the work, or, if the work was made for hire, the employer or other person for whom the work was prepared.
- The copyright claimant. The copyright claimant is defined in Copyright Office regulations as either the author of the work or a person or organization that has obtained ownership of all of the rights under the copyright initially belonging to the author. This category includes a person or organization who has obtained by contract the right to claim legal title to the copyright in an application for copyright registration.
- The owner of exclusive right(s). Under the new law, any of the exclusive rights that go to make up a copyright and any subdivision of them can be transferred and owned separately, even though the transfer may be limited in time or place of effect. The term "copyright owner" with respect to any one of the exclusive rights contained in a copyright refers to the owner of that particular right. Any owner of an exclusive right may apply for registration of a claim in the work.
- The duly authorized agent of such author, other copyright claimant, or owner of exclusive right(s). Any person authorized to act on behalf of the author, other copyright claimant, or owner of exclusive right(s) may apply for registration.

There is no requirement that applications be prepared or filed by an attorney

## *Application Forms*

### For Original Registration

Form TX:     for published and unpublished non-dramatic literary works

Form PA:     for published and unpublished works of the performing arts (musical and dramatic works, pantomimes and choreographic works, motion pictures and other audiovisual works)

Form VA:     for published and unpublished works of the visual arts (pictorial, graphic, and sculptural works)

Form SR:     for published and unpublished sound recordings

### For Renewal Registration

Form RE:     for claims to renewal copyright in works copyrighted under the old law

### For Corrections and Amplifications

Form CA:     for supplementary registration to correct or amplify information given in the Copyright Office record of an earlier registration

### Other Forms for Special Purposes

Form GR/CP:  an adjunct application to be used for registration of a group of contributions to periodicals in addition to an application Form TX, PA, or VA

Form IS:     request for issuance of an import statement under the manufacturing provisions of the Copyright Act

For more detailed information about all these forms, write for Circular R1c.

Application forms are supplied by the Copyright Office free of charge. Photocopies of application forms are *not* acceptable for registration.

*Note: Requestors may order application forms at any time by telephoning (202) 287-9100. Orders will be recorded automatically and filled on an expedited basis.*

## *Mailing Instructions*

All material and communications sent to the Copyright Office should be addressed to the Register of Copyrights, Library of Congress, Washington, D.C. 20559

**The application, deposit (copies or phonorecords), and fee should**

**be mailed in the same package.**

## What Happens If The Three Elements Are Not Received Together

Applications and fees received without copies or phonorecords will ordinarily be returned. Unpublished deposits alone will ordinarily be returned, also. Published deposits received without applications and fees will be immediately transferred to the collections of the Library of Congress. This practice is in acordance with section 408 of the law which provides that the published deposit required for the collections of the Library of Congress may be used for registration only if the deposit is "accompanied by the prescribed application and fee . . ."

After the deposit is received and transferred to another department of the Library for its collections or other disposition, it is no longer available to the Copyright Office; the custody of that deposit has also been transferred to the other department. Then, if you wish to make copyright registration, you must deposit additional copies or phonorecords with your application and fee.

## Fees

Do not send cash. Fees sent to the Copyright Office should be in the form of a money order, check, or bank draft payable to the Register of Copyrights; it should be securely attached to the application.

## Effective Date Of Registration

Please note that a copyright registration is effective on the date of receipt in the Copyright Office of all the required elements in acceptable form, regardless of the length of time it takes thereafter to process the application and mail the certificate of registration. The length of time required by the Copyright Office to process an application varies from time to time, depending on the amount of material received and the personnel available to handle it. It must also be kept in mind that it may take a number of days for mailed material to reach the Copyright Office and for the certificate of registration to reach the recipient after being mailed by the Copyright Office.

If the Copyright Office finds any problem which will delay registration, you will receive correspondence from the examiner responsible for your application. If you want to know when the Copyright Office receives your material, you should send it via registered or certified mail and request a return receipt.

### *Available Information*

This circular attempts to answer some of the questions that are frequently asked about copyright. For a list of other material published by the Copyright Office, write for "Publications of the Copyright Office." Any requests for Copyright Office publications or special questions relating to copyright problems not mentioned in this circular should be addressed to the Information and Publications Section, LM—455, Copyright Office, Library of Congress, Washington, D.C. 20559.

The Copyright Office is not permitted to give legal advice. If you need information or guidance on matters such as disputes over the ownership of a copyright, suits against possible infringers, the procedure for getting a work published, or the method of obtaining royalty payments, it may be necessary to consult an attorney.

**Copyright Office • Library of Congress • Washington, D.C. 20559**

August 1981—200M *U.S. GOVERNMENT PRINTING OFFICE: 1981-341-279/106

# 8

## *My Way*

**F**rom the moment this book was conceived, I knew this was going to be the last chapter. Perhaps it was just a case of saving the best for last or providing the obligatory pot of gold at the end of the rainbow, or perhaps I wanted to be sure of a solid ending (how could you not be interested in what these people had to say about their careers and yours?), but whatever is the case, I don't think this chapter will disappoint you.

If you have read through to this point without skipping, you have earned a reward. You have learned a great deal, and I know it hasn't all been easy. You have also come to grips with many unfamiliar concepts, not all of which are logical.

The artists and writers interviewed for this chapter were not chosen at random. Their choice was dictated by a desire to present as broad a spectrum of excellence as possible within the space available. Each participant has attained the zenith in his or her respective area of entertainment and each had demonstrated an uncommon ability to communicate his or her experiences and points of view in a manner that is clear, candid, and entertaining. I will be surprised if you don't find at least one you can relate to on a personal level.

If you've been with us from the beginning, sit back and relax: school is out. If you're cheating a bit, that's okay, too; perhaps you will find the inspiration to go back and do your homework.

To speak of the graciousness and sincerity of those who participated would be redundant—the interviews speak for themselves.

# Interview With
# Ashford and Simpson

*Established as Gold Recording Artists with ten LP's behind them, Nickolas Ashford and Valerie Simpson have also written such standards as "Ain't No Mountain High Enough," "You're All I Need to Get By," "Ain't Nothing Like the Real Thing," and "Reach Out and Touch." In addition to producing their own albums they also produce artists, including Diana Ross, Marvin Gaye, Stephanie Mills, and Gladys Knight.*

AHS: The title of this chapter is "My Way." Could you very briefly tell me what "your way" was, a short synopsis of how you came to be artists, producers, and writers?

SIMPSON: Well, in short, I think we used the direct approach, which was actually just walking into a publisher's office and saying "Do you have a piano?" and going over and beating out a song and waiting for approval or disapproval. This actually worked for us because even though we were pushing our writing, we were pretty good singers and we were real good entertainers, so we'd sell people things they didn't even want. . . . So, I think that the direct approach . . . just coming right on, worked for us.

AHS: Was that before Motown?

SIMPSON: Before Motown.

AHS: You were selling songs from one . . .

SIMPSON: One publisher to the next, yes.

AHS: When did Motown come into it, after you had some success?

SIMPSON: Yes. We went from publisher to publisher until we wrote "Let's Go Get Stoned," and our publisher then was . . .

ASHFORD: Ed Silvers.

SIMPSON: Ed Silvers—we signed with him and we'd take two, three songs to him every week, and he would give us an advance.

It would keep us going. One week we went there and we didn't have anything. . . .The night before we had been writing to kind of come up with the three songs for the advance, and we just couldn't do it, so we said, "Oh, we'll do it later; let's just go get stoned"—and it was like a big joke. The next day, when we were supposed to present these songs to our publisher, he asked, "Well, do you have anything for us?" and Nick said, "Well, why don't we just strike up that thing we were doing last night?" and we improvised a chorus of "Let's Go Get Stoned" and Ed Silvers said, "You know, I really hear this for Ray Charles." We said "What? Are you kidding?" So we finished up the song and he sent it to Ray Charles and that's how we got our first hit, and that was the real beginning of our career.

AHS:      Already I have something I think nobody else has . . . this little anecdote. . . . Then Motown picked you up?

SIMPSON:  Yes.

ASHFORD:  Well, they sent scouts to New York to look for new talent, and someone had given them our names and they called us. I went over to the hotel and they made me wait so long I thought it was bull, so I went to the elevator. . . . I was leaving; then Brian came up to me and said, "Hey, we really want to hear your stuff." So they got me back in the room; they listened to the demonstration record and they were very impressed. They were impressed that we did everything; the lyrics, the background, and the music, because at Motown at that time, they were doing a lot of it separately. That's what they called "producing." We didn't know it was "producing" at the time. They were willing to fly us out to Detroit to talk, so we just went out there and signed the first paper they put in front of us. [Laughter.]

SIMPSON:  We signed away, quickly signed away, seven years.

AHS:      Val, I heard Nick mention that you had a session and that you couldn't go to the Motown meeting.

SIMPSON:  Yes.

AHS:      Was that as a background singer or doing commercials?

SIMPSON:  Oh, yes, a combination of both.

AHS:      Was that a factor in sustaining you while you were searching. . . .

SIMPSON:  Oh, all in all, I think some of the first money we ever made in this business was doing—remember a hand-clapping session? We got paid $45 to do handclaps. We said, "Well, this is phenomenal." Between that and the background singing and occasionally getting a song published, it was enough to carry you over, and if one wasn't working, the other would kind of hold you over.

AHS:     Question: now, looking back—sitting as we are in this most magnificent home, obviously a home of affluence—when you started working in the music business, was it with a profit motive in mind, or did you feel that you just had to do music?

ASHFORD:  It was definitely that we just had to do music, because I know I could have done other jobs instead of starving and hoping we could get in the back door somewhere. It was definitely for the love of the music. We would work night and day sometimes, just having fun, because it was something we really loved to do.

AHS:     I suspected that would be your answer. Val, when you were at Motown, you had a record or two as an artist.

SIMPSON:  Yes.

AHS:     Motown didn't bring them home for you, they weren't successful. How did you react to that? Perhaps I should ask Nick how you reacted to it.

SIMPSON:  I think it was traumatic, but I always felt that there was an unspoken law at Motown which this kind of . . . just reinforced, that there was only going to be one lady at Motown during that period, and that was Diana Ross. So when my records didn't happen, it just kind of reinforced that idea. I received good reviews and all of that, and people loved the album, but it just didn't really get going.

AHS:     You didn't get down on yourself because of it, because you saw other reasons for that happening?

SIMPSON:  Yes. I mean by that time I knew how the business worked, and that sometimes for reasons unknown or for reasons known, you just couldn't get your thing across. Also, I had other things to do . . . the writing and producing that we were doing kept me busy. I wasn't depending on being an artist . . . it wasn't as if I was *just* an artist; I think that helped, too.

AHS:     Nick, you're not going to get off any easier. The first night I met you, like Harry Truman, you were in the haberdashery business. I met you at an opening of your clothing emporium, and, as I recall, you were very shy and kind of reticent. When I see you on stage now, I don't see the same image. Did you have to change yourself to become a performer, or was it always there underneath that façade?

ASHFORD: I always wanted to perform. I'd had some experience. I sang a lot in the church. . . . I love to sing. I like that kind of freedom of expression; that's why I love to write, but I don't know if I've changed or not. It might have been just lurking underneath somewhere waiting to explode . . . just waiting for the right opportunity.

AHS: The persona was there; you didn't have to work consciously at developing it?

ASHFORD: Entertaining in the pop world, I did.

AHS: That's what I meant, because you struck me as a very private person.

ASHFORD: Oh, yes. Getting out there in front of an audience is totally differect to criticism. When you get out to sing in public, you're singing in the studio. When I sang in church, I wasn't subjeup against the critics and what people think of you and all of that. It had been just a spiritual outlet for me; then it became real entertainment for people. . . . That was quite another thing to deal with. I had to learn about that and train myself to be an entertainer, that's for sure.

AHS: Bill Wyman indicated during his interview that the trouble with many young artists today is that they go into a studio and they do an album before they have any idea how to perform, and then it all falls apart when they get out into the world.

ASHFORD: That's usually the case.

SIMPSON: Absolutely.

ASHFORD: That happened to us. You just don't know. You just don't know what it's like until you first do it and then you realize, God. . . .

SIMPSON: It's so different, yes. You might even assume that they're going to fall all over you, they're going to love you because they loved your record . . . and then there's no reaction. . . . You just don't know what to do with yourself!

ASHFORD: Once you get up there you become a visual; they're not listening anymore, they see *and* they hear, and you have got to fill both of those needs, so it's quite different.

AHS: You have reached the pinnacle in all areas of the music world. You're successful writers, you're successful producers, you're successful recording artists and entertainers. If you had to pick one of the areas that you consider yourself to excel in, which would it be?

ASHFORD: Hmmm . . .

AHS: Do you consider yourself a writer who produces and performs or do you consider yourself a performer who also writes and produces? I told you it wasn't going to be an easy interview.

SIMPSON: A writer who . . . who does the others as well.

AHS: Nick?

ASHFORD: I would say writing because that's how we started.

AHS: You had been very successful as writers and producers and were, I think, enjoying considerable income when you launched your careers as artists. Didn't you feel it was taking a risk? Did you feel that you were sticking your necks out?

ASHFORD: I really didn't feel we had anything to lose. I thought it was time to grow. Since we had become successful as writers and producers, we needed another outlet for our energies. I think it was a natural step.

SIMPSON: I think too that being a writer and producer is like a backup for being a singer. I always feel on the stage that once you let them know that you wrote some well-known songs, they will forgive you a lot of things. [Laughter.]

ASHFORD: They won't forgive some things.

SIMPSON: You know, if you're *just* an artist, they expect you to be *the artist* and you're supposed to be singing impeccably. . . . But because we do these other things, it's kind of like we have this little cushion, you know. . . . "Oh, well, maybe they hit a flat note . . . *but* . . . they really do write well. [Laughter.]

AHS: I'm going to ask you a question, and you can cut the answer out of the interview later on if you choose. Was any of your motivation in becoming performers fostered by a sense of frustration that perhaps others obtained fame and glory using your songs?

ASHFORD: I never, never once, felt that way. I mean, I was so honored to have other artists do the material we wrote that it never entered my mind.

SIMPSON: That's right.

ASHFORD:   When you're a writer, which we basically started out as being, you don't think such thoughts; you just want to get that tune out there and you want the world to hear something you had to say, and when they hear it, you're satisfied.

SIMPSON:   And I think it helps if you have a healthy appreciation of what it takes to be an artist. I mean there's no way we could equate ourselves with Diana Ross. We realized what it took for her to become Diana Ross and knowing what it took . . . I mean, you just don't equate that. There's no way I could feel that we could sing "Ain't No Mountain" and it would have been the same thing. Maybe it would have, but it just doesn't even cross your mind, you know so. . . . It's like a separate hat that you wear.

AHS:   You guys are terrific, because you lead right to where I want to go. You've been in the business a lot of years now.

SIMPSON:   Yes.

AHS:   Have you noticed any particular change in the business as songwriters? Putting yourself in the shoes of a young writer today, as opposed to when you were breaking in, do you perceive a difference? For instance, the availability of prospective users of your songs? What I'm really getting at is: has the advent of the singer/songwriter such as you are now cut the potential market for writers?

SIMPSON:   Regular writers?

AHS:   Yes. Do you consider that a factor in the industry today?

SIMPSON:   I think it has, but . . . I don't see anything the matter with it. I think a singer/songwriter feels a definite emotional need for the public. With the singer/songwriter, you get that two-in-one effect right away, and it does something that maybe just a writer in some respects is not able to do. He's hoping that the artist's talent will blend with him. But a singer/songwriter already has the blending because he is the artist and his is the emotion that created the song, so it comes out right away and there's something very strong there when it works. I just think it's something that the public has been lucky enough to get a lot of, and I think it's been good. But it has cut the market down for just writers.

AHS:   What I was getting to really. . . . You indicated before, you took the direct approach, you walked into the publisher and sat down at the piano. Do you think young writers

|            | today could pull that off as easily as you could back then? |
| ASHFORD:   | I really don't think so because . . . you could call it a writers' inflation. I mean there are so many writers now. At the time when we were coming up and doing the music we were doing, there were relatively few of us. *Now* it's not *just* us. . . . The white writers are able to do black music very well, so that limits the opportunity for other black writers. |
| SIMPSON:   | There are just more folks out there doing it. |
| AHS:       | When you're putting together an album, do you ever consider doing songs by other writers? |
| ASHFORD:   | No, not really. |
| SIMPSON:   | Occasionally. |
| ASHFORD:   | On occasions, yes. But we prefer to do our own material. I do particularly because it's difficult for me to sing other material. [Laughter.] Not being a true singer, being primarily a writer, it's easier to sing your own music. . . . You know how to fluff it up. |
| AHS:       | How important do you consider it to have a manager at the inception of your career? I know you're well managed now, but could you have profited by having a manager earlier than you did? How do you feel about management from the perspective of the young artist, or the artist coming up? |
| SIMPSON:   | That's interesting. |
| ASHFORD:   | You mean as artists, not as writers? |
| AHS:       | Yes. |
| ASHFORD:   | I think it's absolutely necessary, at least to a certain degree. . . . |
| AHS:       | Val, you said it was interesting. I saw wheels turning in your head. |
| SIMPSON:   | Gee, I don't know. I think a little bit of fumbling around is not bad, for maybe a year or so, because I know that in the beginning your own ideas aren't formed. To immediately have someone tell you or push you in a direction could be destructive. It depends. . . . Certain people know who they are. Are you going to be somebody else's creation or somebody else's idea or are you strong enough as an individual so young to say, " This is what I want to be, help me be it"? If you can be strong enough, then a manager's good, but if the manager's going to say "I see you as this," and point you in a direction that might not be right for |

you, then it's not so good. If you've had time to at least have a hint or a glint of where you're going, then I think management can help you get there, but I don't see somebody just leading you.

ASHFORD: Some artists have a natural aptitude or instinct for their business as well as their art. ....Others, such as myself, are just really artists—don't care about business and don't want to know about it. I can't deal with it. I can't wake up in the morning and write checks and do things like that; it destroys me.

AHS: What about when you have a record deal? Don't you find that a manager acts as an insulator between you and the record company?

SIMPSON: Oh, yes. I think it's imperative that you always remain the good guy. [Laughter.]

AHS: That's why lawyers and managers were invented.

SIMPSON: Oh, absolutely, and I really, really feel that way. Your manager should go in there and fight those battles, and you should still be able to talk to everybody at the record company, even though he's not speaking to half the people at the company anymore.

AHS: Everybody makes mistakes. There must have been some mistakes you made along the way that, if you had the opportunity, you might not make today. Perhaps some young people could profit from your past experiences. Any mistakes you'd like to confess to?

ASHFORD: Don't count any money you haven't got. [Laughter.] You have all these dreams, you're sure this record is going to do this, and so . . . but you just wait and see, because you never know how the tide is going to flow against you. I've made bad mistakes by making plans on the dreams that didn't come true. [Laughter.]

AHS: I don't think that's unique to performing artists. [Laughter.] Val, what mistake do you recommend not making?

SIMPSON: Probably fear of high places. I think that in the beginning, you're just so afraid, you want to do something so badly that you're willing to do it for nothing. You don't realize that when a person or a company is investing money in you, they're investing it because they expect a return. You don't appreciate that you have value. When we did our Motown deal, we didn't have to sign for seven years, but we were so eager . . . and no one told us that we *couldn't* have a lawyer look at the paper, but we were just that green. I can't believe that we ever did that, but we really did do that, and I would hate to think that people would do that today. I mean, if they want you, they will want you even when you suggest the necessary changes to make it right for yourself and to feel like a human being. You don't have to just take the first offer they throw at you. That's the mistake that we made; we just wanted it so bad that we accepted it no matter how uncomfortable it was for us.

AHS: You might have been more prudent had you had a little more experience. Your new album is doing very well. It's on the pop charts, and I believe this is really the first time you're crossing over into the pop field. It that true?

ASHFORD: There seems to be a strong indication that we are at this time.

AHS: To what do you attribute that cross-over? Has your music changed, is there a change in your attitude as performers, or is there a change in your environment professionally, in your record company? To what do you attribute this?

ASHFORD: It's like a song we wrote called "It's the Long Run." I think it's a combination of things. We gathered a following through the years, a following that's started to grow a little, to the point where it's crossing over to more whites.

SIMPSON: I don't even know whether the cross-over's really there yet. I think that there are some artists who have such large sales that it seems as if they're cross-over sales, but they may not actually be so. Take Rick James, for instance. I doubt that he has a cross-over, a real cross-over, but he just gets so many sales that it looks like, well, since it's way up on the pop charts, it must be crossed. You know, to some extent it is, but you're never really sure who really is buying those records.

AHS: Do you feel a sense of frustration at not crossing over, at being relegated to a particular market? Does that bother you as performers?

ASHFORD: I hate the labels too, especially this is "Black Music," this is "White Music"; I hate that. And there is a frustration, but I don't think we yield to it. I think we feel strong and confident enough that if we hold on to our brand, our particular feeling about the music, that it will succeed. In

other words, we're not going to sell out. We can write a lot
of different ways, we can write white or whatever they say
is black, but we really go by our own particular feeling as
to what kind of ideas we want to offer, and we hope that it
will grab and pull the people more or less. We don't say,
"Well, this is marketable today, so this is what we'll write."
We try to stick to what really moves us, which isn't always
going to be commercial.

SIMPSON: But I think you owe it to yourself to do that. We signed
with our new record company, Capitol, feeling they were
fans of ours, so I feel like we have to give them what we do
to the maximum. It's like a God-given opportunity to
come up with something that's really *you*, and make that
happen. I think that's probably the biggest hit you can ever
get, when you really get your identification out there
strongly, which is what we're trying to do.

AHS: Is your record company being very helpful?

SIMPSON: Oh, absolutely, absolutely. We go by funny things; it's not so
much the deal that's structured—I mean, all that's good . . .
once I know that George, our manager, tells me that it is a
good deal and he runs the figures by me, I can figure that
out, but the most important thing is that the enthusiasm is
there, that they really believe. . . .

ASHFORD: In *our* music, not something else.

SIMPSON: Yes, believing that they're going to run with something they
like really turns us on

AHS: I'm sure that as producer, you're very often approached by
young people trying to break into the business, and I'm
sure you see they're making a lot of mistakes. Are there any
particular things you see the youngsters coming up doing
that you would admonish them not to do? . . . I'm sure
you're deluged with cassettes and requests for appraisals
and whatever. . . .

SIMPSON: Oh, yes.

AHS: What are the most universal mistakes that are being made?

ASHFORD: I think the big mistake is to think that there's a format or a
set pattern that you can follow. I mean, there's only one
heaven, but there are many ways to get there, so you can
tell young writers and entertainers a lot of things, but in the
long run, it's still the individual endeavor and approach
that counts. The basic thing is to really believe that you

have the energy to do or die, and sometimes it gets mighty lean. . . . Some people will go off to another side career and it will take over their lives as opposed to standing firm and waiting for that inspiration to get them into their career the correct way. There's no formula, no pattern; you've just got to get out there and say "I believe in this, I'm working on this," and go for it. That's all I could ever tell them. I couldn't tell them to be a busboy and then see the light and then go over here . . . no way.

SIMPSON:      I think too that it's gotten to the point . . . I remember from the early days when we first started, there was more respect for what a song is and what a song can do than there is now. I mean, everybody thinks they can write a song. . . . "Well, let me do something that's going to lead me from my mundane life; let me write a song; anybody can write a song" . . . and there are a lot of songs on the radio that sound like anybody wrote them. . . . [Laughter.] So I can understand how they get this feeling. There's no quality anymore to the thought, and there should be quality.

ASHFORD:      Saying something no one else has said . . .

SIMPSON:      Or saying it in a special way, or thinking, Has this been done before? They don't seem to care about these things. It's almost like they do want to copy whatever is out there. That was never our thought; in fact, if we hear something on the radio that sounds like something we're working on, we just say, "Oh, forget it." . . . I think that's the kind of individual feeling you have to have, and it's probably the kind of person you are. It takes a little integrity, I think.

ASHFORD:      Look into your own material! After we write our songs, on occasion we've asked ourselves, "Ah, does anybody care?"

SIMPSON:      "Who cares about this?"

ASHFORD:      We'll analyze the song; we'll listen to it and say, "Um, does anybody care?" And if we both say "No," we just . . .

SIMPSON:      We just dump it.

ASHFORD:      Dump it, because it's probably not important enough. You can write a thousand songs, but what's the point if nobody cares about what you're saying? Is it important enough to merit attention?

AHS:          I think I have a super interview. You mentioned that your energy level drove you to become performers; that you weren't content with just writing and producing. Now that you're approaching your goal as performers, is there anything else percolating in the Ashford & Simpson collective mind?

ASHFORD:       Naturally, we have our ideas, mainly because you know you have to grow. One phase was writing and then it was writing and entertaining; now I feel that we should go to musicals. . . . We're thinking about getting our heads into that now because it's another growth; it's another challenge; it's another form of expression that we haven't tried.

SIMPSON:       Yes.

AHS:           Are you of similar mind, Val?

SIMPSON:       Oh, absolutely. The idea of seeing it happen and hearing it at the same time is exciting. I think probably, because of our performing too, we may have a little edge.

ASHFORD:       We're not the kind of entertainers who want to be out there past our time. [Hearty laughter.]

AHS:           I think you still have a lot of time to be out there.

ASHFORD:       Yes, but . . . we're always reaching out to try something we haven't tried. It keeps the juices flowing. Even if we fail, we like the idea of being able to say, "Well, we tried to do it."

SIMPSON:       Where's the new goose bump going to come from?

AHS:           I thank you very much. I think my readers will really enjoy this.

# Interview With
# Marvin Hamlisch

A Chorus Line. *Pulitzer Prize. Nine Tonys.* The Sting. *Academy Award.* The Way We Were. *Two Academy Awards. Four Grammys.* "Nobody Does It Better." "What I Did for Love." *Theme for ABC-TV's* Good Morning America. *Motion-picture scores. Pop contemporary songwriter. Musician. Conductor. Composer. . . . Gentleman. . . . Marvin Hamlisch.*

AHS: I would appreciate a thumbnail sketch of your career.

HAMLISCH: Around the age of nine or ten, I wrote a song with my cousin and we thought it was a very good song, and we took it to a publisher.

AHS: At age ten?

HAMLISCH: At about ten or eleven or something like that. We made a little demonstration record and we took it to a publisher because that was the way we had heard it was done. The song was called "What Did You Get Santa Claus for Christmas?" It was a very novel idea. Nothing very much happened until months later, when a neighbor said she had heard my song on the radio. I wondered how that was possible. No one told me anything about it. I found out that the song that she'd heard on the radio was called "Let's Give a Christmas Present to Santa Claus." At the age of eleven or whatever it was, I was already the victim of an infringement. . . . As my mother would say, "It was stolen." That was my introduction to the music business and the world of popular music. It became clear very quickly that I was going to get burned a lot unless I could figure out how not to get burned. After I wrote, God knows, two hundred songs and got nothing published and nothing going on . . . just making demonstration records . . .

AHS: At the ripe old age of maybe fourteen?

HAMLISCH: Fourteen, fifteen, something like that. I kept writing songs and nothing really was happening, even though at that time more singers were looking for outside songs. This was before the advent of the singer-songwriter, which has in a way hurt the writer per se (which is one of the points I want to make). In those days, most singers were looking for material. So I went around and I finally found a publisher that I thought was nice, just a nice person. It was Pinkus Music.

AHS: George Pinkus?

HAMLISCH: That's right. He seemed very nice, very reputable. I remember when I finally got a song recorded, it was by a total fluke, having nothing to do with any publisher I knew or anything like that. My ear, nose, and throat doctor knew Georgia Gibbs. She was looking for a very up song. I wrote a song with my cousin called "Sunshine, Lollipops and Rainbows." I presented it to her and she didn't like the song, and turned it down. The doctor was so incensed by the fact that she turned it down after I had written the song and done the demo and worked so hard that it became his mission in life to get that song recorded. He also knew Quincy Jones, and one day Quincy said he was looking for a song for a beach-party movie which could be used to get a girl from one side of the beach to the other. Lo and behold, the girl was Leslie Gore, and that's how the song got recorded. It had nothing to do with the work of publishers or anything like that. It became clear to me even then that the more personal contacts you had, the less you had to depend on publishers. The chances were that if you could meet the right people, the artist, the artist's manager, the producer of the record, whoever, you had a much better shot than if you let your song pile up with the thousands of other songs that were piling up with the publisher. So I wrote a few more songs and the turning point in my career came when I was about eighteen. Having had Leslie Gore's hit, "Sunshine, Lollipops and Rainbows," and then having another hit with her called "California Nights," I walked into her producer's office with the third song that I had written for her, hoping that this would also be a winner. The record producer let me wait in his office for about an hour and a half before he saw me. When I got into the office, I said to him, "I always thought you made me wait because I never had a hit song and I was a 'nobody,' but now that I have a hit song, you still made me wait an hour and a half." I didn't play the song; I left, and I haven't written another song "just for the heck of it" since then. I realized that that was not the business for me. My whole approach to the music business after that was directed to getting projects, to finding movies, to doing a show . . . whatever. What I learned in terms of basic songwriting (and this is not now background; this is more philosophy for today) is that most artists, if they're even accepting outside songs, stick to a certain writer. In order to have that artist continue using their songs, those writers are making deals whereby they're practically selling their souls. Therefore, it's not the most lucrative business to go into if you're just going to be a "writer." If you think there are millions in just writing songs without either producing the record or without being the artist, or somehow having more control, you would be wrong. I don't think you could find a writer to agree that just writing songs is a lucrative business . . . because it isn't, and it's becoming an increasingly difficult business because the number of artists who are looking for outside songs is dwindling. And, of course, as you know, practically no song gets recorded without making some sort of a deal. All of a sudden someone walks in and says, "Well, we'd love to do the song; however, you're going to have to lose some of your 'this' or some of your 'that.' So, by the time you take . . .

AHS:          You must have read my book. . . .

HAMLISCH:     By the time you take your royalty and you divide it among everyone who was involved, either artistically or not artistically, it becomes rough. So my idea was to circumvent all of that and to determine how I could best get into what I really wanted to do, which was writing Broadway shows. When I was nineteen years old, no one was offering me Broadway shows to write! So I became a rehearsal pianist for Broadway shows and stuff like that. Around the age of twenty-two, I was sent to play at a party for the producer Sam Spiegel. He was producing a film called *The Swimmer* and he liked the way I played the party and asked me if I was a composer. He showed me the script, and I went home, and, sight unseen, I wrote the theme music that I thought would be right for that script. He liked it, and he sent me to Hollywood, and that was my first picture. And again, it had nothing to do with agents or publishers. I was at the right place at the right time.

AHS:          You saw to it you were at the right place by taking the job as a rehearsal pianist.

HAMLISCH:     Whatever. I find that the letters I receive from people who are trying desperately to make it in the music business usually go like this: "Hello. I'm from Iowa and I want to know what I'm doing wrong." And I say, "The first thing that you're doing wrong is that you're not in New York, Los Angeles, or Nashville." I have no faith at all in a song that is just sent to a publisher or to an artist, because I know myself that I get tons of stuff here, and I'm not even an artist, but people want to know my opinion. The truth is you don't have time to listen, and even if you do, let's face it, what are you going to do? Number one, you've got to get to the source; you kind of need a publisher, but what you really need to do is to find the artist, to crack into that wall somehow, and to make sure that at least you were heard on that song. The other thing that I think is very important is to write songs that suit many artists. If you pin all your hopes on a song that would be great for Streisand and if you don't get Streisand, what happens? The song just dies? If the song dies 'cause Streisand said "no," then how good a song could it be? If the song doesn't have a life of its own beyond one artist, you're in trouble, because the minute that artist says "no," you're dead. As you can probably tell, I've been burned a lot. It's very funny; people think I'm a hit songwriter. I'm not. I've had only three or four hits in my life in terms of individual songs. I've had hit projects and hit shows, which I much prefer for about ninety-seven reasons. Because the truth is that the trip of getting a hit song is so fraught with glass on the road that by the time you get to number one, I'm not sure any more how much joy there's left in Mudville. You know what I mean. It's a difficult trail. So I tend to say to upcoming writers: don't make your goal to be just a hit writer. If that's your goal, to just have a hit, then you're going to be in a lot of trouble, because you're not going to be able to sustain yourself financially. There aren't enough pieces of the pie to go around. Get into it in a whole way. I mean get into it as a producer, as an artist . . . . To get into it just as a writer alone is very difficult. And most writers, even hit writers, even writers who've had a lot of hits, tend to agree with me. I would recommend to you, even though you want to get writers that have had hits or that are well known to the public-at-large for your book, that you should interview people who have had hits, but who are unknown to the public . . . real journeymen writers. Yes, Neil Diamond has had hits, but how many hits would he have had if he had been just a writer and not recorded them? I'm always very jealous of, say, Billy Joel. Billy Joel can write whatever he wants to and he knows it will be recorded. Who will record it? Billy Joel! There's no problem. I am always the middleman. I'm the guy who writes it and then has to wait and see who will record it. And I could write what I thought was the greatest song in the world, but if it gets turned down by fifteen artists, it couldn't be the greatest song in the world. Now, if I were Billy Joel, I could just record it tomorrow and it might be a big hit. So, therefore, it's a very difficult road you follow if you are just a writer. I no longer even try going down that road. I don't even write songs per se. I have just written (because my publisher said *please*) two songs out of context, meaning just for the heck of it. These will probably be the only songs I write this year that won't be part of a project such as a show or a movie. So I would suggest to you to see writers who basically do this for a living and nothing else, because I'm very lucky. If you took the money that I made as a "writer of songs" . . . there isn't much of it. Where I made my money was in writing shows, writing movies, and getting involved that way. My actual income from songwriting without those other sources is nearly nil. I got frustrated writing songs for people and then having them constantly either turned down or recorded as other than an "A"-side single. One of the things that's happening in the business now is that there are not so much songs as there are records. I think you should talk about that in your book, about the difference between what a good song is and a good record. Ideally, when a good song and a good record come together, you've got something. Earth, Wind & Fire's last big hit was just incredible, as was "Takin' It to the Streets"—you know, Mike McDonald and The Doobies. A good song stands on its own. You play it—it's a good song. A good record, where the record is just fantastically produced, can be made out of a bad song. I mean, you can have a bad song that is so brilliantly produced that it goes number one because the production values of the record are just incredible. The ideal is to have a good song with a good production. You can start with a good song, and what happens many times is you get a bad production and the song will not become the "A"-side single. They could have gone into the studio thinking the song is going to be the "A" side, but by the time they finish at two o'clock in the morning, after making the record, they conclude, "This just doesn't groove, man; we'll go with the other song." Well, if you've been the writer who's thinking you're going to have the "A"-side single and, because of nothing to do with you, the record just didn't come out well, then what do you do? There were so many pitfalls that I finally gave up. I didn't have the stomach for it. I really didn't. I just didn't have what it took to continue. If I had a son and he said, "Daddy, I want to be a songwriter," I'd say, "Never; forget it!" But if he said, "I want to do that *and* I want to produce records," I'd say "Fine!" Because it's becoming a closed shop. I could write the greatest song for Stevie Wonder, but what would it matter? Stevie Wonder does not record outside songs. By the time you take away Stevie Wonder and you take away Neil Diamond, Elton John, Billy Joel. . . . Of course, there are always some people who are going to listen. There are always the Barry Manilows of the sect, but because there are fewer of them, the competition has become ferocious. Start looking at records and see whose names are on what records. It's very interesting. In fact, take a look at the "B" side and see whose name is on it. You'll see a lot of familiar names. [Laughter] I would say for a writer to help himself today, the first thing I would do is try to have him sign an AGAC contract. I think that is always helpful. Because, at least, then you can't get totally overrun by the whims and wishes of everyone else. I think an AGAC contract is at least a strong, good, minimum basic agreement.

AHS:          But most publishers won't sign them.

HAMLISCH:     Right; well, that's the other thing. Or then just be in it for the thrill and not for the money. Just be in it for the fact that your song got recorded . . . Wow!

AHS:          You didn't start off at eleven as an accomplished musician. I understand that you've had some extensive formal training.

HAMLISCH:     Yes, I was a Juilliard student, and I studied and everything like that. But I could play pretty good already at eleven or twelve.

AHS:          How important do you think technical training is?

HAMLISCH:     I don't think it's important at all. I think it helps if you can put it down on paper, because you can save some money there. But I mean most kids pick up a guitar, they learn a couple of chords, and they start drifting away on their own. I sometimes find that being able to play well can be a hindrance, in fact, because you can't "get down" on the piano. Trying to write rock-'n-roll on the piano is not an easy thing, you know. It's easier on the guitar, or a Fender Rhodes piano, or something like that. But I don't think it matters how well you play. I think having a good lyricist is very important. I think the big change in music is that lyrics have become much more important in the last twenty years, and having the "good hook" can be very helpful. When I write, I write to a lyric. But I really think that it would be very helpful if, in your book, you include, among the big-name people the journeymen writers, the people who write songs for a living. I think it would be interesting to include some interviews with writers who have not yet made it or had very scattered success. . . . What are they doing? They've got to be doing something else besides just writing.

AHS:          Right. As a matter of fact, I am interviewing a young client of mine this afternoon who just had interest from a record company. He's been supporting himself writing jingles and playing background.

HAMLISCH:     Right. It's not an easy task.

AHS:          Did you ever do any of that to support yourself?

HAMLISCH: I was a rehearsal pianist for Broadway, and then I became a dance-music consultant, and then I played for ballet schools, and I just kept doing it that way, but I never played in a band or anything like that; that wasn't my thing.

AHS: Was there anybody in your career that you felt helped you a lot?

HAMLISCH: Well, Quincy Jones was very helpful because he went for that song and he was very friendly and very nice. It's nice to meet somebody whose first reaction to a song after they like it isn't "Okay, we've gotta have this and we gotta have that." It would be nice if we could at least have a drink first. It's a very funny thing. I'm not in the business of getting records. The songs that I've had recorded are mostly from movies and shows. To get individual songs recorded requires peddling, and I don't want to peddle songs. You see, the beauty of being Billy Joel is that when you write something, you know it's going to come out if you want it to come out. That's what I do with shows. I know if I write a show and we get a producer, I know on a certain date it's going to be there, and I'm thrilled about that.

AHS: I understand that. One of the points I've made in the book is that if you're not a singer-songwriter, it's very tough.

HAMLISCH: Very tough. I recommend it to no one. I don't care how talented you are. If you're that talented, write a show. If you've got ten great songs, write a show, because at least then it's yours. You're one of the owners.

AHS: You mentioned that you have a publisher. I don't want to pry. . . .

HAMLISCH: Chappell.

AHS: Oh, you work with Chappell. Do you own your copyrights?

HAMLISCH: Nope. I own some of them, not all of them.

AHS: A piece?

HAMLISCH: A piece of it. Right.

AHS: I would think that Marvin Hamlisch today would own his own copyrights, but those were show tunes . . . you have to give a taste. . . .

HAMLISCH: Yes. Right.

AHS: That is really a problem today for youngsters. They've been taught don't give up your publishing. You have to give to get today . . . at least while you're paying your dues.

HAMLISCH:   You're always paying your dues. I know writers who have written big hit songs and have been offered annual advances or guarantees from publishers of no more than $100,000. . . . That sounds like a lot of money, but if that's it after having big hit songs, it's not worth it.

AHS:        Publishers are not known to be overly generous.

HAMLISCH:   Also, publishers are not doing what publishers used to do. Publishers used to be the people who went from door to door selling the songs and getting records. Publishers basically to me now are huge collection agencies. I mean they just get the checks and then they send you the money.

AHS:        In other words, you're questioning, with Harry Fox and with ASCAP and BMI, why do you need a publisher? I mean, they're going to collect most of your money for you.

HAMLISCH:   Right, because . . . I guess it's your dream that occasionally, once out of thousand times, they'll say, "Dionne Warwick's recording; I can get it to her" . . . boom! And they go and they get it. For that one out of a thousand, you stick with them. The reason I'm being down on all this is because I think up to now there has been a tremendous distortion of what young kids think is a glamorous business. Now it may be glamorous for the Billy Joels—I think it's very glamorous—and even then it's hard because they still have to tour like crazy and they have to get on the bus and keep going.

AHS:        Do you use an agent when you're doing motion pictures?

HAMLISCH:   Yes. I have an agent. That's one thing I do believe in. I have an agent for movies and I have an agent who takes care of me for public appearances. I have been able to divide it up a little bit, and I think that's very important. I don't think one person can do it all. I think it's good to surround yourself with experts. Yes, they get a piece of the pie, but that can be very well worth it. . . . And always have a lawyer around.

AHS:        Amen!

HAMLISCH:   Always be one step away from a lawyer.

AHS:        You've been more than generous with your time. Thank you very much.

# *Interview With*
# *Barbara Mandrell*

*Consummate musician, established recording artist, television star, and a peerless performing artist, Barbara Mandrell has won more awards than can be listed here. She is nevertheless exploring new areas in which to excel.*

AHS: Barbara, the title of this chapter is "My Way." I wonder if you could give our readers a brief synopsis of what "your way" was.

MANDRELL: First, I think it was just loving music and wanting to sing music and play music and be a part of anything that *made* music, and it never occurred to me to be doing what I'm doing today or to make *money* doing it. You know that old saying "You have to love this business to be in it"? I really think that's true. At first I just wanted to learn to play instruments. I watched a friend of mine play steel guitar for Merle Haggard. I didn't want to be a singer; I just fell in love with that instrument. I was eleven years old and I asked him to teach me. I started studying, and God had given me an ear and it came sort of easy for me. I had some previous experience with music, because my mother was a music teacher. She taught piano, and she taught me to play the accordion and to read music when I was five. I learned to read music before I learned to read "See Spot Run," but I never thought of it as a way of making a living; it was always something I did "for the love of it." Then, later, especially as a teen-ager, I found that it was a good way to make money to buy clothes and to have extra spending money.

AHS: How did you make money as a teen-ager? It wasn't through records.

MANDRELL: No. I was lucky. I was in a little band. It's as I often tell young people today: be organized, be rehearsed, know your keys, know your numbers, and be as professional as you can, and then find a group that appeals to you, that you think's good, and ask for an audition. Find somebody to work with, or create your own group. I remember in my high-school days, there were always teen-age bands that played for dances. Whether it's a dance or a PTA meeting or a church function or whatever, the primary teacher in the music business, as far as I'm concerned, is experience. It's marvelous if you have the time and have the opportunity to go to a university and study music, and I'm not belittling that—that's marvelous and I wish I had that sort of knowledge—but if you want to be a performer, the only school is the school of experience. You learn the most by actually doing. There are so many things that happen to me today—situations that I find myself in—where I know that the only reason I am able to do the appropriate thing in a way that seems to come naturally and that "works" is because I've been at it so many years.

AHS:     You mean you're not an overnight success?

MANDRELL:     I'm thirty-three; I started when I was eleven. I also do a lot of watching. I watch people that I work with. A lot of people won't watch a performer they don't particularly like. I watch every performer that I haven't seen before, whether it's the opening act or the closing act. I watch because I learn by watching. I can learn from a newcomer in the business as well as from veterans. I can learn because you are dealing with a creative subject when you're dealing with music. No two people are alike, and if they're worth their salt, I can learn from them. You sometimes learn what *not* to do as well as what *to* do. I think in the beginning I did it all "for the love of"; now, I am a quote "businesswoman" and I do it for the love of and the profit of, because, unfortunately, sometimes profit is a gauge of success. You know, how well are you doing? How many records are you selling? How many people are you drawing? ... And that sort of thing. But that "love of" has to be first, and that's where the heart comes from. I did an eight-day tour one time about four years ago. When I got home, I went into the hospital—I was nearly dead and I didn't even know it was pneumonia. You know, that old thing of "the show must go on"—that's not because somebody *said* it; that's because you love the business and you have a feeling for the audience and you have a feeling for the whole atmosphere of being a performer, and somehow or other, whatever's within you makes you do it.

AHS:     I think most people don't realize that Barbara Mandrell had a professional life before MCA and ABC. You had an earlier record deal that I recall. The world would certainly not know about it. That must have been a disappointment to you. How did it come about, and how did you react to the fact that nothing happened?

MANDRELL:     At first it was a joy just to get a record deal—especially with a major label—but I was really lost in the shuffle, although it never discouraged me. I never had any doubt that it was going to continue, but I'm like everyone else, I get impatient, and I sort of felt like *I* knew I had something to offer. I just wanted the other people who controlled my destiny, as a record label seems to do sometimes, to have as much faith in me as *I* had. I would get on the phone and I would call the disc jockeys and do anything I could think of to do to make progress. There were times when first starting out—my father and I have always been in business together—that we really went through his funds just to pay the bills and to have food and to pay for the diesel for the bus, but I *never*—and I think this is the most important of all the things I could tell newcomers, because it's not press, because it's from my heart and from knowing—I can honestly say, I *never* doubted for one minute that I'd be doing what I'm doing today. I may not have known the path I would take or exactly what the story would be as it unfolded, but I never doubted.

AHS:     How did the first record deal with CBS come about?

MANDRELL:     Well, each artist has a different story, but if you really analyze each story, you find a lot of similarities. A friend of mine, Gordon Terry, was singing in a small club in Printer's Alley in Nashville. I was living with him and his wife at the time; they were old friends of mine and I couldn't afford my own place. He was appearing and she just said "C'mon, let's go down and watch Gordon tonight," and we went down there and he asked me to come up and sing, and the club owner liked what he heard and he booked me in there for a week. During that week, different people within the industry—musicians and various people—began to talk a little bit and pretty soon record producers came in to see me. One night there were, I think, representatives from four major labels, and Billy Sherrill of Columbia Records was one of them, and I signed the Columbia contract. It was no big contract, but it was a big label, and it was a chance to make records and to at least have people hear me. It was a shot; it was a chance. I was sitting on top of the world then, but I was very quickly to find out that just having a record doesn't make for success. Everything happened very slowly for me; I think we're all so impatient today. As a beginner, if you had offered me an overnight smash-hit record—you know, first record out, big hit—I would have said, "Yes, give it to me." But in retrospect I think it was marvelous the way things happened for me, because everything happened very slowly. People within country music knew who Barbara Mandrell was before I had a number-one record, so they weren't going into record stores and saying, "I want such-and-such a song; I don't know who the girl is." . . . You know, sometimes a record gets in front of the artist. I had to *crawl* a lot before I was able to walk in this business, and I think it did two things: it helped establish me on a solid foundation as far as my ability went, and it also made the public more aware of me. Of course, the television show has changed a lot of that; a lot of people have now heard of me who had never heard of me before.

AHS:        But you were established before the television show happened.

MANDRELL:   Yes. In fact, I won Entertainer of the Year on a Tuesday night and came out to L.A. on the following Sunday to start the show.

AHS:        But when things didn't work out on the first record deal and you didn't feel that the record company was doing right by you, you didn't just sit back and lament. You raised hell!

MANDRELL:   No! I came off a number-one record and I said I want off the label because I didn't feel I was being treated right. I thought I was a *very* small fish in a big pond, and that I was being very much overlooked. I think no matter what career you choose, but *especially* in the music business, positive thinking is very important. You must never listen to the people saying, "It's too tough; you don't want to do this" or "It's too hard to achieve" or "There are too many people trying for record contracts"—you cannot give any credence to that kind of garbage. It doesn't mean that you walk around being cocky; it simply means that within your inner self, your own feelings about yourself, you believe in yourself and you know that ultimately you will have success. If you don't have that, if you don't have the guts, the determination, and the belief in yourself, you might as well forget it and save yourself the trouble, because you'll never make it.

AHS: Do you feel there are any things in your career that you would do differently if you had to do them all over again? Are there any mistakes that you made? Are there any things you would do differently?

MANDRELL: No. I mean, I've made some mistakes, but I don't think I've made any major career mistakes, because—this is going to sound very philosophical—I followed my "instincts," and I surrounded myself with wise people, starting with my father. I didn't have to worry about being swindled or misled or someone choosing things for the wrong reasons. I've been fortunate with my record producers. My lucky breaks have been the people in my life, and one steel-guitar player named Lloyd Green, who's a session musician in Nashville. He is the man who spoke to Billy Sherrill and said, "You've got to go see this girl playing in the Alley . . . she sings, she plays all these instruments, go see her!" After I signed the Columbia deal, I said to him, "How can I ever repay you?" He told me that when he came to Nashville, he was making a living as a shoe salesman, and some guys in the session work helped him, and he asked the same question, and he said he was told that by helping somebody else you sort of repay your debt. There are a lot of crummy people in our business, but the majority of our people care about each other and they help young talent. That's why I get a little up in arms when people belittle show-business personalities and say that they're selfish and self-centered. I think a lot of them try to put back a little bit of what they take out. I've been fortunate in being around good people most of the time, and wise enough to stay away from the ones that were not good people. But I . . .

AHS: That's a little bit what the book is about—how to choose the right people. . . .

MANDRELL: I was approached to do my own session in Nashville and pay for it, but at that point in my life, Merle Travis, who wrote "Sixteen Tons," said to this person, "Aw, c'mon . . . ." People watched out for me, and I had the time to watch out for me, too. I sort of would take each step as it came, or each opportunity, and sort of stand back and look at it and think, Now, should I do this or should I not? Would this be a mistake? . . . And God gives you horse sense, you know, and you just kind of look at the situation. You think, Does it make sense for *me*? I mean, I'm the one that's singing—should I go in and pay for the session? No! If you want me, *you* pay for the session, and if it sells any records, then you give me some money; if it doesn't you don't. Just my horse sense told me that. But unfortunately some people are conned. I think young people are so anxious and so eager that they don't want to take things slowly. I took them so slowly, not necessarily by choice, that it was a struggle just meeting the bills. You beat your brains out and do four or six shows a day at fairs and Vegas and lounges, and have nothing really to show for it as far as profit, but I didn't mind because for some reason I knew that was what I had to do to get where I wanted to be.

AHS: You're highly respected among the professionals in the industry, not only for your vocal talents, but also as a musician. Do you have any sense of how important that was in your development or how important it was to your career?

MANDRELL: In my case, I think it was very important, because I'm not the greatest singer in the world—and I think the fact that I'm a musician and I'm a woman made me different. You see, each of us needs to be unique. That's a very important factor.

AHS: In being successful?

MANDRELL: If you sing just like Ella Fitzgerald, if you sing just like Roy Acuff, we don't need you . . . we've got those people. You've got to be whoever you are and be special and have something to contribute, and if you do, there's room for you and nobody's going to throw you out. I think the fact that I played the instruments and that I had all the years of experience—I had nine years of performing before I ever had a chance to record—was a big factor in my success. I've heard kids say, "Well, I've been playing music, but, you know, I *only* play down at the Elks Lodge," or "I played in a thing over at the city park," like it's nothing. . . . It's *everything*!

AHS: Have you ever had an inclination to write your own songs? To express yourself through writing?

MANDRELL: I really am interested in writing, but I've done very little . . . not even enough to mention. I found that when I did achieve something—you know, to actually finish a tune and record it and everything—it was because I was in a unique situation, where I didn't have anything else to do. I think at this point in my life I probably can't write, because I am too occupied—maybe later. I find that to write I have to be not busy and not preoccupied.

AHS: Are you attuned to the prevalence of singer-songwriters in the business today?

MANDRELL: Absolutely. I was lucky with the instruments and being a woman; it made me different. But if you can write and create your own songs, and if you have a gift of voice, something that makes you sound different, to sing those creations with, I think that is a foot in the door with a record label. But so what if you get a recording contract; so what if you have a hit record; where do you go from there? You better make darn sure you know what to do when you hit that stage. What are they going to do if they can't do something when they hit the stage? You might as well sit there and listen to a record. Now that's my own personal viewpoint, and a lot of people disagree with that, but that's why I say don't underestimate working in drama class in school and working in choir in school. All these things that seem so insignificant are enormously important. I can think back to my schooldays—I was the first one to raise my hand when it was an oral book report for English, because I wanted to perform, to get up in front of somebody and have their attention. If it was a written book report, I was lucky if it got in on time—and that's the performer in me. Now, as a recording artist, I find I love going into the studio, because it demands something different from me. You have to concentrate on audio, strictly on what those people are going to hear and whether it is commercial—all of those things.

AHS: How do you screen songs, Barbara? How do you decide what you're going to sing, since you don't write most of your songs?

MANDRELL: First impression, really. I've never really thought about this . . . first impression. If I do say so myself, I have a real good ability to listen as a fan. The mistake so many people who are gifted make is the mistake of playing over people's heads or playing things that are non-commercial. I think I have a good ear for what's commercial. Is that what the public will buy? And I don't look for a ballad; I don't look for an up-tempo; I don't look for a positive or negative; I just look for the *magic* in the song. Is it a possibility in the commercial sense?

AHS: This is a tough question. To what extent are songs screened before you ever hear them? I imagine hundreds and hundreds of songs are sent to you and to your producer, and you certainly don't have the time to listen to all of them.

MANDRELL: Okay. I don't sit there and listen myself, so this is based strictly on what people tell me. I'm told that there are many, many of those grocery-store cardboard boxes full of tapes. I'm also told, and I believe, that they are all listened to. Those that surface as having potential and as songs that I should listen to are given to me and I listen to them. At the point I am now in my career, time's the most valuable commodity—and you have to learn how to delegate authority.

AHS: As a rule, you do ten songs on an album. How many songs do you select those ten from? From the hundreds that are submitted, how many ultimately do you listen to in choosing the ten? Ball-park figure? I'm not going to hold you to this.

MANDRELL: Well, because I've got a good producer, I would say I probably only listen personally to about thirty, maximum.

AHS: That's thirty out of hundreds and hundreds?

MANDRELL: Hundreds and hundreds. Young people and older people alike will send me material, and I listen or I make sure it's listened to. What bothers me is that a songwriter may have what I perceive to be a real potential, but *that* particular song may not be it for me. . . . And there is no way to tell them not to be discouraged—that established songwriters send me songs that are not it for me.

AHS: I know—I've sent you those. . . .

MANDRELL: It's hard to choose the words. I think this is important to say to songwriters: don't be discouraged because a certain artist or a certain producer did not take your song if you believe in it, because I—and it's true of every artist— personally turned down hit songs. I think the one that I most regret was a great country hit called "What a Difference You've Made in My Life" that Ronnie Milsap did. I turned it down. I thought it sounded like a Gospel song. . . . I said, "Yeah, when I do my Gospel album, maybe" and then it went on to be a very big hit for Ronnie Milsap. I think every singer you talk to can tell you about a hit song that they turned down. More important than anything— more important than anything I can think of—talent is only 40%, maybe—you have to *believe.*

AHS: It's that attitude, plus all of the hard work that you barely mentioned.

MANDRELL: The work is unbelievable, and I wouldn't want any young person to think it's glamorous. It's not a glamorous business. It is *not*; it's just like anything you do. It's not handed to you; you have to make it happen. I don't believe there's so much luck in this business. There's something to be said about meeting the right people and being in the right place at the right time, but I think you make your own luck.

AHS: They say, Barbara, the harder you work, the luckier you get.

MANDRELL: I believe it.

AHS: I think that's your story, really.

MANDRELL: And I also believe that an important factor was that I tried so hard along the way to earn whatever love and affection the audience gave me. I had this need to feel that I could earn their respect. I used to love being the opening act—the challenge of having the audience, who came to see whoever the headliner was, leave talking about you because your show was so good, your music was so good, and you were so together. The next time around, they're going to come back to see *you*.

AHS: Of course you'll be fronting for another headline act if you're that good.

MANDRELL: Well, another thing—here again I'm skipping around—I'm probably not supposed to tell this, but I'm going to tell it—I don't care—I've had PR people with my record label say that they've had some of my "fellow acts" on the label complain that I get such good PR with the magazines and the newspapers, etc. Now I'm going back years ago, too, not just today, and they've said that they told them the truth, and the truth was the reason I got good PR was because when they could arrange for an interview or an appearance for me, I did it. A lot of people will have a little bit of success and a little bit come their way and they take it for granted and they feel "I don't need that; I don't need to do interviews." Well, I genuinely feel that I'm fortunate to have a big spread on me in a magazine or an interview on a television show or on a radio station. . . . It's very valuable. I used to—I wish I had the time today, I don't—really visit the radio stations, and they were kind enough to interview me. When I had my first hit on rock stations, I started all over again like a beginner. I knew the country jocks on the major stations, but now I did something like six cities in four days, going to rock stations. Here I was, a fairly major force in country music having to start from letter "A" again with the rock stations, but I think if you think of yourself as a working-class person—and believe me, if you're going to be in show business, that's exactly what you are, a workin' man—you must pay your dues. People pay dues for a reason. It's not because you have to do it to earn the money; it's because you have to do it to *learn your trade*.

AHS: Well, this interview certainly isn't for mass media, so I must assume it's for me, and I thank you very much.

MANDRELL: Is any of that going to work for you?

AHS: I think it's going to work for me beautifully. I thank you very much.

MANDRELL: Thank you.

# Interview With
# Bill Wyman

As co-founder and bass player for the Rolling Stones, Bill Wyman
needs no introduction. An active and successful record producer,
songwriter, solo artist, and composer of film scores, he also enjoys
many interests outside the world of music.

AHS:     Bill, after a very solid and enduring career, one would
         think you would be content to rest on your laurels, yet you
         seem to have chosen to start an entire new career as a solo
         artist and songwriter. What is your motivation?

WYMAN:   In the Rolling Stones, I'm really a bass player, and apart
         from contributing to arrangements in the recording studio
         and various business decisions and artistic decisions within
         the band, there's very little else I can do creatively within
         the Rolling Stones. I find that my frustrations are building
         up regarding ideas I have musically for songs of a different
         kind than the Rolling Stones record. I always found it very
         difficult to find an outlet for that thing inside me . . . that
         energy; so one alternative was to go out and try to sell
         songs to other people, but I didn't think that was going to
         be very successful, because the obvious reaction would be,
         "Well, if the song's that good, why aren't the Rolling
         Stones doing it?" But I thought, Well, I may as well do it
         myself and see what happens, and I did that reasonably
         unsuccessfully in the mid-70s. The records were pleasant to
         make, and although I had a great time and gained a lot of
         experience arranging, recording, and working in the stu-
         dio, they weren't the right kind of songs, and I wasn't
         singing very well, and I concluded that that was not the
         avenue to explore. Then I started becoming interested in
         writing music for descriptive things. I was thinking maybe
         I could get a small TV special on Stonehenge or some

archeological program like that and I could do the music and slowly work up until maybe I could do a movie score one day. So I started writing descriptive music, and along came a song (completely wrong) called "(Si, Si), Je Suis un Rock Star," and everybody tried to persuade me to record it even though I didn't really want to do solo recording any more. However, everybody was so persistent that it could be a hit (and I did have a gut feeling it might be) that I decided, Okay, well then maybe I won't do another album, maybe I'll just do a single or something and pop that off and see what happens. That's what I did, and it was a success, and consequently there was a need to do another single and then an album, and so on. I'm in that situation now. About the same time, I was offered the opportunity to score the music for *Green Ice,* which I accepted. Suddenly I found that there were a lot of avenues I could explore musically that I hadn't thought about before, such as songwriting for other people with another writer, for instance, and starting to build a music publishing company. More avenues opened relative to various other hobbies that I had. It's just progressed, and of course I *am* a workaholic. I suppose the main reason, to answer your question in a nutshell, is that the Stones don't work as frequently as they did five and ten years ago, and I do have more time on my hands to venture into other things. I do find now that my ventures are successful and that there is a *result* instead of just a chance that something might happen. Now I can see that I'm doing that thing for *that* movie, and I'm doing this thing for *this* album, and I'm doing *another* for a book, and so on. There's always an end product, which so far has been commercially successful.

AHS:        Have you noticed an appreciable change in the industry over the last five or ten years, especially from the point of view of somebody who's trying to get a toehold; do you find it more difficult now than it was then?

WYMAN:        Well, I find it difficult, yes, and I have a name. I would prefer not to be a name and hope to be successful just on material, but the name is valuable as far as getting TV shows and articles written and going on radio shows and things, but for the average newcomer to music, I think it's *really* tough because of the depression, mainly caused, I think, not by lack of money in the kids' pockets, but probably by the purchasing of tape cassette machines. Who's going to go out and buy the top thirty singles for $30 or whatever it costs, when they can sit at home and tape them off the radio in an hour? . . .

AHS:  I know . . . I've fathered two infringers of my own!

WYMAN:  [Laughter] Which I don't think really is that bad, because I think if the kids particularly like an artist, then they will go out and buy that artist's album. But they certainly are more selective in what they buy these days. They just don't go in and say, "I want the latest So-and-So album," just because of the name. They really have to like it now.

AHS:  Do you feel that the advent of the singer-songwriter, artists who primarily sing only their own songs, has dried up the marketplace for writers who don't perform themselves? Do you think that you as a songwriter would have greater difficulty in placing songs with artists today because they sing their own material?

WYMAN·  I think you have to look for the right publishing company. Many publishing companies will not work on trying to get cover versions of songs. Most artists record their own material as much as possible because it's very lucrative, but there is, at least in Europe, which I'm more familiar with than America, still quite a fair number of songwriters who have their material covered by other people and who are not performers or recording artists as such. I think that some of these terrible things that go on, like the Eurovision Song Contest, which I think is really very badly done, do give people a chance of having a song put forward. . . . In England they usually have about six or seven hundred entries from amateur songwriters which get whittled down to thirty, and then twelve and then six, and then one is chosen. So people do get the chance, you know, somebody's mom living in Halifax . . . no, I better not say Halifax . . . [laughter] . . . you'll think it's Canada . . . all right, Huddersfield, in northern England, can write a song, and it could become the biggest record in Europe. A lot of songs are recorded in Europe by people who didn't necessarily write them.

But home recording does hurt the recording companies, who lose an enormous amount of revenue and therefore don't have the money to experiment in other music and new artists. New artists find it very difficult to get recording contracts and advances to buy good equipment and go on the road. That's the problem.

AHS: I find most of the record companies are hurting very badly, or are at least crying "poor boy" and whittling down their deals. The president of a major record company told me today that he made eight deals with new artists in the last nine months, which is really very, very few.

WYMAN: Yes, but don't you think that's also caused by the artists over the last fifteen years "wising up" to what is available in record companies, because in the 60s, when we started, if anybody got 8%, it was phenomenal. You know, the average artist off the street was getting 1% and 2%—3%, if you were lucky. . . . The Beatles were on 1%, I believe, when they first started . . . for five years! We managed to get about 6% out of Decca. Now, even a band off the street is going to go in and ask for 12% or 10%.

AHS: In today's marketplace, I don't think they're going to get it. Maybe a group . . .

WYMAN: They have in the last ten years.

AHS: Oh, in the last ten years, yes. As a matter of fact, it was going up to twelve and fourteen, but this week [laughter], this year, it's gone into reverse.

WYMAN: But the record companies in those days did make an awful lot of money, and although the artist didn't get so much, the record companies were able to experiment and take chances on new acts and now they can't, because everybody's going for the top price when they do a deal.

AHS: I think you've really zeroed in and pinpointed it. I couldn't agree with you more.

WYMAN: It's a shame for the new acts . . . all the young kids out there. . . .

AHS: They have to work harder at it.

WYMAN: Then you get the new little indy labels coming out. In England there are an awful lot of them. Kids just record their single in a back room on a TEAC four-track or an eight-track or something they can borrow for the day or rent for the day, and they go in with a record like they did in the 50s . . . the way all the early rock-'n-rollers did it, like Eddie Cochran and people like that. Gene Vincent and

Buddy Holly went into garages and just cut a dub and sent it to a deejay in those days, and he played it and if it was a hit, then suddenly they had a recording contract. Now they take it to small independent labels like Stiff Records or people like that; there was one just a few months ago who had a really, really big hit home-dubbed, so there's still a chance there for it, but you've really got to come up with the goods now.

AHS: When you said you really have to come up with "the goods," what did you have in mind? Do you believe that the song is the prime factor as opposed to the performance?

WYMAN: That's a tough one. . . . I think a *great* song will always come through. I think an artist, somebody clever, can do a mediocre song, an average song, and make it a great record, as is proven by the Kim Carnes record "Bette Davis Eyes," which was recorded by Jackie DeShannon about five years ago and was a very mediocre, ordinary kind of song as it was rendered. I like it—it's pleasant—because now I know it, but I wouldn't have really gone out and bought it then. Listening to it now, it sounds quite interesting, but the way it was done by Kim Carnes made it a fantastic record, and it made the song sound even better then it probably was. It can go both ways, but I don't think a *bad* song can ever be a hit, a real bad one. . . . Well, there I go; there are some [laughter]. . . .

AHS: [Laughter] But, in general . . .

WYMAN: The comedy value of the bad ones gets in . . .

AHS: I imagine a lot of aspiring artists and writers try to get your ear. Do you perceive anything in the attitude of today's new artists that differs from the attitude of artists five or ten years ago? What I'm really asking is, do you think they're doing anything wrong?

WYMAN: Yes, they're trying to make records before they tour, before they go out and play in front of the public. They think, Oh, let's get four good-looking guys together . . . he can play bass, he can play guitar, he can play drums, and he can sing, and let's go and make a record. They make a record, and then suddenly it's in the charts and they've never played in front of the public. I'm not saying *everybody*, but it happens quite a lot these days. It doesn't really work that way. I think they have to go out there. Most of the really big acts that have come out over the last twenty years have actually worked a lot in front of the public before they made records . . . including the Rolling Stones. The Beatles were out there four years before they made a hit record; we were luckier than that, but we played an awful lot. We used to play two shows a day, you know, for months. A lot of bands just go in and make a record, have a hit, and then they can't follow it on stage. They go out on stage, and they're a disaster. That also helps to make touring more of a problem these days as well, because touring bands do not sell out, and everybody wants the front line. In the 60s, you'd do anything to go on the road and do a tour with a Roy Orbison or Chuck Berry or anybody that was touring England. You'd give your right arm to be sixth on the bill. We were fifth on the bill, the first tour we did with Little Richard, Bo Diddly, Everly Brothers, and so on, and we thought it was an amazing honor. If that was today and it was a new band that had just made a record like we had then, they'd say, "No, man, we don't want to go out with them; we want to headline our own tour" . . . then they go out there and they don't sell tickets. People don't go out to see bands unless they're really, really top bands and they know they're going to get their money's worth. Today no one wants to be second on the bill to anybody else. There used to be package tours, but there don't seem to be so many of them now. We used to have four, five really good acts going out together. You could sell out and you could make money. Now you've got one average band backed by a local band, and it doesn't do the industry very much good at all. I saw Crystal Gayle in Australia, who I think is really good, I like her music and she makes great records. She was doing a show of her own in Australia, and she wasn't selling out. In Australia, for instance, people won't go to see a Crystal Gayle concert. Now if it had been Crystal Gayle and Dolly Parton or Crystal Gayle and Jerry Reed, it would have been sold out, but someone of that stature cannot sell out in places like France or Australia or Germany. They might in Nashville. And I felt really sorry for her, you know; it was obviously the mistake of the promoters and management, and it happens all the time. That doesn't help record sales either.

AHS: What I gather you're saying is that the new acts today are not as willing to pay their dues as . . .

WYMAN: They're not as humble as they should be, I don't think. It's the old adage, you know, you've got to starve before you can succeed, and all the great artists, like Otis Redding and Little Richard and Chuck Berry and Marvin Gaye and the Stones and the Beatles and so on and so on and so on, you can name them forever, all starved. . . . They all went through a real tough time at the beginning. They really had to work their asses, you know, to get there. In the 70s particularly, it was so easy for people just to put a couple of musicians together and get a recording contract, have a hit record, and then . . . nothing.

AHS: I know; it was very easy to make deals then. It's no longer easy to make deals. Tell me, are you thinking now of writing songs for other people as well as for your own performance?

WYMAN: Yes. I think it's an interesting thing to do. I don't write music that is of Rolling Stone style, but I do think I can write songs for many other kinds of artists.

AHS: Do you target your songs? When you write a song, do you think, Hey, this would be great for So-and-So?

WYMAN: No. I just do it and see what it comes out like, and then I think, Oh, that sounds a bit like So-and-So, or maybe that one could have been good if I'd sent it to Ian Dury or whatever.

AHS: I'm going to ask you a kind of loaded question.

WYMAN: Go on then.

AHS: It's really not that bad. In preparing an album, your own album, under what, if any, circumstances would you consider performing somebody else's song?

WYMAN: Only if I like it enough to do a good job on it, really. I don't think of myself as a singer, you see, so my rendering of a song by somebody else would probably not be as good as they might hope. They'd probably sing better on the demo they would give me than I do. Then I have to think, Well, am I going to improve on it musically and get away with not singing it quite as well? . . . And most of the time I think to myself, No, I'm not. . . . [Laughter] So I tend to stick to material that I find that I can sing successfully. On my new album, I tried a few ballads and things and they came out quite well, and people say, "Hey, he can sing after all," but I never practiced singing like I practiced playing bass and keyboards. I never do it, even in the bath, and you've *gotta* practice if you want to do it. Because I've never thought of myself as a singer and I never wanted to be a singer, I use my voice as an extension of my instrument really, I suppose, as another instrument in the music rather than as a solo thing, and sometimes it's quite difficult to get it together.

AHS:        You've been described to me as a true Renaissance man, and I'm wondering to what extent do all your outside interests play a role in your music? You kind of anticipated me and mentioned it peripherally at the beginning of our discussion when you said your "other interests" have caused you to do things. I understand you're a photographer of some reputation. . . .

WYMAN:        I wouldn't say "some reputation." I don't think I've got a reputation as a photographer yet, although I've had the opportunity to do a photo-and-text book of Chagall which is coming out shortly, which is very nice. It was a project, and I never had a photographic project before. I've always taken photos, but no one's ever asked me to do anything specifically for a project that was interesting. On my album I've got one song called "Nuclear Reaction," which is really, I suppose, a song about my interest in astronomy because it's a factual . . . It's not nuclear *reactors*; it's *reaction*, which is, as we all know, what happens on the sun and in space, and I do talk about all the strange objects in space. I liked very much to do that, because it did express my interest in astronomy, for instance, but my other interests don't really get into my songs apart from the odd time like that. I mean space-sounding music is kind of interesting and it's been popular over the last ten years, so I found that one easy, but I couldn't really write a song about archeology, could I? [Laughter]

AHS:        [Laughter] I don't know; perhaps you could. . . .

WYMAN:        [Singing] "I found her in a hole. . . . " [Laughter]

AHS:        I don't know what part management has played in your career, or in the career of the Stones. Do you have any opinions or feelings about the necessity of management for new acts?

WYMAN: Yes, management's very important for new artists who are inexperienced in the business. The difficult thing to find is an honest one. I would say the majority are dishonest in varying degrees. Sometimes they're slightly dishonest, but if the group becomes big, the small dishonesty becomes a large one because it escalates with the earnings. Then you have the big dishonest managements that really tie everything up, and the group ends up with nothing after three years, which has happened to a lot of other bands in their careers. You just have to try and find the one you most trust and you think can do the best job for you, and you will always make mistakes. The Stones ended management in 1969 after two attempts and two failures, and since then we've had no management whatsoever, and we find that in our position we can adequately manage ourselves, but of course we do know the business a lot better now then we did in 1963 and '65, when we made the two signings and the two mistakes. It's very difficult to advise or suggest what to do. If you don't know the business, you've got to have somebody. Now we can employ anybody we want for any project we want, and that's a really good way of doing it. If we want a tour done, we employ a tour manager to organize it (or hire three and find out which one's the best), and if we want a cover done, we employ a photographer. If we want anything done like that, we employ a man for the job instead of a manager overseeing all that, because he really only has to follow your instructions anyway. It's strange in our business about management, because if you run any other business, I think I'm correct in saying, your manager works for you, looks after your business, and is responsible to you. In the music industry, it usually turns around after about three months, and you find that the artist is working for the manager, which is a very strange role, and he's not saying, "Would you like to do this show on Thursday night?" He's saying, "I have booked you for this show on Thursday night and you have to be there at 7:30," you know, and "You are on that television show and you will be going in the studio on Wednesday week." It's not an extension of the artist any more, generally speaking; it's a takeover of the artistic decisions, I think, that the artist should really make, and that's not very good for the artist. So you end up working for your manager, and you end up doing things you don't want to do, and going in directions that you don't want to go in as well, and being committed to doing things that you haven't agreed on in the first place. Then you get the frictions and the breakups of the groups and the managements, and the lawsuits and the things that keep you people in business. [Laughter] There's a strange thing in America about lawyers as well. I won't say they're dishonest, but they take percentages of things, don't they?

AHS: We don't.

WYMAN: I know you don't. That's why I employ your people to look after me, or one of your people, but many, many do. Many lawyers are very unreliable, and many of them have bad reputations. . . . Am I going to get myself shot here? . . . [Laughter]

AHS: [Laughter] No, because you're going to read it before it's printed, so you don't have to worry. . . .

WYMAN: There are a lot of dishonest lawyers in America.

AHS: I think you use the term "dishonest" almost synonymously with "overreaching" as opposed to actual dishonesty.

WYMAN: Yes.

AHS: I get that impression.

WYMAN: Well, you're probably right, because when somebody walks in and takes a cigarette without asking, I think of that as dishonest, or borrowing a book and never returning it. I mean it's nothing, but it's dishonest. Dishonesty to me includes something that's done without permission and, yes, it's a very general term the way I use it. It's not as heavy and as evil as it might sound or look on notepaper.

AHS: All those fellows who are taking percentages are hurting now because the deals aren't coming through from the record companies.

WYMAN: But even trying to settle things . . . I mean, the European lawyers, mainly English, 'cause I know more about them, are so tied up with their oaths and things that they will ask you (if there's something that they're not supposed to hear that's slightly dishonest), please don't tell them, and they're very, very reliable. They might not be the most efficient lawyers, but they are straightforward, and I would say, as far as principles are concerned, more honest than the average American lawyer, who will . . . (I'm saying honest and dishonest again) . . . who will be in on something for what he can get rather than looking after his client first, and then thinking of his salary. You know . . . "If I settle this lawsuit, I want 20%." You never get an English lawyer to say that. He will say, "You will get my fees and charges. They might be a bit expensive, but . . . " And sometimes lawyers and accountants as well, in the music industry in America, do try to get into the same situation as the manager does. That's the rest of what I mean by "dishonest."

AHS: That's my next question. . . .

WYMAN: They like to get involved for a piece of the action, rather than doing a specific job for specific expense and salary.

AHS: I was going to ask you whether you felt lawyers in this country tended to act as managers. . . .

WYMAN: Yes, I know people who have had lawsuits against other people for not being paid for records or for playing in a band, or someone ran off with the advance from the album, and so on, and the lawyers have said to them, "All right, I want that much of the action if you want me to proceed with it, and if I get it for you, you pay me that much," and guys have said, "Okay!" because, you know, a bird in the hand is worth two in the bush. You wouldn't have it that way dealing with it in England, for instance.

AHS: Don't you think that most of those situations arise where the client is bereft of funds and the attorney is taking a risk in expending his time and effort . . . and that would be his compensation?

WYMAN: Yes, sometimes.

AHS: I don't find that as distasteful in those circumstances as . . .

WYMAN: No, he's taking a risk.

AHS: You know, we do have a great deal of experience with not getting paid by artists, especially those who haven't made it or aren't able to make it. . . .

WYMAN: Artists have a lot of experience in not getting paid as well. [Laughter]

AHS: I'm sure they do. . . . [Laughter]

WYMAN: I think there's something on both sides. . . . [Laughter]

AHS: Do you look forward to getting into the business end of the music business?

WYMAN:     Not really. I don't consider myself a businessman. I can make artistic decisions fairly adequately, and I can involve myself a little in the legal aspects, but I need experienced people to advise me and suggest what to go for if we're going to do a deal . . . what is possible, what isn't. I have to employ a lawyer to do a deal with a music company for a sound track. I've *no* idea of what's appropriate. I don't know whether I should get $5,000 or $500,000. I just don't know. I don't know what the percentages might be. They know better than I do. They've got similar clients and experience. I'm always ready to listen to professional advice. I mean, that's what I'm paying for when I employ a lawyer or a business consultant or whoever he might be to do a specific job. I'm paying for their advice and experience in a situation I'm not experienced in, so they're very necessary people and some of them do a wonderful job.

AHS:     Thank you. You've been more than generous with your time.

# About The Author

Alan H. Siegel, an entertainment lawyer since his graduation from Harvard Law School, began his career as house counsel to a leading international music publisher. He later entered into private practice, and has been a partner in an eminent New York entertainment law firm for the past thirteen years.

Siegel, who confesses to a "healthy schizophrenia" induced by "sitting on all three sides of the bargaining table," enjoys an eclectic entertainment practice. He has represented clients in virtually all areas of the entertainment world, including a galaxy of stars ranging in diversity from rock 'n roll to Grand Opera. In addition to his law practice, Mr. Siegel has lectured extensively on entertainment subjects for the Practicing Law Institute, the American Bar Association and law schools in the United States and Canada.

In addition to *Breakin' In*, Siegel's literary efforts include several magazine articles and a screenplay which "taught me to empathize with clients whose talent is not yet recognized." He is now working on two additional screenplays "to demonstrate the tenacity I preach in *Breakin' In*."